D1560066

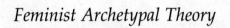

Feminist Archetypal Theory

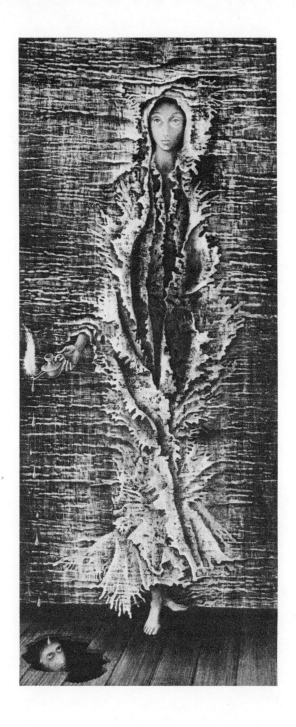

Feminist Archetypal Theory

INTERDISCIPLINARY RE-VISIONS OF JUNGIAN THOUGHT

*Edited, with an Introduction
and a Theoretical Conclusion,
by Estella Lauter and
Carol Schreier Rupprecht*

The University of Tennessee Press / Knoxville

The paper in this book meets the guidelines for permanence
and durability of the Committee on Production Guidelines
for Book Longevity of the Council on Library Resources.
Binding materials have been chosen for durability.

FRONTISPIECE: Remedios Varo, *Emerging Light (Luz emergente)*, 1962, oil on masonite, 25½ x 11 in. Courtesy of Walter Gruen.

Library of Congress Cataloging in Publication Data

Main entry under title:

Feminist archetypal theory.

   Bibliography: p.
   Includes index.
   1. Jung, C.G. (Carl Gustav), 1875–1961 — Addresses,
essays, lectures.   2. Archetype (Psychology) — Addresses,
essays, lectures.   3. Feminism — Addresses, essays,
lectures.   I. Lauter, Estella, 1940–   .   II. Rupprecht,
Carol Schreier, 1939–   .
BF173.J85F43   1985   105.19'54   84-12007
ISBN 0-87049-447-3

To all the women who have enriched my life by their creativity, intelligence, and caring.

ESTELLA

To all the women, real and imaginal, in my life, and especially to my mother — Caroline Comstock Schreier, my aunt — Priscilla Comstock Wells, and my grandmother — Gladys Kibbe Comstock Slye.

CAROL

Contents

Illustrations

Preface

Although this collection is the product of many minds, the introduction which begins the book and the theoretical chapter which concludes it are the result of an exchange between only two persons, co-editors Estella Lauter and Carol Schreier Rupprecht. (Our contributors have enriched that exchange beyond measure but cannot be assumed to agree with all or any of what we say when speaking together.) Our idea for an anthology emerged in June 1979 at a conference on "Creativity and the Unconscious" at Miami University of Ohio, but our dialogue actually began in 1976. That was the year the panel on "Women and Psychology," comprised of Naomi Goldenberg (*Changing of the Gods*, 1979), Madonna Kolbenschlag (*Kiss Sleeping Beauty Good-bye*, 1979), and Carol Schreier Rupprecht, took place at the annual C.G. Jung Conference at the University of Notre Dame. As a result of our activities in the seven years following the Notre Dame conference we have come to believe that no discipline is better suited than archetypal theory to our need as women to study the patterns in our dreams, fantasies, memories, associations, verbal and visual images, stories, songs, rituals, myths, and philosophies.

In 1977 Carol lectured on androgyny and language in dreams at the C.G. Jung Institute in Zurich where she reiterated her proposal, first brought forward at the Notre Dame conference, that we abandon the concept of animus. This proposal elicited from female analysts and analysands the startled response: "Then how would you describe a woman's thinking?" Carol knew then that more vigorous steps had to be taken to revise Jungian theory. At the same time, through teaching and lecturing in New England and New York State, she became aware that her interests were shared by women like Sylvia Brinton Perera of New York City and Jean Shinoda Bolen of San Francisco, both practicing analysts with feminist concerns. (Bolen was also head of the American Psychiatric Association group, Psychiatrists for ERA.)

Also during the late seventies Estella gave slide lectures and papers and organized sessions on poetry and visual art by women at various professional meetings. She was continually impressed by the number of women doing what she considered to be archetypal studies despite their wariness of Jung. In 1978 she chaired a symposium at the annual Jung Conference at Notre Dame, now called the "Conference on Jungian Psychology and Archetypal Theory," that included twelve presentations by both academic and nonacademic women. The symposium proved that academics' reservations about psychology and analysts' and analysands' discomfort with ego-directed academic discourse could be overcome through a shared commitment to understanding women's experience.

In 1979 we began to formulate a plan to draw together the diverse work of colleagues in several fields under the rubric "New Directions in Feminist Archetypal Theory." The first session bearing that title was held at the National Women's Studies Association meeting in June 1980 and included ourselves, Naomi Goldenberg, and Annis Pratt (*Archetypal Patterns in Women's Fiction*, 1981). A thoroughly interdisciplinary audience of close to one hundred people again demonstrated the burgeoning interest in our topic. In December 1981 Carol presented some of our findings and theories and those of our contributors at the First International Interdisciplinary Congress on Women at the University of Haifa in Israel. She was surprised and heartened to find that our work was readily grasped and supported by similar efforts among feminist psychologists around the world.

In the process of soliciting, reading, and editing essays and shaping our own theory, we have identified several problem areas in our enterprise. One is the division between academics and analysts. For example, Sylvia Brinton Perera's essay on Inanna has been published in a longer version by the Toronto Jung Society, but it remains unknown to feminist scholars and women in general. Another problem is the tendency for many writers to become stuck in the feud between Freud and Jung, so that using the concepts of one seems to preclude using the concepts of the other. Linked to this problem is the tendency toward discipleship in both the Jungian and Freudian camps even when such loyalty negates women's lived experience. We also discovered a bias in many women against theory (in favor of the personal and experiential) and against male theorists.

We hope that this group of essays drawn from the study of religion, literature, art, mythology, therapy, neurophysiology, analytical psychology, and archetypal theory will provide some principles for addressing these problems. We hope by overcoming divisions and bridging gaps, we will be able to work more effectively together to value our shared experiences of being female.

Acknowledgments

We are grateful both to our contributors and to those who shared their ideas with us in early stages of the project, most notably Naomi Goldenberg, Dr. Jean Shinoda Bolen, and Karen Petersen. Several organizations gave us opportunities to test our ideas in public forums, among them the C.G. Jung Conference at Notre Dame (1976–80), the Mid-West Women's Caucus of the Modern Language Association (1977), the National Women's Studies Association (1980, 1981, and 1983), and the First International Interdisciplinary Congress on Women (Israel, 1981).

We thank the University of Wisconsin-Green Bay for the sabbatical leave in 1980–81 that allowed Estella to draft Chapter iii, and for its contributions to the incidental expenses inevitably associated with long-distance collaboration. We are grateful to Hamilton College—through Dean C. Duncan Rice and the Academic Council, Associate Dean Peter Millet, and Carol Bellini-Sharp and Nancy S. Rabinowitz of the Advisory Committee on the Kirkland Endowment—for generous support, particularly for the travel grant that allowed us to finish the first complete draft of the book in January 1983 and the Faculty Fellowship leave that enabled Carol to oversee its revision in the fall of 1983. Peter J. Rabinowitz, Chair of the Department of Comparative Literature, offered unflagging encouragement as well as timely advice. Two typists deserve recognition here for their helpfulness: Karen Lorge in Menasha, Wisconsin, and Julie Kisiel in Clinton, New York. Teresa Stasio was a meticulous proofreader and good-humored companion to Carol.

Thanks are also due to Director Carol Orr and Acquisitions Editor Mavis Bryant of the University of Tennessee Press, whose editorial judgments helped to make this a better book. Estella's colleagues Kenneth Fleurant and Raquel Kersten gave generous assistance in securing the rights for photographs to be reproduced. We have benefited also from comments by Douglas A. Weldon and J. Diane Mowrey at Hamilton College. Special thanks go to Sidney H. Bremer at the University of Wisconsin-

Green Bay and to Richard P. (Peter) Suttmeier at Hamilton for their thorough reading of Chapter iii and Chapter vi respectively. Finally, we appreciate the love and forebearance of our families and friends, especially from Chuck, Kristin and Nicholas Lauter, Edna and Judson Loomis, Jody and Whitney Rupprecht, Betsy Adams, Paul Drobin, Jane and Dick Lewis, and Jeff Klugman.

Permission to reproduce photographically the mixed-media sculpture of Escobar Marisol, *The Family*, has been granted by Memphis Brooks Museum of Art; it was commissioned for Brooks Memorial Art Gallery through a grant from the National Endowment for the Arts and matching funds from the Memphis Arts Council, Brooks Fine Arts Foundation, and the Brooks Art Gallery League.

For permission to reprint parts of her *Descent to the Goddess: A Way of Initiation for Women* (Toronto: Inner City Books, 1981), we give special thanks to Sylvia Brinton Perera.

Grateful acknowledgment is also made to the following individuals and publishers for permission to quote from the works cited:

Samuel Noah Kramer for excerpts from his *The Sacred Marriage Rite: Aspects of Faith, Myth and Ritual in Ancient Sumer*, Indiana University Press, copyright (©) 1969.

Susana Ortiz for excerpts from "Dreams in Pregnancy," M.S. in Nursing thesis, Yale University, 1977.

Princeton University Press and Routledge and Kegan Paul, London, for excerpts from *The Collected Works of C.G. Jung*, trans. R.F.C. Hull, Bollingen Series XX. Vol. 7: *Two Essays on Analytical Psychology*, copyright (©) 1953, 1966. Vol. 8: *The Structure and Dynamics of the Psyche*, copyright (©) 1960, 1969. Vol. 9, I, *The Archetypes of the Collective Unconscious*, copyright (©) 1959, 1969. Vol. 9, II, *Aion: Researches into the Phenomenology of the Self*, copyright (©) 1959. Vol. 10: *Civilization in Transition*, copyright (©) 1964, 1970.

The University of California Press for excerpts from *From the Poetry of Sumer: Creation, Glorification, Adoration*, by Samuel Noah Kramer, copyright (©) 1979.

The lines from "Transcendental Etude" from *The Dream of a Common Language, Poems 1974–1977*, by Adrienne Rich, reprinted by permission of the author and the publisher, W.W. Norton & Company, Inc. Copyright (©) 1978 by W.W. Norton & Company, Inc.

Yale University Press for excerpts from Thorkild Jacobsen, *The Treasures of Darkness: A History of Mesopotamian Religion*, copyright (©) 1976.

J. Allan Hobson, M.D., and Robert W. McCarley, M.D., for excerpts from "The Brain as a Dream State Generator: An Activation-Synthesis Hypothesis of the Dream Process," *American Journal of Psychiatry*, 134, No. 12 (Dec. 1977).

Contributors

DEMARIS S. WEHR completed her Ph.D. in Religion and Psychology at Temple University in 1983, with a dissertation on "Jung's Religious Psychology: A Feminist Perspective," and teaches in the Department of Religion at Swarthmore College. She also holds an M.A. in Religion from Temple and an M.A. in French from the University of Pennsylvania and has taught at Connecticut College and the Pendle Hill Quaker Center. She spent one year at Harvard Divinity School as a research-resource associate in Women's Studies. One of her goals is to evolve a feminist vision of peace on our planet.

ESTELLA LAUTER received her Ph.D. from the University of Rochester in 1966. She is Associate Professor of Humanistic Studies at the University of Wisconsin-Green Bay, where she teaches several interdisciplinary courses in women's studies and aesthetics. Her essays and reviews on the visual arts and poetry have appeared in *Spring, Fiber Arts,* the *Woman's Art Journal, Soundings, Women's Studies Quarterly, Women's Caucus for Art Newsletter,* and *Feminist Collections.* Her essay on feminist aesthetics is published in *Philosophical Issues in Art,* ed. Patricia Werhane (Englewood, N.J.: Prentice-Hall, 1984). She is the author of a book of feminist archetypal criticism, *Women as Mythmakers: Poetry and Visual Art by Twentieth Century Women* (Bloomington: Indiana Univ. Press, 1984).

ANNIS V. PRATT holds the Ph.D. in English from Columbia University. She emerged as the leading feminist archetypal literary theorist with the publication in 1981 of *Archetypal Patterns in Women's Fiction* (Bloomington: Indiana Univ. Press) and had previously published books on Dylan Thomas and Doris Lessing. She is a poet, author of numerous scholarly articles, and Professor of English at the University of Wisconsin-Madison. She is currently at work on a companion volume to her last book, on archetypal patterns in women's poetry.

SYLVIA BRINTON PERERA completed her analytic training at the C.G. Jung Institute of New York where she is now a member of the faculty. She also has a private practice in New York. Her article "The Scapegoat Complex" appeared in *Quadrant*. Before becoming an analyst, she worked in the field of art history as a curator, researcher, and teacher; she holds an M.F.A. degree from Princeton University. Her current interests include exploring Celtic mythological themes as they illuminate psychological dynamics and postpatriarchal ego styles. Her chapter is based on her book, *Descent to the Goddess: A Way of Initiation for Women* (Toronto: Inner City Books, 1981).

CAROL SCHREIER RUPPRECHT received her Ph.D. from Yale University with the continuous support of a Merrill Fellowship from the Bunting Institute of Radcliffe College. She began her teaching career at Kirkland College and is now Associate Professor of Comparative Literature at Hamilton College. She has written for *Spring, Women's Studies Quarterly*, and other journals, and has lectured on psychology and literature in the United States, Israel, the Netherlands, and at the Jung Institute in Switzerland. She is also a founding member and lecturer in the Connecticut Association for Jungian Psychology. She is at work on a book that combines her two major areas of interest: dreams and the Renaissance in Italy, France, and England.

Feminist Archetypal Theory

i Introduction

ESTELLA LAUTER and

CAROL SCHREIER RUPPRECHT

Feminist archetypal theory is an interdisciplinary re-visioning of the theories of the Swiss psychologist Carl Gustav Jung (1875–1961). All of the essays collected here review, recast, and freshly conceptualize Jungian thought and its successor discipline, archetypal theory, and the final prospective essay provides a framework for the development of a feminist theory based on such revolutionary work. The purpose of such re-vision is to reformulate key Jungian concepts to reflect women's experiences more accurately.

But why revise Jung? Why not devise an entirely new theory about the characteristics of female experience? We begin with Jung because his psychology embodies a rich, suggestive, timely, and especially comprehensive approach to the psyche. His theories, which he continuously revised throughout his life, were based on his clinical experience, especially with dreams; on his own dreams; and on his voluminous reading (in several languages) of texts from many different periods and cultures. Jung came to feel that many people living in the twentieth century—a post-Enlightenment, technological, scientific, aetheistic age—had lost contact with nature, in the form of human instinct, and with the psyche or life of the spirit. The unconscious was for him "no mere depository of the past, but . . . full of germs of future psychic situations and ideas."[1] As a "natural phenomenon producing symbols that prove to be meaningful,"[2] it was capable of providing energy and direction for the continual renewal of life in instinct and spirit. Through dreams, Jung thought, we gain a "self-portrait" of the psyche as a natural phenomenon which "harbors no intention to deceive, but expresses something as best it can, just as a plant grows or an animal seeks its food as best it can."[3] When we are in contact with these deeper layers of the psyche, we move beyond the limitations of the personal and the psychopathological.

Although he originally based his research and hypotheses on Freud's exploration of the unconscious background of conscious experience, Jung eventually went on to formulate his own concepts, among them the "personal unconscious," the "collective unconscious," the "archetype," and the "individuation process." In contrast to Freud's concept of the id, the personal unconscious was value-neutral and heuristic, and consisted of "all those contents that became unconscious because they lost their intensity and were forgotten or because consciousness was withdrawn from them (repression) and secondly of contents, some of them sense-impressions, which never had sufficient intensity to reach consciousness, but have somehow entered the psyche."[4]

The collective unconscious, which Jung hypothesized on the basis of otherwise inexplicable dreams, was an "ancestral heritage of possibilities of representation," containing qualities that are inherited and not acquired. As such, he said, it was "not individual, but common to all men, and perhaps even to all animals." He thought of it as "the true basis of the individual psyche."[5] It was not, however, an undifferentiated mass of material; instead, Jung claimed, it was organized in its manifestations by recurring patterns called archetypes, or "typical modes of apprehension." We will return to the problem of defining archetypes shortly.

For Jung, psychic life was a continuous, dynamic exchange between conscious and unconscious levels of experiencing and functioning. The psychic system, he thought, was self-regulating, and the dynamic exchange led purposively toward the wholeness of the person, or the realization of "the Self." He called this process "individuation." The Self was a comprehensive center that included the ego as defined by Freud. While Jung accepted the ego as the center of consciousness, he postulated the Self as the center of the greater psyche with its interacting elements.

Jung saw individuation as a lifelong task, an elaborate and subtle process whereby the person brings recessive potentials into balanced relationship with more conscious or highly developed potentials. He thought that all the human attributes were open to development by either sex, and that the "mature" person would balance (or develop in relatively equal proportions) opposing qualities in the psyche. Thus, in one of his favorite explanations, the person for whom thinking was the dominant function would eventually want to experience feeling and integrate that function into the personality.

This aspect of his theory led Jung to value all human qualities as part of the reality of human existence, and to revalue some qualities, in particular those he labeled as "feminine," which he felt had become recessive in culture as well as in individuals. He thought it especially dangerous that modern man has neglected his feminine attributes. (Jung's preoccupation with the feminine has been recognized most recently by publication of *Aspects of the Feminine* in the Bollingen paperback series of selections from his work.) From our point of view, however, the most important implication of this line of thought is that culturally defined masculine and feminine qualities are equally available for development by either sex.

Another valuable feature of Jung's work was his view of analysis as an exchange between two human beings, both of whom are inevitably altered by the experience. He ultimately rejected the term "therapy," with its emphasis on sickness and cure, and replaced the term "patient" with "analysand." He trusted the analysand's experience and insight, de-emphasizing the analyst's authority and insisting that it is more important for an analysand "to understand than for the analyst's theoretical expectations to be satisfied."[6] When resistance in analysis occurred, he believed, the analysand "is not necessarily wrong; it is rather a sure sign that something does not 'click.' "[7] Either the analysand has not yet reached a point of understanding or the analyst's interpretation does not fit.

With so many potentially positive features in Jungian psychology, why do we see a need for revision? The need arises partly because Jung's ideas became codified among the first generation of his followers. Many of the analysts and authors who studied with him personally may have wished to minimize certain ambiguities and inconsistencies in his thought and so turned some of his admittedly provisional formulations into statements of fact and truth.[8] Primarily, however, revision is necessary because of Jung's tendency, despite the remarkable range, complexity, and fluidity of his system, to think in terms of rigid oppositions. For example, he posited that Eros, or the principle of relatedness, was not only associated with females but was dominant in the female psyche; conversely, the analytical principle, or Logos, was dominant in males. Despite all our efforts toward individuation, he said, Eros would remain weaker in most males and Logos weaker in most females. Thus he set arbitrary limits on the development of both sexes and reinforced the stereotypes of man as thinker, woman as nurturer. By associating men with thought, the cultural category with the higher value in the twentieth century in most Western societies, he helped to perpetuate the inequality of women.

Jung's great strength as a theorist was that he usually worked inductively, synthesizing vast quantities of data. In the case of gender, however, he seems not to have taken into account the wide variance in the intellectual capabilities of both men and women, a variance which is receiving more and more documentation. Instead, he moved too quickly from a description of culturally induced gender differences to an assumption about sex differences, undercutting his inductive method with his predilection for dichotomies.

In any theory, such a problem would call for revision in the denotative sense: to look over again in order to correct, improve, amend, or update. Jung's theory, in addition, calls for re-vision in the connotative sense made current by James Hillman in *Re-Visioning Psychology:* to see anew, to *en*vision new possibilities in what has previously been discovered and explained.[9] Revision of either kind is especially important when a theory does not fit the facts of experience it was constructed to explain.

On a controversial panel titled "Women and Psychology" at the University of Notre Dame's annual C.G. Jung Conference in 1976, Naomi Goldenberg, Madonna Kolbenschalg, and Carol Schreier Rupprecht took the first public steps toward substantially revising Jungian theory to include the perspectives of women, as women identified them. They called attention to limitations and gaps in parts of Jung's theory that had previously enjoyed uncritical acceptance. The panelists asserted that his highly reputed reverence for the feminine, though certainly valuable, involved only recognition and support for the feminine principle in

men and did not value the actual experiences of women themselves.

Later that year, in a forceful article based in part on her panel
presentation, Naomi Goldenberg outlined succinctly the major
objections to Jung women were beginning to have. By the midseventies, Goldenberg argued, Jungian psychology had become
increasingly cultish, to the point of being itself "a form of patriarchal religion."[10] The cult fostered unquestioning acceptance of all
of Jung's thought, despite the obvious contradictions, complex-
ities, failures, and evolutionary changes inevitable in the work of
a man who lived for eighty-six years. At the time of his death,
Jung was still writing and editing *Man and His Symbols,* a version
of his theories adapted for the lay reader that was published
posthumously. His *Collected Works* runs to over twenty volumes.
But in the climate of reverence among his followers, statements
such as the following were taken to be incontrovertible truths:

> No one can get around the fact that by taking up a masculine
> profession, studying and working like a man, woman is doing
> something not wholly in accord with, if not directly injurious to, her
> feminine nature. . . . I do not mean merely physical injury, but
> above all psychic injury.[11]

Women followers such as Marie-Louise von Franz, M. Esther
Harding, Jolande Jacobi, and Aniela Jaffé—all highly educated
persons, prolific writers, active analysts, and widely traveled
lecturers—lived their lives in patent contradiction of such a claim.
Yet these women in their writing affirmed Jung's assumptions as
frequently as his male followers did. Women like Goldenberg and
other members of the panel and audience at Notre Dame could no
longer accept such contradictions without question.

Goldenberg also pointed out that Jung's followers had come to
see the archetypes as "unchanging and unchangeable," or as the
material *contents* of the collective unconscious. Archetypal images that Jung had described were frequently understood as
absolutes. Instead of being explanations of reality experienced by
females, archetypes of the feminine had become categories to
contain women. Finally, and most destructively, because of their
reputed origin in a transcendent and religious realm, the archetypes had acquired an irrefutable numinosity and were even

called "past documents" of the soul.[12] Demaris Wehr develops Goldenberg's critique in Chapter ii of the present volume.

Goldenberg concentrated on one particular theory concerning the phenomenon Jung called the archetype of the "animus." This theory drew criticism from all three of the panelists at Notre Dame, both for its inadequacies of articulation and the method of its derivation. Jung introduced the animus as the "contrasexual" element, the masculine aspect of the female psyche, in accord with his tendency to see the world as organized into opposites. But his explanation of this concept is uncharacteristically deductive and conjectural:

> Since the anima is an archetype that is found in men, it is reasonable to suppose that an equivalent archetype must be present in women; for just as the man is compensated by a feminine element, so the woman is compensated by a masculine one.[13]

The method of Jung's formulation cannot be ignored because the concept became an essential feature of his description of the differences between men and women:

> Woman is compensated by a masculine element and therefore her unconscious has, so to speak, a masculine imprint. This results in considerable difference between men and women, and accordingly I have called the projection-making factor in women the animus, which means mind or spirit. The animus corresponds to the paternal Logos just as the anima corresponds to maternal Eros. . . .[14]

The anima is understood in Jungian psychology to mean the man's soul. As Goldenberg pointed out, such a position gave "women and men qualitatively different kinds of unconscious (or soul)—an enormous assertion based on little evidence."[15] The injustice of a theory that undermined women's capacity for conscious thought by making it a matter of archetypal projection was compounded by Jung's habit of deriding the animus. For example, he labeled certain colleges and universities, especially in the United States, "animus incubators," because they turned out opinionated, animus-possessed women who were inferior men; that is, their thinking processes persisted at the level of irritable argumentation, and their intellects were desperate and driven. Since he thought that women's consciousness was by definition "characterized more by the connective quality of Eros than by the

discrimination and cognition associated with Logos,"[16] he concluded that women's performance in activities such as writing
books would necessarily be inferior to men's, although he consistently wrote admiring forewords to books written by his female
followers, books which supported and extended his theories.[17]

In retrospect the contentions of the panelists at Notre Dame
and their subsequent writings seem mild and appropriate
enough, for they represented the inevitable critical reappraisal of
one man's thought by those coming of age in a different culture
and time. There is certainly sufficient material in Jung of the sort
quoted above to testify to a need for re-visioning. But in 1976
these contentions were received as the first salvoes in what was to
become a vigorous debate among feminists and among Jungians
and between both groups. The controversy flared even though
the panelists contended, at the conference and in their subsequent writings and lectures, that the problematic areas they had
identified were not sufficient grounds for discarding the archetypal approach altogether. The heat and the light generated by
this fiery debate prompted the editors of this volume to merge
feminism and archetypal thinking in one work, just as they are
merged in our own minds, experiences, disciplines, and souls.

Indeed, on one level this collection may be seen as a response to
the challenge issued by Naomi Goldenberg:

> Feminist scholars must examine the very idea of archetype in Jun-
> gian thought if sexism is ever to be confronted at its base. Indeed, if
> feminists do not change the assumptions of archetype or redefine
> the concept, there are only two options: either (1) to accept the
> partriarchal ideas of the feminine as ultimate and unchanging and
> work within those or (2) to indulge in a rival search to find female
> archetypes, one which can support feminist conclusions.[18]

Goldenberg feared, as we still fear, that the second alternative
might produce a new set of restrictions on female experience; and
this fear led her to pose the possibility of abandoning the concept
of archetypes, which she understood as "absolute, transcendent
ideals of which our changing experiences . . . are only inferior
copies."[19]

She suggested, following archetypal theorist James Hillman
(whose concepts were presented at the same conference), that we
understand all "imaginal activities, all images . . . as archetypes

to the degree that they move things and partake of what we might want to call 'numinosity.' "[20] As Hillman puts it, all "rich" images, that is, fecund, generative images that merit our repeated attention, are archetypal. We make them archetypal as we extend and value them in our image-making work.[21] In defining what makes an image archetypal, Hillman described a process of attending to the image: "(a) precise portrayal of the image; (b) sticking to the image while hearing it metaphorically; (c) discovering the necessity within the image; (d) experiencing the unfathomable analogical richness of the image."[22] His criteria make it clear that the recognition of an archetype is a *valuing* process. We call something archetypal when we believe that it is basic, necessary, universal; the trouble comes when we begin to believe that what we have valued is the essence of what is real. Hillman is committed to the process of interpretation—making psyche matter—without reducing what is interpreted either to the (merely) personal or the symbolic.

Hillman's revision of the concept of archetype is difficult to maintain in practice, however, because of the tendency we have to turn processes into things. His revision also leaves several key questions unanswered: What makes us give repeated attention to certain images while we discard others as unimportant? Why are some images unfathomable? What determines the "necessity" we find in an image? And so on. Nevertheless, Hillman's approach allows women to value their images more fully (archetypally) than they did as students or analysands of traditional Jungians. Moreover, Hillman's work proves that it is possible to revise the core concept of the archetype as it had come to be known in Jungian psychology.

There were others before Hillman, however, who defined the archetype less rigidly. The view of the archetype as an absolute, transcendent ideal that somehow determines our experiences may not have been as orthodox as Goldenberg assumed. Consider this definition from Erich Neumann's *Art and the Creative Unconscious*, first published in 1959.

> The archetypes of the collective unconscious are intrinsically form-less psychic structures which become visible in art. The archetypes are varied by the media through which they pass—that is, their form changes according to the time, the place, and the psychologi-

cal constellation of the individual in whom they are manifested. Thus, for example, the mother archetype, as a dynamic entity in the psychic substratum, always retains its identity, but it takes on different *styles*—different aspects or emotional color—depending on whether it is manifested in Egypt, Mexico, or Spain, or in ancient, medieval, or modern times. The paradoxical multiplicity of its eternal presence, which makes possible an infinite variety of forms of expression, is crystallized in its realization by man in time; its archetypal eternity enters into a unique synthesis with a specific historical situation.[23]

While we may bristle at the words "eternal" and "eternity," Neumann proposes a very different concept from the one Goldenberg represents as Jungian orthodoxy, or the one Rachel Blau DuPlessis derives from the dictionary in her influential essay on myth in women's poetry:[24] Far from being a "binding, timeless pattern" that exists without change outside of history, the archetype, according to Neumann, is a formless structure of the psyche itself that is known only through its changing manifestations. If it is "eternal," it is also thoroughly enmeshed in history.

Thus in reformulating our concept of the archetype in terms that are enabling for women, we might take from Hillman the notion that the archetype is not an entity in itself so much as a process of valuing an image. From Neumann we might take the idea that the archetype assumes different forms according to the personal and social history of the person who manifests it. We would still need, however, an explanation of why certain images seem rich before we attend to them consciously. And we need to examine the paradox of a "formless structure."

Another Jungian, James Hall, suggests a direction for us when he writes about the dream in Jungian theory:

The most profound contents of the objective psyche are the archetypal images, the archetypes themselves not being observable in their unimagined state. . . . There is no fixed number of archetypes, since any recurrent human experience can be archetypally represented. It is perhaps more nearly correct to speak of an archetypal field, with the observable archetypal images indicating nodal points in which the field is particularly dense. Archetypes are not inherited images; they are part of the tendency to structure experience in certain ways.[25]

Carol Schreier Rupprecht arrived at a similar description of the archetype in 1974 in her article on androgyny in literature: "There is an associative field, and the combined total of the associations, while always shifting and regrouping, establishes certain parameters within which an archetype reveals itself."[26] Hall continues:

> Each complex rests on an archetypal core, since archetypes are simply the ordering structure of the mind. The archetypal core of the complex may be thought of as similar to a magnetic field; it has no physical structure, but it determines the order and relationships of images susceptible to its influence. Jung considered the archetype like a dry river bed—empty, but capable of determining the flow of libido when there is activation of a psychic process.[27]

Archetypes are "part of the tendency to structure experience in certain ways"; they are "the ordering structure of the mind"; they determine the flow of libido "when there is an activation of the psychic process." Hall's theory sounds remarkably like Chomsky's notion that we have a tendency to form a language—a tendency that is triggered by certain needs as we develop and then manifested in different ways depending on the place, time, and talents of the individual. Clearly, the trigger for the archetype to manifest itself is also experience. For example, "there is no inherited image of the mother, but there is a universal tendency to form an image of the mother from the experience of the child."[28]

Still, the word "universal" seems to essentialize the archetype again, or, in Hillman's words, to "literalize" it. It also seems to contradict Hall's earlier statement that there is "no fixed number of archetypes," since the number of experiences as "universal" as the child's experience of the mother is extremely limited.

Hall does speak to the problem of concretizing and fixing the archetype. He notes that the archetypes of anima and animus will undergo change because the distinctions Jung made between them are "patently culturally determined": "It is my own impression that as the roles of male and female become more diversified, as is now happening, the phenomenologies of the animus and the anima will undergo similar change consistent with their functional role in the psyche."[29]

Apparently without knowledge of the work of Hillman and

Hall, Eric Gould proposes, from a vantage point informed by structuralism, psychoanalysis, and phenomenological hermeneutics, that the archetype is "universal" because it presents us with a "fact" that always remains open to interpretation. For the archetype is a "site" or "contact surface" where "inner and outer" meet; it is the

> hypothetical space created by the subject's search for himself as well as by what lies outside himself, through the tradition of language and its meanings. As such, it contains not a fixed reality but a propositional statement which experiments with the literal. The archetypal motif is largely proleptic. It is less useful to us as an object of belief, as a fixed systematic item, than as a *transactional fact*, slowly revealing its form only in language and interpretation. It is objective only insofar as it exists as a semiotic item, leading us to link it to other signs and to modify our assumptions about itself and ourselves. The archetype is subjective in that it depends on interpretation for its very existence.[30]

The archetype, as a "transactional fact" that marks the site where inner and outer meet, gives the appearance of being universal not because of its content but because the various meetings of inner and outer are never complete, never totally bridged by any process, linguistic or otherwise.

What the foregoing theories all have in common is a reluctance to regard the archetype as absolute or transcendent or unchanging. They suggest that the concept of the archetype remains useful even when it is removed from the essentialist (Platonic) context in which it was originally formulated.

Why does it remain useful? Even more to the point here, why might it remain useful to feminist theory? Presumably the concept survives because of our sense that it refers to something real in our experience—whether we describe that reality as a seemingly infinite variety of related forms, as images that are "unfathomable" and "necessary," as nodal points in an energy field that determine the flow of libido, or as the identifying mark of a transaction that is never fully resolved. The concept survives in these forms because it has real explanatory power.

In the case of feminist theory, if we regard the archetype not as an image whose content is frozen but (in the way Estella Lauter suggests in Chapter iii) as a tendency to form and re-form images in relation to certain kinds of repeated experience, then the concept could serve to clarify distinctively female concerns that have persisted throughout human history. Applied to a broad range of materials from women, it could expose a set of reference points that would serve as an expandable framework for defining female experience, and ultimately the "muted" culture females have created.

Suppose, for example, we say that there is indeed a tendency to form and re-form images of "the mother," and that such a tendency is related both to general species-wide experiences of being mothered and to specifically female experiences of mothering, or confronting the biological potential for childbearing. Suppose we consider the repeated images of these experiences—in the reported dreams, journals, poems, visual art, ordinary speech, daily rituals or performances by women—as reference points for the definition of female experience. We are then free to compare images formed by women in various stages or states of psychological development, by peoples of various cultures, or by men and women in the same culture or time of life. We may find, as Lauter does in her essay on visual art by women, that a description of the archetypal mother based on works by women will look quite different from, say, the description given by Erich Neumann in *The Great Mother*.[31] But the concept we are developing here should prevent us from assuming that either set of images is normative. Theoretically, the archetype (as a tendency to form images) cannot be known completely until all its manifestations—past, present, and future—are brought to light. No one set of images, whether Greek, Renaissance, or modern, can be synonymous with "the mother." No set gives privileged access to the experience of mothering. Nor does the existence of a tendency to form such images either prescribe or proscribe motherhood (much less a particular kind of motherhood) for all women. Feminist archetypal theory will allow us to uncover a complex, changing figure of the mother, richly informed by history, which we may use consciously in a variety of ways. And as with this archetypal image, so with others.

The archetype we uncover may be universal in the sense of being a tendency that is shared by great numbers of women across time, space, and human culture. It is probably a species-wide tendency, like the tendency to learn a language. Thus, the resulting images are transpersonal; that is, they partake of the history of the image as well as the individual's subjective experience. They are often "numinous" because of their cumulative energy. But the archetype is not unchanging. The experiences of human gestation and birth have already changed drastically, and along with them the archetypal images of such experiences have changed. Even the archetype of the mother could fade away from disuse, or become dormant, since it cannot continue to manifest itself apart from collective human experience.

Our proposed concept of the archetype requires that we consider the experiential context in which the image occurs. A central tenet of our theory is that image and behavior are inextricably linked; our images of possible behavior inform our actions, and our actions, in turn, alter our images. The body, of course, is the place where these two facets of experience are joined. We need to understand the extent to which our female bodies determine our images and actions. Nancy Chodorow has proposed, for example, that girls develop less firm ego boundaries than boys do because of their differing early experiences of being mothered and their continuing experiences of the permeable boundaries of their bodies in menstruation, intercourse, pregnancy, and lactation.[32] Our theoretical orientation will encourage a search through female images and behavior for information concerning women's experiences of these boundaries, such as the recent study of the dreams of pregnant women cited in Carol Schreier Rupprecht's essay.

It is important to clarify that in this theoretical enterprise we do not seek to reify a phenomenon of female consciousness as distinct from male consciousness. In fact, we find questions concerning such differences less interesting than questions concerning the content of actual experiences. We regard the patterns in works and acts by women as important regardless of their degree of closeness to or distance from patterns created by men. Such patterns are part of the human struggle to order existence, and they are created by half the population of the world.

We must learn what women imagine, dream, fantasize, feel, and think. We need to be free to study large bodies of material by women just for the sake of describing the content, without any intent of proving or disproving gender differences. But if we are not simply to filter the experiences of women solely through established categories of culture, we need an appropriate principle of organization for such study. The principle we have chosen is the archetype as defined here and as written about in the essays that follow. In these essays the archetype becomes a feminist tool for re-examining and re-evaluating patterns in women's experiences as they are revealed in psychotherapy, studies of the arts, myths, dreams, religion, sociology, and other disciplines as well. This use of the archetype opens the way for a theoretical framework that will be complex and supple enough to illuminate the multiple phenomena we presently call "female experience."

We must pay attention to theory, for we know that there is no such thing as raw data. If we go without an adequate theory to the documents of experience prepared by or gleaned from women, we will repeat the errors of oversight, underestimation, exclusion, projection, and devaluation made by our (mostly male) predecessors, or we will fall into new errors of exaggeration, distortion, and overestimation. Feminism offers us a system predisposed to validate women, whether women's experience is congruent with or radically different from men's. Archetypal theory offers feminism a general sanction to look at women's images, as well as at their social, economic, or political behavior, and to value all kinds of material, not just those kinds currently privileged in contemporary culture. Thus images in quilts and needlework and dreams are as important as images in paintings and poems; all, taken together, are essential to the preparation of the theoretical ground.

We need a theory that will allow us to take seriously the patterns we find in women's thoughts and images while preventing exaltation of any detected patterns. In such a theory the archetype cannot be defined as an image whose content is frozen but must be thought of as a process, a tendency to form and re-form images in relation to certain kinds of repeated experiences.

The essays included here were written independently, only later being selected for inclusion in the collection, and they exemplify several possibilities of feminist archetypal theory. The theory charted in these essays is an expandable framework; it need not become a prescription or a proscription. Feminist archetypal theory will eventually embrace many studies of patterns in women's lives and works that are not now labelled "archetypal."

This collection, however, has been designed to surmount several important stumbling blocks to the systematic interdisciplinary study of women's experience: the concept of the archetype itself; the possibility of using methods and ideas developed by previous archetypal theorists without adopting their ideologies; and the necessity of reformulating the relationship between images and reality, between the unconscious and the material world.

The first essay, "Religious and Social Dimensions of Jung's Concept of the Archetype," by Demaris Wehr, looks at the way in which Jung's concept of the archetype has been ontologized and therefore has tended to support the status quo of women in society. Although Wehr's field of specialization is religion and psychology, she uses methods from the sociology of knowledge developed by Peter Berger. She shows that Jungian descriptions of gender-linked archetypes (such as the anima and the feminine) serve as useful descriptions of socially constructed reality only as it is experienced in a misogynist and patriarchal culture. She recommends that we see Jung's work as a richly reflective mirror of our cultural stereotypes and fears and use it to exert a corrective influence on society. She finds the concept of the collective unconscious ingenious and believes that we can not discard a psychology that describes so well the inner experience, fantasies, moods, compulsions, and pulls that beset us in our daily lives. The danger in Jung's concept of the archetype, Wehr argues, lies in its essentially theological origin and uses. To the extent that we can avoid making neurotic inter-human and intrapsychic phenomena into theological constructs, feminists may find the concepts of both the archetype and the collective unconscious liberating.

Estella Lauter's essay, "Visual Images of Women: A Test Case for the Theory of Archetypes," offers a more stringent critique of Jungian descriptions of gender-linked archetypes. She hypothesizes that if such descriptions are true to the realities of women's experience, they ought to correspond with the patterns of images we find in works of visual art by women created outside the clinical setting. Thus she turns to visual art by twentieth-century women and examines three categories of images: the widely accepted archetype of the mother, which was described at great length in Jungian theory by Erich Neumann; the Jungian construct of the animus; and an extensive pattern of images in art by women that has not yet been described as an archetype. The mother, she finds, does appear in works of art by women with sufficient frequency and intensity to suggest that the images are rooted in experiences women share, but the pattern of mother images she finds differs substantially from the archetype described by Neumann and others. Where the animus is concerned, she finds very few images in art created by women that fit the best Jungian definition of the animus. Images of men do exist in women's work, however, and she suggests that we examine them to find any patterns they may contain.

In marked contrast to the paucity of animus images, Lauter finds a significant number of images of what she calls, for want of a better name, "independent women": women engaged in productive tasks, alone or with subordinates, who present aspects of female strength. These images are not adequately described by the Jungian categories of "medium" or "amazon." Rather, they describe a figure who marshalls her creative energy on her own behalf and on behalf of others with passion, intelligence, and responsibility. With this working description of the archetype of the strong woman, we can identify her presence in our history and prepare for her increasing importance in a world where the necessity of zero population growth will require the continuing development of new roles for women.

Despite its inadequacies in describing many of the patterns in women's works and lives, Jungian theory is presented by Lauter as a map to be redrawn rather than abandoned in the exploration of still unfamiliar territory. Like Wehr, Lauter asserts that the map is not sacred; she further argues that it does not accurately reflect women's experience, at least as such experience is recorded in visual art. She hopes to encourage others, whether they are academically or clinically trained, to explore images created by many women before accepting any psychological theory as valid.

Annis Pratt's essay begins with a caveat, essential in any evolving discipline, about becoming stuck in any one theoretical perspective or methodology. She then shows how she is redrawing the maps provided by Jung, Northrop Frye, and Claude Lévi-Strauss; all in limited ways can serve as models for feminist archetypal theory. She not only demonstrates multiple "ownership" of the concept of the archetype, but shows how feminists can "spin among fields," gathering ideas from several disciplines, as they develop new theories. Indeed, the metaphor of spinning (borrowed from Mary Daly) seems more appropriate than any other for the enterprise of feminist research.

Beginning with Jung, Pratt shows how his description of the archetypal rebirth journey must be altered in order to serve as a guidepost to similar journeys in women's fiction. From Jung she takes the propensity to value the materials of the unconscious, while she rejects the Jungian tendency to conceive of the feminine as a pole in a dualistic system of absolutes. From Northrop Frye she takes an inductive approach to the materials of literature and the tendency to see archetypes simply as recurrent images in the "total order of words" that is literature, while she rejects some of the categories Frye himself derived from his inductive study of literature in the European tradition written by men. In particular, she shows how basic assumptions within that tradition about the connection between men and culture on the one hand and women and nature on the other led to the development of categories that are inappropriate to the study of women's fiction. Indeed, she observes that Frye himself had to turn away from those categories in order to deal with his native Canadian literature, which evolved in opposition to the European tradition. From Lévi-Strauss she takes the notion that various activities in a given culture are organized in similar ways, and that these "invariant elements" or "bundles of relations" reflect the substructure of the culture, while she rejects his "dualistic and imperial" tendency to swallow up the phenomena under study into a logical system of signs. An overvaluation of concepts, Pratt says, may finally endanger not only the intellectual life but the earth itself.

Feminism need not abjure reason, but it does need to reject absolutist commitments to theories and disciplinary boundaries. The model of "spinning among fields" that Pratt suggests involves making connections between psychology, art, and culture in a virtually endless cycle. In large part, Pratt finds, our task is to disentangle feminine archetypes from the masculine warp of culture. The task is complicated because men can write without gynophobia and women can be possessed by it. Our freedom to spin among fields is blocked both internally and externally. We need the help of many more hands and minds; we need time; we need patience.

Sylvia Brinton Perera gives us an analyst's perspective on an ancient female version of the archetypal descent to the underworld and compares it to contemporary women's quest for wholeness. From among many myths of descent made by or to a female goddess, Perera chooses the oldest, the Sumerian "Descent of Inanna," recorded on clay tablets during the third millenium. She argues that the myth provides a many-faceted wholeness pattern of the feminine that goes far beyond the maternal. Inanna symbolizes all the ways the energies of life confront each other and flow together, including connections and disjunctions that are both loving and passionate. Her sister Ereshkigal, goddess of the underworld who exacts death from Inanna, symbolizes the energy that allows a woman to survive alone. Both are necessary for the full development of the female person.

In addition, Perera claims that Inanna's descent into Ereshkigal's realm offers a model for disidentification with patriarchal values which she believes are encoded in the woman's animus. If a woman is to claim her own creativity and strength, she must detach herself from animus ideals.

Perera intersperses her psychological commentary on the Inanna myth with anecdotal accounts of her experiences as a therapist, especially with successful-in-the-world women, like herself, whom she calls "daughters of the patriarchy." She believes that such women have often repudiated their own full feminine instincts. Only by returning to a model such as Inanna's descent and by redeeming the aspects of it that have been judged "terrible" can they expect to become psychologically healthy. Perera suggests that Geshtinanna, the loyal sister of Inanna's consort who saves him from death by alternating with him in the underworld, provides a potential model of the equilibrium (that "never-ending play" or "balancing act" without a predetermined end) that constitutes wholeness.

As a practicing analyst continually made aware of the uniqueness of each individual's life, and the necessity of recognizing and valuing that uniqueness, Perera is even more wary of theory than Pratt is. As Perera says at the end of her essay:

> There are no paradigms that exactly fit our situation. The ancient
> tale of Inanna tells us only what forces we must serve. How each of
> us is to find her own individual balance as we descend-ascend and
> ascend-descend—that is still to be lived and written.

Yet her essay exemplifies the process Annis Pratt describes of
disentangling the feminine archetypes from the masculine warp
of culture. Perera uses Jungian concepts freely when they fit the
female patterns revealed by the myth; she abandons or revises
them just as freely when they do not fit female experience. Her
recommendation concerning the animus is a case in point. Similarly, her presentation of a female descent without reference to
similar descents by male figures (Odysseus, for example) departs
significantly from the Jungian tendency to regard males and
females as mirror images of each other. Furthermore, her awareness of the role patriarchal values have played in the development of women's consciousness is decidely feminist. Her work
not only dovetails with other feminist projects (such as Lauter's
account of images of the independent woman in visual art) but
has fascinating implications for feminist psychological theory,
which we will discuss in our final essay.

Carol Schreier Rupprecht's essay addresses the necessity of
reformulating the relationship between the unconscious and
material reality. She takes the position, most recently articulated
by psychiatrist-neurophysiologists J. Allan Hobson and Robert
W. McCarley but long held by Jung, that dreams, far from being
the products of conflict and repression, are "naturally occurring,
undistorted, accessible phenomena of mentation." As Hobson
and McCarley put it: "Dreams are the obligatory and relatively
undistorted psychological concomitant of the regularly recurring
and physiologically determined brain state called 'dreaming
sleep.' " The principal value of Hobson and McCarley's work for
feminist archetypal theory lies in their laboratory validation of
elements of archetypal dream theory and in their insistence on
the unity of mind and body. Their work challenges the authority
of Freud in dream theory by stressing the ontological naturalness
of dreams and emphasizing the creative rather than the pathological side of dreams. They pose the possibility of continued con-
gruence between archetypal dream theory and neurophysiological discoveries and hypotheses.

Rupprecht applauds Rosalind Cartwright's statement that a twenty-four-hour perspective on the stable elements across the three states of waking, sleeping, and dreaming allows a more holistic view of human experience, including gender-linked experience. Research on dreams to date, however, has been gender-biased in many ways. Rupprecht calls for a "non-sexist environment for the study of dreams" and more careful studies of the correlation between dreams and behavior in women and in children. Finally, she encourages women not specifically trained in either neurophysiology or psychology to attend to their own dreams and follow developments in these two rich fields of investigation.

The essays included here treat the subjects of traditional archetypal theory: archetypes (and their manifestations in society, art, and literature), myth, therapy, dream, the unconscious. Collectively they represent the first steps toward the formation of a coherent yet flexible framework for a feminist archetypal theory and a post-Jungian approach to the female psyche. As archetypal theory, effectively revised, moves into feminist scholarship, it will allow women, as an inquiring community, to stay in touch with the sources of energy and meaning uniquely available through the unconscious. It will make room in women's awareness for what Adrienne Rich has called the "many-lived, unending forms" of women's experience. The ultimate justification for this book (far more important than any theoretical framework that may emerge) is the commitment that runs through all of these essays to the diverse experiences of women and the reality of the unconscious. As Annis Pratt said in an early stage of our project, "It would be ironic if Women's Studies scholarship should assimilate the dualistic insistence on the primacy of reason which has been so destructive both to women and to the earth itself, to the extent that its scholars turn away from the empowering treasures of women's thousands of years of dreams and fantasies and creations."

ii Religious and Social Dimensions of Jung's Concept of the Archetype: A Feminist Perspective

DEMARIS S. WEHR

In recent years, feminist discussion of the usefulness of C.G. Jung's theories, notably the theory of archetype, has been wide-ranging, with some of the most intense debate taking place in the field of religion. Conferences and journals have been the usual forum for this debate. Feminist authors like Carol Christ and Naomi Goldenberg have criticized Jung's psychological model from a feminist perspective, and Jungians have responded by either updating the theory or defending Jung against what they perceive to be misinterpretations of his theory.[1] This essay is my contribution to the debate.

Using a methodology informed by feminism and drawn from the sociology of knowledge, specifically the work of Peter Berger, I will examine the religious and social dimensions of Jung's concept of the archetype. This broad sociological emphasis allows us to uncover the central problem and the potential value of this concept. The central problem is this: Jung ontologizes what is more accurately and more usefully seen as socially constructed reality. Even though Jung and Jungians at times describe the archetype as simply a propensity or a predisposition to act or image in a certain way, the category of archetype is often used as a category of Being itself. Thus Jungian theory can function as quasi-religious or scientific legitimation of the status quo in society, reinforcing social roles, constricting growth, and limiting options for women. Seen for what they actually describe, however, in other words, deontologized, Jung's archetypes can be useful.

A PARADIGM FOR UNDERSTANDING: SOCIOLOGY OF KNOWLEDGE

The sociology of knowledge is a subfield of sociology that emphasizes the role of institutions (religious, psychological, scientific and others) in molding human behavior and emotions. It also stresses the enormous human need for the ordering principles that institutions provide and the seemingly exorbitant price paid by individuals who defy established boundaries. Although human beings have created these institutions, the institutions have acquired an objective character, hiding the fact that they were created by humans in the first place. People collude with these structures because of the suffering they would incur if they did not and also, more importantly, because the very structures of consciousness itself come to be isomorphic with the social structures. By a similar process, one which Jung seems to have overlooked, the archetypal images of the collective unconscious and social structures, institutions, and roles also become congruent with one another.

In *The Social Construction of Reality,* written with Thomas Luckmann, and *The Sacred Canopy,*[2] Peter Berger has elaborated his sociology of knowledge as it applies to the individual in society. In *The Sacred Canopy,* a sociological study of religion, Berger concentrates on the interaction between a human being and society and on the role of religion in ensuring that society's mandates gain the necessary, sacred legitimation that will ensure their enforcement. Berger emphasizes that a society is nothing but a human product, and yet this product attains an objective status which allows it to "continuously act back upon its producer."[3] While it is obvious that society is a human product, it is perhaps not so obvious that each human being is also a product of society, and not merely in a simple and benign sense; for society is not only an objective reality but also a coercive force in the lives of individuals. Although human beings are entirely responsible for creating institutions, they come to perceive institutions as something that can act over and against them. Their role in the creation of these institutions becomes entirely lost to them and their relationship to institutions is thus characterized by alienation and even self-deception. The socialization process occurs in three phases—externalization, objectivation, and internalization:

> Externalization is the ongoing outpouring of human being into the world, both in the physical and the mental activity of men. Objectivation is the attainment by the products of this activity (again both physical and mental) of a reality that confronts its original producers as a facticity external to and other than themselves. Internalization is the reappropriation by men of this same reality, transforming it once again from structures of the objective world into structures of the subjective consciousness.[4]

Externalization, the first phase, takes place almost on the level of instinct. It is an "anthropological necessity." Human beings, by definition, must pour themselves and their activities into the world and, by so doing, create the world. This necessity springs from the unfinished character of human beings and the "relatively unspecialized character of our instinctual structure."[5]

Objectivation, the second phase, refers to the process by which the human outpouring of activity in the world attains an objective character so that human products come to confront human beings over and against themselves. These products then seem to have what Berger calls a "facticity" outside of the factor of human agency. "The humanly produced world becomes something 'out there.' It consists of objects, both material and non-material, that are capable of resisting the desires of their producer."[6]

The third phase, internalization, is the process whereby human beings come to be determined by society. Internalization refers to the "reabsorption into consciousness of the objectivated world" so that the structures of the world and the structures of consciousness are isomorphic. In other words, society produces people with structures of thought that coincide with the social institutions people created in the first place. "Internalization, then, implies that the objective facticity of the social world becomes a subjective facticity as well."[7]

Berger uses the metaphor of a conversation to explain the socialization process. He says that socialization is an ongoing conversation between significant others and the individual. World-maintenance, Berger points out, is a precarious affair and depends on this ongoing conversation with other people who live within the social structures and institutions and take them for granted, thereby giving them legitimacy. If this conversation is disrupted, the world begins to lose its "subjective plausibility." "In other words, the subjective reality of the world hangs on the thin thread of conversation."[8] The reason we do not recognize either the necessity of maintaining the conversation or the precariousness of the socially created world is that most of the time the conversation goes on undisrupted and unnoticed. The maintenance of this continuity is one of the most important imperatives of social order: "The socially constructed world is, above all, an ordering of experience. A meaningful order, or nomos, is imposed upon the discrete experiences and meanings of individuals."[9]

For Berger, two of the strongest structurers of human experience are language and religion. Religion is the "sacred canopy" which lends sacred status to socially constructed reality. Language is a strong reinforcer of social reality because it bestows an objective and apparently permanent status on humanly produced institutions, making them resistant to change. Descriptive language becomes prescriptive and helps to ward off change, thus maintaining and protecting our fragile social existence. Drawing heavily on Alfred Schutz's view that language is rooted in everyday life, Berger situates language within the stage of objectivation since it has the qualities of objectivity and coerciveness. Language tells us what is and religious language tells us what is in the realm of the sacred or the inviolable:

> All legitimation maintains socially defined reality. Religion legitimates so effectively because it relates the precarious reality constructions of empirical societies with ultimate reality. . . .
> Religion legitimates social institutions by bestowing upon them an ultimately valid ontological status, that is, by locating them within a sacred and cosmic frame of reference.[10]

As we will see later, the mythological language used by Jung and Jungians locates the archetypes within a sacred and cosmic frame of reference. Furthermore, since the language of Jung's psychology contains both scientific propositions and religious overtones, it fits well within Berger's framework.

Jung and the Jungians seem to think that by seeing irrational modes of behavior as being "possessed" by an archetype, or by viewing social role definitions as archetypes of the feminine, that is, by "seeing archetypally," they have freed people from the power of stereotypes. As feminists we claim that precisely the opposite effect occurs.[11] Using Berger's paradigm, we see that the third phase, internalization, is the phase at which the problem is no longer recognizable by us, the phase at which we are almost self-deceived, or alienated. When religious or scientific language names the world, it bestows an objective and sacred validity and fits Berger's second phase, objectivation. Such language is the tool of the most powerful legitimating process: the creation of a symbolic universe which gives us a matrix of meaning.

Seeing certain modes of behavior and role definitions as symbolic is especially dangerous when archetypal images of the collective unconscious serve to legitimate and perpetuate painful experiences in the world. Consider the prostitute, for example. Were such a woman to consult a Jungian analyst, the analyst's goal would be to free her from an identification with this archetypal image. But there is danger in archetypalizing her experience in the first place. It is not far-fetched within the Jungian framework to describe her experience as a living-out of the archetype of the fallen woman, a form of the Hetaira archetype, and thus lend her socially created role a kind of sacred status:

> Being given over to the concern with individual feeling, with its everchanging fluctuations, this type of woman may find it difficult to commit herself to any permanence in outer relationships. Indeed she may, like her male counterpart, the *puer aeternus*, shy away from any concrete commitment and forever lead a provisory life of emotional wandering. The mythological images which express this type are the love deities, hierodules and priestesses dedicated to the service of love; the seductresses, nymphs, beautiful witches and harlots also express its unadapted aspect.[12]

Surely there is a problem with a psychology that identifies certain ways of being in the world as archetypal and then makes no real distinction between types of archetypal experiences. If an experience is "numinous," it is archetypal and in some way partakes of divinity. This elevation has the effect of cosmic endorsement. The Jungian framework, while it gives us a way to integrate unconscious and conscious contents, shows very little awareness of the social conditions that have created certain character types and offers no explicit criticism of traditional female and male roles.[13]

Another hazard in understanding certain experiences, psychic images, or behaviors as archetypal is that one thereby excludes the possibility of any real freedom from these compulsions. Jung said, in discussing the mana personality:

> It is indeed hard to see how one can escape the sovereign power of the primordial images. Actually I do not believe it can be escaped. One can only alter one's attitude and thus save oneself from naively falling into an archetype and being forced to act a part at the expense of one's humanity.[14]

II JUNG, JUNGIANS, AND DEFINITIONS OF THE ARCHETYPE

Jung's understanding of the archetype evolved during his lifetime and his conceptualization of it became clearer. His use of the term remained persistently ambiguous, however, because he failed to distinguish between "archetype" and "archetypal image." His lack of precision in using these two terms led to frequent attempts at clarification by his disciples and students. In the beginning, a certain fuzziness, as Jung formulated his concept, was perhaps natural. Also, Jung seemed to be motivated by a strong desire to be accepted by the scientific community. This may account for his use of medical language, equating archetypes with instincts. The instincts, he said, "form very close analogies to the archetypes, so close, in fact, that there is good reason for supposing that the archetypes are the unconscious images of the instincts themselves, in other words, that they are patterns of instinctual behavior."[15] While the biological model may have been useful in legitimizing Jung's theories, the analogy with instincts has not added clarity to the concept of the archetype, which continued to be associated with images.

When associating the archetype with motifs from literature, myth, and folklore, Jung arrives at a much clearer definition:

> The concept of the archetype . . . is derived from the repeated observation that, for instance, the myths and fairytales of world literature contain definite motifs which crop up everywhere. We meet these same motifs in the fantasies, dreams, deliria, and delusions of individuals living today. These typical images and associations are what I call archetypal ideas. . . . They impress, influence, and fascinate us. They have their origin in the archetype, which in itself is an irrepresentable, unconscious, pre-existent form that seems to be part of the inherited structure of the psyche and can therefore manifest itself spontaneously anywhere, at any time.[16]

This definition makes a distinction between archetype and archetypal image (idea), a distinction so crucial to Jung's thinking that it is unfortunate that he was not careful to speak of "archetypal images" every time he meant them, rather than lapse into the linguistically simpler "archetypes." Even if this distinction had been maintained, however, the concept of the archetype is still problematical in ways having to do with Jung's particular use of "numinosity"—a quality attributed to the experience of the archetype. As Jolande Jacobi explains in her study of the archetype, the archetype has a "dynamism which makes itself felt in the numinosity and fascinating power of the image."[17] In another book, Jacobi follows Jung in linking the archetype to the biological model, which she calls the "concern of scientific psychology." She distinguishes between the biological aspect of the archetype and the picture of the archetype when viewed from the inside, where its most important aspect is its numinosity, "that is, it appears as an experience of fundamental importance."[18]

III   ON NUMINOSITY: JUNG AND OTTO

Jung borrowed the concept of numinosity from Rudolf Otto's *The Idea of the Holy* (1923). There are some interesting implications of this borrowing. Otto's premise is that the rationalist conception of God lacks something essential, leading to a "wrong and one-sided interpretation of religion."[19] Otto thought that orthodox Christianity had failed to recognize the value in the non-rational and hence had kept that element out of its interpretation of God. His aim was to restore to the understanding of God the element of the non-rational. Thus Otto brings us to the category of the "holy" or "sacred." He calls the "holy" a category of interpretation and locates it squarely within the sphere of religion.

Otto suggests that there is something special about the "holy" which is "above and beyond the meaning of goodness." To describe this something, he uses a word, "numinosity," coined from the Latin "numen." Numinosity implies first of all, for Otto, creature-feeling. "It is the emotion of a creature, submerged and overwhelmed by its own nothingness in contrast to that which is supreme above all creatures."[20] The numinous is felt as objective and outside the self; it is the "Wholly Other." It also carries with it the feeling of *mysterium tremendum*. Otto is poetically eloquent in his description of this feeling, comparing it to the "sweeping of a gentle tide" or the bursting "in sudden eruption up from the depths of the soul with spasms and convulsions."[21]

The numinous also has an element of awefulness. Otto associates the kind of awefulness that accompanies the numinous not only with the perfectly familiar and "natural" emotion of fear but with a particular kind of fear. "Its antecedent stage is 'daemonic dread' . . . . It first begins to stir in the feeling of something uncanny, 'eerie' or 'weird.' "[22] This fear of the *mysterium tremendum* is accompanied by shuddering, which "is something more than 'natural,' ordinary fear. It implies that the mysterious is already beginning to loom before the mind."[23] The numinous, too, is characterized by *majestas*, which means "might, power, absolute overpoweringness." Otto connects the qualities of creature-feeling, awefulness, dread, a sense of the weird or uncanny, and the element of overpoweringness with mysticism and its annihilation of the self and understanding of the transcendent as the whole and entire reality: "One of the chiefest and most general features of mysticism is just this *self-depreciation* . . . and the estimation of the self, of the personal 'I', as something not perfectly or essentially real."[24]

The numinous contains an element of energy or urgency: "It [the numinous object] everywhere clothes itself in symbolical expressions—vitality, passion, emotional temper, will, force, movement, excitement, activity, impetus."[25] The numinous also has the power to fascinate:

> The daemonic-divine object may appear to the mind an object of horror and dread, but at the same time it is no less something that allures with a potent charm, and the creature who trembles before it, utterly cowed and cast down, has always at the same time the impulse to turn to it, nay even to make it somehow his own. The 'mystery' is for him not merely something to be wondered at but something that entrances him. . . . he feels a something that captivates and transports him with a strange ravishment.[26]

Throughout his descriptions of the numinous, Otto is talking about the experience of God. Jung applies the notion of numinosity to the experience of archetypal images residing in the collective unconscious, but his use of the term remains very close to

Otto's. In carrying over a concept that pertains to the experience of the Divine and applying it to human (psychological, mythological, imaginal, fanciful, and social) interaction, is Jung divinizing the human psyche, or at least part of it, the unconscious? His use of the word "numinous" to apply to an experience of the archetype is congruent with Otto's description of an experience of the "holy," a category of interpretation and valuation peculiar to the sphere of religion.[27]

Jung is careful in some of his statements to separate the psychological and theological dimensions of inquiry, claiming that theologians are the only ones who can legitimately speculate about Reality or the Beyond. He states that as a psychologist he can only speak of human psychological experience and claims only to have demonstrated that a God archetype exists in the human psyche. In his theoretical explanation of the concept of God, however, he comes close to collapsing the distinction between the psychological and theological realms. In the following passage Jung gives religious legitimation to irrational behavior such as "an inexplicable mood, a nervous disorder, or an uncontrollable vice" by equating "autonomous psychic contents" with what has previously been labeled in our culture as divine, or even daemonic.

> When, therefore, we make use of the concept of a God we are simply formulating a definite psychological fact, namely the independence and sovereignty of certain psychic contents which express themselves by their power to thwart our will, to obsess our consciousness and to influence our moods and actions. We may be outraged at the idea of an inexplicable mood, a nervous disorder, or an uncontrollable vice being, so to speak, a manifestation of God. But it would be an irreparable loss for religious experience if such things, perhaps even evil things, were artificially segregated from the sum of autonomous psychic contents. . . . If we leave the idea of "divinity" quite out of account and speak only of "autonomous contents," we maintain a position that is intellectually and empirically correct, but we silence a note which, psychologically, should not be missing. By using the concept of a divine being we give apt expression to the peculiar way in which we experience the workings of these autonomous contents. We could also use the term "daemonic," provided that this does not imply that we are still holding up our sleeves some concretized God who conforms exact-

ly to our wishes and ideas. . . . by affixing the attribute "divine" to the workings of autonomous contents, we are admitting their relatively superior force.[28]

In the following passage Jung goes even further in conflating psychology and theology:

> It is only through the psyche that we can establish that God acts upon us, but we are unable to distinguish whether these actions emanate from God or the unconscious. We cannot tell whether God and the unconscious are two different entities. Both are border-line concepts for transcendental contents.[29]

The admission by Jung of a possible fusion, or at least a possible confusion, of God and the unconscious is crucial for our understanding of how the collective unconscious can serve to legitimate socially constructed roles for women.

On the negative side: the quarrel I have with Jung is with his willingness to consider archetypal phenomena as manifestations of the Divine and with his assertion that we lose something valuable psychologically if we do not see them as such.[30] While a plunge into Jung's theology is outside the scope of this essay, it is enough here to note that Jung's theory confers religious and ontological status on behaviors, moods, and even uncontrollable vices, which can be explained on other grounds. These grounds do not involve us in categories of the sacred as we try to understand ourselves and others, to change our behavior, and to become free from stultifying roles and compulsions.

On the positive side: although the theological underpinnings of Jung's psychology are fundamentally flawed in this way, and although he mixes the levels of psychology, ontology and theology to a confusing degree, his *method* of differentiating oneself from unconscious contents has much to recommend it. It gives us a greater awareness of the unconscious pulls operating on us—greater self awareness in other words—and a measure of freedom from those irrationalities. The consequent absence of moralistic condemnation as a response to the evil in ourselves is also valuable, and indeed, is the first step toward self-acceptance and transformation.

Jung's perception of the numinosity of certain moods and the irresistible pull of certain psychic responses is convincing. There is no doubt that our inner world often contains powerful compulsions and Jung describes very well the inner experiences, fantasies, moods, compulsions, pulls, that beset us in our daily lives. Nor is there any doubt that we experience these things as autonomous, coming from somewhere other than our own conscious will. In fact, our own conscious will alone is insufficient to free us from them. The process which Jung called individuation (both the goal and the natural outcome of life) is one in which we become more truly ourselves. It demands that we increasingly differentiate our conscious selves from a sort of murky identification with unconscious contents. In other words, we become more aware of moments when inner voices, archetypal images, or complexes, are pulling on us and we learn not to identify with them. We can also engage with them, as personifications (shadow, animus and anima) and gain the benefit of their perspectives. As individuation proceeds, we become increasingly free of such compulsions, since we perceive them as autonomous, collective, and impersonal. Archetypes, used in the sense of a compulsion, mood, or psychic pull, are part of a vast sea of mental influences, from which the process of individuation gives us at least some measure of freedom. That element of Jung's description is part of the genius of his psychology.

IV   ANIMUS AND ANIMA

Our understanding of archetypes can illuminate the way women's and men's psyches both reflect and conflict with images of women and men given to us by a patriarchal society. In particular, the experience of "being possessed by an archetype" (acting out of an unconscious identification with an archetypal image, so that a man acts like the anima and a woman acts like the animus— both of which are inferior "feminine" and "masculine" ways of acting), when viewed in cultural context, exposes the human tendency to internalize imprisoning and oppressive images. But understood ontologically, as archetypes often are, Jung's concept has the capacity to imprison us further. Because of his gift for grasping fantasy and dream images, Jung offers a more imaginal description than Freud does of the inner world of women and men bound by a patriarchal culture. Women caught in seemingly isolated individual struggles are acting out the culture-wide struggle of all women to realize their full humanity (one that includes, for example, a strong intellect) in a society which devalues them and offers no complete vision of their possibilities of empowerment.

The anima and the animus are two especially powerful archetypes. Both Emma and Carl Jung used the terms anima and animus to indicate the unconscious contra-sexual element (the anima being the feminine component of the male psyche and the animus the masculine component of the female psyche) in the male and female personalities. These are lopsided concepts given that the cultural positions of men and women differ, with men generally having and women generally lacking, power and respect. This inequality is not discussed by the Jungs, although Emma Jung comes close to recognizing it. Jung summarizes the distinction between anima and animus as follows:

> If I were to attempt to put in a nutshell the difference between man and woman in this respect, i.e., what it is that characterizes the animus as opposed to the anima, I could only say this: as the anima produces *moods*, so the animus produces *opinions*.[31]

Emma Jung's version of the animus was clearer and less pejorative than C.C. Jung's. She describes the animus in terms more likely to resonate with women's inner experience. For example, with respect to the way in which the animus functions within the female psyche, Emma Jung says:

> The most characteristic manifestation of the animus is not in a configured image (Gestalt) but rather in words (logos also means word). It comes to us as a voice commenting on every situation in which we find ourselves. . . . As far as I have observed, this voice expresses itself chiefly in two ways. First, we hear from it a critical, usually negative comment on every movement, an exact examination of all motives and intentions, which naturally always causes feelings of inferiority, and tends to nip in the bud all initiative and every wish for self-expression. From time to time, this same voice may also dispense exaggerated praise, and the result of these extremes of judgment is that one oscillates to and fro between the consciousness of complete futility and a blown-up sense of one's own value and importance.[32]

Had Emma Jung gone one step further in her analysis, she would have realized that the animus can emerge as harsh self-criticism in a male voice and that this internal, critical voice is an accurate reflection of the culture's derogatory view of women's motives, intentions, and self-expressions.[33] Since, from a Jungian standpoint the psyche operates by compensation, the animus's exaggerated praise is the opposite of devaluation. The woman's inner evaluation of herself swings back and forth between these two extremes. But this phenomenon, too, reflects the polarized images of women that our society offers. As many scholars have noted, images of women presented by modern media, as well as in fairy tales, myths and religious stories, tend to be extreme rather than balanced, fragmented rather than holistic.[34]

Emma Jung describes another facet of the animus:

> And now we come to the magic of words. A word, also, just like an idea, a thought, has the effect of reality upon undifferentiated minds. Our Biblical myth of creation, for instance, where the world grows out of the spoken word of the Creator, is an expression of this. The animus, too, possesses the magic power of words, and therefore men who have the gift of oratory can exert a compulsive power on women in both a good and an evil sense. Am I going too far when I say that the magic of the word, the art of speaking, is the thing in a man through which a woman is most unfailingly caught and most frequently deluded?[35]

Again, without a sense of the social dimension, Emma Jung did not realize that women are spellbound by the power of the word precisely because that is the power which has been denied them. An awareness of this double bind is essential if women are to be liberated from their sense of powerlessness. Mary Daly's description of the problem is characteristic of the large body of feminist theory about women and the power of the word.

> Women have had the power of *naming* stolen from us. We have not been free to use our own power to name ourselves, the world, or God. The old naming was not the product of dialogue—a fact inadvertently admitted in the Genesis story of Adam's naming the animals and the woman. . . . To exist humanly is to name the self, the world, and God. The "method" of the evolving spiritual consciousness of women is nothing less than this beginning to speak humanly—a reclaiming of the right to name. The liberation of language is rooted in the liberation of ourselves.[36]

A positive contribution of Jung's concept of the anima is that it offers us a unique view of the inner world of the male who struggles to accept a side of himself which is devalued by society. It is interesting that no devaluation of the man by his anima like that of the woman by her animus is presented. Rather, the anima in men appears to work primarily by seduction (again, a replication of the way in which society has encouraged women to behave). This seduction takes many forms—bewitchment, frozen feelings, dangerous fascination—but it is seduction nevertheless, and not devaluation. There are many examples of the anima's gentle art of seduction in Emma Jung's article on the animus and anima. Here is one:

But swan maidens and nixies are not the only forms in which elemental feminine nature shows itself. Melusine is scolded by her husband for being a "serpent," and this figure, too, can embody the primal feminine. It represents a more primitive and chthonic femininity than the fish does, for example, and certainly more than the bird, while at the same time cleverness, even wisdom, is ascribed to it. Moreover, the serpent is also dangerous. Its bite is poisonous and its embrace suffocating, yet everyone knows that despite this dangerousness the effect that it exerts is fascinating.[37]

While Emma Jung's treatment of the anima and animus archetypes may be offensive to some feminists because it starts from an assumption of differing feminine and masculine natures, it is internally consistent and speaks of the necessity of integrating the other side of one's nature. Unlike female followers of Jung such as Toni Wolff and Ann Ulanov, Emma Jung does not make the mistake her husband does of identifying real women with the anima.[38]

Carol Christ has astutely observed that "the strength of [Jung's] theory lies in its insight into the psyches and psychic tasks of educated (and culture-creating) white males in Western culture."[39] Christ feels that Jung's eros/logos model does seem to account for white males' underdeveloped eros function and highly developed intellect, and suggests that the model be kept as a "useful tool for analyzing white males and the culture they have created."[40] I agree with Christ here, and I also think that the archetypal model of the psyche has some value for understanding women as well as men if the model is seen in relationship to society and its values, in other words, if it is contextualized and hence deontologized.

Jung and the Jungians omit from their descriptions of the animus and anima three crucial elements: the ubiquitous nature of patriarchy, the equally ubiquitous and persistent problem of misogyny, and the dialectic relationship between the individual and society.[41] If these three phenomena are explained and incorporated in the Jungian system, we discover a useful description of our culture as it is *experienced inwardly*, and as it is reflected by the psyche in dreams, fantasies, and moods.

Jung not only ontologizes a socially constructed reality, his emphasis on religion, religious experience, and the numinosity of the archetypes gives divine sanction to psychological experiences that are culturally-based. These psychological experiences, or images, need to have the divine sanction removed from them.

Naomi Goldenberg has suggested that the Jungian concept of the archetype as an absolute must be discarded or revised.[42] Nonetheless, she thinks that there is much of worth in the Jungian schema, particularly Jung's understanding of the symbolic reality of religion and of the religious value of inner experience. Goldenberg is helpful in directing our criticism to the concept of the archetype, the central Jungian concept. Without it the Jungian system loses its very foundation.

Feminist readers have asked, "Why retain the Jungian model at all?" "Why bother about its 'uniqueness' if the theory is corrupt?" Part of the answer is that Jung's psychology does give us a workable view of the unconscious. Jung's understanding of the unconscious is positive and creative in many respects. That this concept has been used, like many others, to reinforce existing stereotypes about women does not warrant throwing out an idea which gives the study of soul some of its soulful dimension. Our understanding of what the unconscious is can be rescued from the notion that it is a stagnant, static eternal entity. Furthermore, the volumes and volumes of work Jung did on the collective unconscious do illustrate the ways in which it mirrors the culture. Assimilation and integration of archetypal images can be understood as an experience of wrestling with the demons of a sexist culture. Gender-linked archetypes can be seen as inner representatives of socially sanctioned, seductive but oppressive roles and behavior patterns.

V   THE ANIMA AND THE FEMININE:
TWO ARCHETYPAL IMAGES ILLUSTRATED

The socially constructed nature of the archetype as it affects women is best illustrated by comparing the concepts of the anima and the feminine. The anima is a component of male psychology, and the feminine a component of female psychology. Although both terms seem to refer in some way to women, "anima" is not synonymous with "the feminine." The anima is the soul-image of men's imaginations which they often project onto real women. Men must disentangle themselves from the anima in order to be able to relate to real women and to allow real women the space to be themselves. The feminine, on the other hand, is a way of perceiving and being in the world as lived out by women. The latter is a social role definition, although it becomes archetypal in Jungian thought. This essential distinction between the anima and the feminine is not always made by Jungians.[43]

Men's experience of the quality of their own souls, according to Jung, is primarily a "feminine" experience; that is, it has an emotional quality that reminds them of what they think women are like. Jung intends to make it clear that the anima is a part of male psychology. This "soul-imago" is composed of three elements. The first is the experience of real, adult women whom the particular man has known; this experience is registered as an "imprint" on his psyche. The second is the man's own femininity, usually repressed; the more repressed his own femininity, the more traditionally feminine his soul-image will be and the more likely it is that the women he is attracted to will carry that projection. ("Carrying the projection," in Jungian terminology, means being the one on whom the image is projected.) The third is an *a priori* category, an archetype, an inherited collective image of women.[44]

Though Jung placed the anima in the male psyche, he frequently mixed a discussion of the anima with a discussion of the psychology of women:

> Woman, with her very dissimilar psychology, is and always has been a source of information about things for which a man has no eyes. She can be his inspiration; her intuitive capacity, often superior to man's, can give him timely warning, and her feeling, always

directed towards the personal, can show him ways which his own less personally accented feeling would never have discovered.[45]

This quotation is taken from the chapter "Anima and Animus" (*CW* VII) in which Jung attempts to explain the way the feminine soul-imago is formed upon the male's experience of real women. Jung fails to acknowledge, however, that what he has written is *his* experience of women, a reflection of *his* anima, and, no doubt, that of many men. While attempting only to describe the anima in men, he has attributed all of its characteristics to "woman."

A similar mixing of levels arises when Jung explains man's own repressed femininity:

It seems to me, therefore, that apart from the influence of women there is also the man's own femininity to explain the feminine nature of the soul-complex. There is no question here of any linguistic "accident," of the kind that makes the sun feminine in German and masculine in other languages. We have, in this matter, the testimony of art from all ages, and besides that the famous question: *habet mulier animam?* [Does woman have a soul?] Most men, probably, who have any psychological insight at all, will know what Rider Haggard means by "she-who-must-be-obeyed," and will also recognize the chord that is struck when they read Benoit's description of Aninea. Moreover they know at once the kind of woman who most readily embodies this mysterious factor of which they have so vivid a premonition.[46]

This last sentence again illustrates Jung's confusion of the anima and all women. In discussing "man's own femininity" he has lapsed into talking about actual women. No wonder later readers have had such a hard time deciphering the meaning of the anima. Jung himself alludes to the difficulty of the concept: "I do not expect every reader to grasp right away what is meant by animus and anima."[47]

With respect to the third component of the anima, the *a priori*, or inherited, collective images of women, Jung does not slip into a discussion of real women, but keeps to the issue at hand:

As we know, there is no human experience, nor would experience be possible at all, without the intervention of a subjective aptitude. What is this subjective aptitude? Ultimately it consists in an innate psychic structure which allows man to have experiences of this kind. Thus the whole nature of man presupposes woman, both physically and spiritually. . . . The form of the world into which he is born is already inborn in him as a virtual image. Likewise parents, wife, children, birth, and death are inborn in him as virtual images, as psychic aptitudes. These *a priori* categories have by nature a collective character; they are images of parents, wife and children in general, and are not individual predestinations. We must therefore think of these images as lacking in solid content, hence as unconscious.[48]

While Jung in this passage does not equate women with male projections onto them, he does take an androcentric perspective. Female psychology, while mentioned frequently in his writings, always has a clearly derivative character.

Another Jungian, Marie Louise von Franz, in *The Feminine in Fairytales*, provides an example of the way Jungians have confronted and rationalized inconsistencies in Jung's theory such as the ones noted above. Unlike Jung, von Franz seems at least to recognize the mixing of levels as she describes the feminine in fairytales:

The authors of these religious writings are men known to us. Under such circumstances, we can say that the figure of Sophia represents certain aspects of the man's anima. At other times, however, we could just as well say that the figures represent feminine psychology. The whole problem becomes in one way more, in another less, complicated if we try to concentrate on how the psychology of the feminine and the psychology of the anima are intertwined. . . . Thus some women give in entirely to the anima projection. . . . If he only likes her as an anima figure, she is forced to play the role of the anima. This inter-reaction can be positive or negative, but the woman is very much affected by the man's anima figure, which brings us to a very primitive and simple and collective level where we cannot separate the features of anima and real women. Frequently they are mixed to some extent and react upon each other.[49]

Von Franz's description has the advantage of clarity on one level—she is undoubtedly correct about the effect of male projections on female behavior and attitudes—but this passage shows the same androcentric bias found in Jung's writings. Neither does it account for the social element in this interplay. There do not seem to be any accounts of the man's character being shaped and formed by women's animus projections, other than the descriptions of the man who has been plunged into an anima mood because of conversing with a woman's animus.

Like Emma Jung in *Animus and Anima,* von Franz failed to realize that men's projections shape female character and behavior to the great extent they do because women are relatively powerless in society. As Jean Baker Miller shows in *Toward a New Psychology of Women,* dominants have very different psychological characteristics from subordinates, and subordinates absorb much of the dominants' viewpoint because it is the norm. "Tragic confusion arises because subordinates absorb a large part of the untruths created by the dominants."[50]

Much about "women's nature" has crept into what is reputedly a discussion of a component of male psychology, the anima. This mixing means not only that readers must make a continual effort to clarify Jung's ideas, but also that the usefulness of the anima as a concept is seriously undermined. Disparaging comments about women can be found throughout Jung's writing and feminists who examine Jung's theory of the anima in its present state will reject all Jungian statements about female psychology.

If we consider Jung's concept of the anima in light of Otto's description of the numinous, we see that the effect of the numinous is remarkably similar to the feeling of being gripped by an archetypal image. The element of fear, whether it takes the form of dread, awe, horror, or fascination, is important in both. The experience of the anima in men seems to contain all of these elements, and parallels men's attitudes toward women in our culture and toward the feminine element in themselves. In our society men are often alienated from their own emotions and from relationships generally.[51] In this condition, they do indeed project onto women both exalted and debased images of the kind Jung describes and then are captivated by these projections.

The crucial element in these descriptions is fear. Fear (awe, dread, horror, bewitched fascination) must surely be the basis of misogyny and misogynistic projections such as the devouring mother. Fear functions in the psyche as an agent of distortion, preventing one from truly seeing the other, as of course, Jungians know. Yet their descriptions of the anima contain these very distortions of women's nature. The concept of the anima can still be useful, however, if it is recognized for what it is: a picture of romantic alienation in men, or, to put it another way, a psychological response arising from men's ambivalence toward women, which is a form of fear.[52]

The archetypes of the feminine were first elaborated by Toni Wolff, a member of Jung's inner circle. Drawing on Jung's own description of feminine archetypes, Wolff names and describes them: the Mother, the Hetaira, the Amazon, and the Medium. For Wolff, these four archetypal images represent the major ways in which women experience the world. Ann Ulanov explains this tetralogy in *The Feminine in Jungian Psychology and Christian Theology*:

> These fundamental archetypal forms of the feminine are described in the myths and legends of all cultures throughout history, as for example in the recurrent tales of the princess, the maiden, the wise woman, the witch, etc. In our everyday speech, when we describe women we know or know about, we often resort to typing them, unconsciously using archetypal imagery. Common examples are the references to a woman as "a witch," "a man-eater," and so forth. The archetypal forms of the feminine describe certain basic ways of channeling one's feminine instincts and one's orientation to cultural factors. They also indicate the type of woman one is or the type of anima personality a man is likely to develop.[53]

Notice that in this passage certain social categories are unquestionably accepted as categories of Being. The feminine, a social role definition and a way of relating to the world, has acquired ontological status. Moreover, archetypes of the feminine, with their aura of the numinous, have entered the dimension of religious experience.[54] They have become part of the meaningful order, or nomos, that is "imposed upon the discrete experiences and meanings of individuals. . . ." "It may now be understandable if the proposition is made that the socially constructed world is, above all, an ordering of experience."[55] Role definitions and behavior as well as neurotic character types have become legitimated by their relationship to the sacred.

According to Berger's framework, it is impossible for human beings to live without a nomos, or an ordering principle in their lives. Society is just such a giver of order, and it follows that socially defined roles which order and legitimate our lives in the social realm also partake of the character of the nomos. Berger's dialectic shows that an individual becomes that which she or he is addressed as being by others. On the other side of the dialectic of identity formation and society lies "anomy," a word Berger took from Durkheim's "anomie" but spelled in the Anglo-American manner. "Anomy" means "loss of order." At its most extreme, anomy leads to disintegration, fragmentation, and chaos; on an individual level this can mean mental illness, suicide, or extreme anguish. These are the consequences, Berger believes, of trying to live outside of the social order (nomos). To criticize, doubt, or otherwise threaten the identity-creating conversation with others is to risk anomy, but anomy must be risked if social change is to be effected and the truth about our institutions be known.

The concept of the archetype protects and shields us from the terror of anomy. This concept gives order to our experience, giving archetypal experience the blessing of the gods. Yet a confrontation with nothingness, Mary Daly tells us, is essential if women are to become authentic: "This becoming who we really are requires existential courage to confront the experience of nothingness."[56] Speaking of a space set apart from the prevailing "nomos": "it is important to note that this space is found not in the effort to hide from the abyss but in the effort to face it, as patriarchy's prefabricated set of meanings, or *nomos*, crumbles in one's mind. Thus (this space) is not 'set apart' from reality, but from the contrived nonreality of alienation."[57] Many societies punish members who dare to live outside the prescribed roles. However, the confrontation of anomy is the first step in creating not only an authentic self but a new social order.

A possible way of confronting the experience of nothingness is to attempt to live outside nomic structures which legitimate damaging or limiting social roles and identity concepts. The experience of nothingness to which Mary Daly refers must surely be the consequence of stepping outside the parameters of the ongoing conversation. In spite of the risk of anomy, feminists must dare to step outside of the nomizing conversation. On the other hand, all of the works cited, as well as Jung's, understand the inherent human need for order. Feminists, being human, do not escape this need.

What, then, is a possible solution? Goldenberg suggests the breaking down of mental hierarchies; Daly proposes the radical bond-breaking bonding between women; Miller stresses the need for the courage to embrace conflict with men, with other women, and with outworn self-images whose fraudulent hold on our psyches nonetheless exerts a formidable grip. All of these are sign-posts. None of these is a total solution. We do not and cannot know the full direction in which we are moving, as we continue to see through and reject nomic solutions with sexist implications.

From the point of view taken in this essay, Jung's and Jungians' explanations of archetypes of the feminine and of the anima are descriptively, and also prescriptively, limiting images of women in a patriarchal society. There *is* room, however, within the theory for a creative working-through of one's relationship to certain archetypal images. This working-through must be done with awareness of the patriarchal imprint which the archetypal images bear.[58] Jung's and the Jungians' explanations of archetypes of the feminine and the anima, therefore, are not useful to women unless deontologized and they may be dangerous as originally conceived and presented.

Archetypal images are really considered by Jung to be the stuff of which revelation is made. They also constitute the symbolic language of the unconscious. Jung is concerned with our increasing symbolic impoverishment and the consequences of this for human life and relationships; many feminists share this concern. The problem, then, lies in the divine status which is given in Jungian theory to certain symbolic expressions.

I see gender-linked archetypal images as inner compulsions, psychic pulls, to be part of a collective view of women and men. My evaluation of Jung's concept of the gender-linked archetypes finally rests on two bases: one negative and one positive. On the negative side, it carries the potential for lending sacred legitimation and ontological status inappropriately to neurotic behaviors. The ontological-theological language about archetypes paradoxically serves to reinforce existing stereotypes about women and men rather than freeing us from them. Seen ontologically, the concept is stultifying and romantically compelling; it tends to make social change difficult. On the positive side, the method of differentiation is useful and the concept of the collective unconscious with its archetypal images is ingenious, original, and unusually effective in describing people's inner states. When it is deontologized and seen as a reflection of cultural taboos and fears, the concept of gender-linked archetypes is a very helpful one. As a way of understanding the manner in which our psyches wrestle with socially constructed images of women and men, it is liberating.

iii Visual Images by Women: A Test Case for the Theory of Archetypes

ESTELLA LAUTER

Do the archetypal images Jung described as characteristic of female development appear in works of visual art by women? If so, do they take the form Jung's theory leads us to expect? Do other images or patterns not accounted for in Jung's theory occur? Is the concept of the archetype compatible with feminist thought regarding female development? These are questions that should concern every student of female psychology, for until we have a theory that encompasses the images that women themselves have created, we have an impoverished theory. If the archetypes as Jungians have described them reflect the realities of female experience, they ought to turn up in visual art by women.

While this essay challenges widely accepted Jungian assumptions about women, it does accept the basic Jungian premise that works of art, like dreams, furnish material from the unconscious. One need only glance at the plates in *Man and His Symbols* to see how heavily Jung and his colleagues relied on both the fine and the popular arts for verification and communication of the theory of archetypes.[1] As far as I know, however, no previous effort has been made to assess the relationship between images created by professional women artists and existing theory regarding female development. Indeed, my project contradicts assumptions articulated by the two women who were closest to Jung, his wife Emma and his companion Toni Wolff. Both stated with conviction that the creativity of women is expressed primarily in the sphere of living, in relationships, in the spontaneous dreams, fantasies, and phases of everyday life, and among the arts, in drama, but *not* in the "objective" language of visual art. There, Wolff asserted, women merely imitate the prevailing style and "remain on the surface" or "within the personal sphere."[2] No doubt these ideas were reinforced by the culture's tendency to believe that an artist is something of a freak and a woman artist is doubly so; but such positions are no longer credible. The books and slides cited in my notes afford ample evidence of women's creativity in virtually every medium, and a recent issue of *ART news* even suggests that women have assumed the leadership in several fields.[3] Moreover, new biographical information reveals that women artists differ less from "ordinary women" than our biases would lead us to suppose.[4] The time has come to consider the substantial body of work created by women as seriously as we take the work of Greek, Renaissance, or Modernist masters.

I propose to answer the questions I have raised by interpreting representative examples of several hundred relevant works in the visual arts by women. Visual art, compared to other creative media, offers more direct access to women's images. Dreams are reported in ordinary language even in the most frank diary, and ordinary language carries with it centuries of cultural devaluation of women. In therapy, images and dreams may be represented in drawings, movement, or extraordinary uses of language, but they are filtered through the therapist before they become available to us; we would need to see video tapes of the actual sessions in order to have the same access to the images that the therapist does, and even then our access would be limited to what the machinery could record. Visual art bypasses words and offers a record that is accessible to anyone who can perceive aesthetically. Because the cost of reproduction prevents the inclusion of more than a handful of images here, I will restrict my discussion to images in books or in commercial slide collections that are likely to be available in public or university libraries, so that others may retrace my steps and compare my observations with their own.[5]

To be sure, the conventions of art operate as filters for both the artist and the viewer. Since such conventions are less binding in our own century than in any other, for the most part I have based my generalizations on the interpretation of twentieth-century works. It is also true that not every artist delves deeply enough into her own images to touch any level of the psyche that Jungians would call archetypal, and some styles of art prevent the viewer from knowing the artist's references. One cannot tell if the "hard edge" painter, for example, is concerned with a specific psychological subject. Most of the women I have studied, however, have been deeply self-reflective, and many have worked in styles that provide a wealth of psychological information. Archetypal images do turn up in the body of work I have studied, but not in the way we have been led to expect. Because Jungians have viewed masculine and feminine potentials as shared by men and women, though distributed in different proportions or with different emphases, they have assumed that the archetypes, apart from the animus and anima, are fully shared. Thus they have thought it appropriate to construct their ideas of "the feminine" primarily from male sources. Emma Jung even turned to male writers for examples of the animus.[6] Toni Wolff validated her description of the "structural forms of the feminine psyche" by claiming that they can be traced back in the male-authored history of culture and also that they "correspond to the aspects of male Anima."[7] If the differences uncovered here between the images created by women and Jungian descriptions of the archetypes that accompany human development turn out to be collective rather than merely individual, they will necessitate radical changes not only in the content of Jungian thought, but also in the mode of constructing archetypal theory.

To make a fair test of the theory of archetypes, I have chosen to interpret three categories of images. In the first part of my essay, I will examine an obvious pattern of images of the mother to see if the images fit the description of the archetype provided by Jungian theorists such as Erich Neumann and Toni Wolff. In the second part, I will describe the results of my search through visual art by women for evidence of the archetypal animus described primarily by Emma Jung. In the third, I will discuss by far the largest pattern of images to appear in five centuries of art by women: the independent woman, a potential archetype that is not adequately described by Jungian theory. On the basis of these explorations, I will suggest some directions that feminist archetypal theory might take to encompass images by women.

In order to prepare for this discussion, let us settle on a workable definition of the term "archetype." Demaris Wehr has suggested that the one from Jung's *Civilization in Transition* is the clearest because it distinguishes between archetype and archetypal images or ideas. It appears in the glossary of *Memories, Dreams and Reflections* in the following form:

The concept of the archetype . . . is derived from the repeated observation that, for instance, the myths and fairy tales of world literature contain definite motifs which crop up everywhere. We meet these same motifs in the fantasies, dreams, deleria and delusions of individuals living today. These typical images and associations are what I call archetypal ideas. The more vivid they are, the more they will be coloured by particularly strong feeling tones. . . . They impress, influence, and fascinate us. They have their origin in the archetype, which in itself is an irrepresentable unconscious, pre-existent form that seems to be part of the inherited structure of the psyche and can therefore manifest itself spontaneously anywhere, at any time. Because of its instinctual nature, the archetype underlies the feeling-toned complexes and shares their autonomy.[8]

If the definition is clear in its distinction between archetype and archetypal image, however, it is unfortunate in its implication that the "form" Jung had in mind was solid. Though he tried to correct this impression, most notably in *The Archetypes and the Collective Unconscious* (CW IX, part 1, par. 4), he never succeeded in finding the right words to convey his meaning.

A few useful qualifications can be salvaged. Jung seems to have had in mind something like the innate tendency to learn a language; just as the tendency does not predetermine the specific language to be learned, so the form of the archetype does not predetermine the specific content of the images. The archetype, we might say, is a tendency to form images in response to recurrent or widely shared experiences. It is meaningless to say that the archetype is "unchanging," as many have thought, because we know it only in its changing manifestations. If it is by nature "empty," or only "a possibility of representation," as Jung says, it is in no way binding.[9] Still, it is easy to see how the images produced over hundreds of years might be similar enough to *appear* relatively unchanging.

I suggest here that we continue to use the concept of the archetypal image to identify images with recurrent attraction and the concept of the archetype to refer to the tendency to form images, in relationship to patterns of development that are widespread and relatively constant through the centuries. There would then be many more archetypal images than archetypes, and the archetypal images would be our sole means of inferring the presence of archetypes. The reason for retaining the concept of the archetype at all is to accord recognition and dignity to certain widespread developmental tasks, and to confirm the connection between the imagination and the biological and psychological processes of development. The patterns that imply the existence of an archetype, then, are the ones that most deserve investigation in behavior studies and other kinds of psychological research. And archetypal images can be used to corroborate such research, or to test its validity. The search for archetypal images should present no problems for feminist theory as long as we regard the process as a virtually endless search for insight into human experience, which is constantly evolving while we are searching.

I   IMAGES OF THE MOTHER IN VISUAL ART BY WOMEN

What does it mean then, to approach a work of art archetypally? At bottom, it involves regarding each separate instance of an image as part of a larger pattern extending beyond the boundaries of art history, so that the context for interpreting the images becomes not only the artist's work, life, and society, but also other manifestations of the image. Even in cases where the pattern of images has been exhaustively described, however, the interpreter is never justified in ignoring the immediate context in which the particular image occurs; in one of Jung's most famous dicta, only the dreamer can interpret the dream.[10] Just as the analyst serves the dreamer by providing amplification of the image in a dream, the critic serves the perceiver of art by enlarging the context in which the art can be understood; neither can disregard the history of the image itself. The point must be stressed because Jungian thinking has the deserved reputation of being ahistorical. Its blindness to the social origins of gender differences is one of the reasons for this book. But the theory itself actually requires a degree of historicity.

Let us consider the implications of this historical conception of the archetype in relation to the image of the mother, which has been solidified, perhaps more than any other, by Erich Neumann's compelling treatment of it in *The Great Mother*.[11] The constellation of images he describes has at its core the idea of female relationship to the child and to the male. The specifically maternal aspect of the archetype involves bearing and/or caring for children, and is evaluated positively or negatively according to the mother's willingness to let the child achieve independence. But the "Great Mother" also contains the capacity to inspire or awaken another adult, who is always male in Neumann's description; in other words, it contains within it the archetype of the anima. Whereas in Neumann's view the mother encompasses the entire range of the feminine, in Toni Wolff's description it is only one of four possibilities of female development. In her schema the figures of the mother and the "hetaira," or eternal companion, appear in the sphere of intimate relationships, while the amazon and the medial woman appear in reference to the woman's possibilities in the impersonal social world.[12] Still, at the core of all Wolff's descriptions is the idea of relationship, the *sine qua non* of Jungian ideas of the feminine. The mother for Wolff, and for other Jungians, is the embodiment of an ideal of self-sacrificial caring for "all that in man [sic] is in the process of becoming."[13] Both of these theorists had clinical data at their disposal, although neither exposed much of it in the theoretical essays. Neither had much access to art or literature by women. The question of accuracy was resolved by reference to ancient sources, probably composed or transcribed by men.

Until recently their descriptions may have seemed apt because they correlated so well with the ideal mother who has dominated Christian art and religion. A quick perusal of Jean Guitton's *The Madonna*, which documents the image of Mary in painting and sculpture from the medieval period to the twentieth century, will make the point.[14] The positive mother figure, in the context of Western art at least, is scarcely aware of herself at all except insofar as she is a vehicle for bringing the child (and in the Christian story, the Word made flesh) into the world. Jean Guitton puts it this way, intending a high compliment: "Mary's face is the least imperfect figure of Thought, I mean of that Thought which acts through love."[15] But the mother's thought is mysterious to the viewer. Inevitably it is her body we focus upon, luxuriously wrapped in color except for her ideally rendered face, neck, shoulders, breasts, and hands—a body she seems to understand only as a vessel of love.

Without arguing for rigid differences in male and female points of view, I want to show the difference that female sources make in the contours of a theory by asking how the image of the mother looks to women who are themselves mothers, or who must consider their potential to become mothers, even if only to reject it. How is the ideal of female nurturance treated in works by women? To ask the question is to restore the image to a historical context that has been ignored. If we find that the poles, axes, and values of the image in this context are different from the ones Neumann and Wolff describe, we will at least need to redescribe the archetype.

Until the twentieth century most women artists were painters of religious subjects, portraits, still-life, and genre subjects. Within these categories, images of the Madonna, the Pietà, the royal matron or the "happy mother"—all positive in their presentation—are so numerous that they are impossible to tally. Not until the nineteenth century do we begin to see images by women that relate more to the painters' experiences or their observations of contemporary women than to the conventions of art.[16] Mary Cassatt (1844–1926) is perhaps the best known of these artists. Eleanor Munro calls her "the last serious artist in history, with the exception of Picasso and Henry Moore, to do homage to the life-preserving mother as the ground of being."[17] And Adelyn Dohme Breeskin says that her "incomparable renderings of the mother and child theme will probably always be considered her main contribution to the history of art."[18] From Breeskin's point of view, Cassatt's paintings, pastels, and prints are incomparable precisely because they differ from the more ideal renderings of the subject of the mother and child by her male and female predecessors: "Her mothers and children are wholly of the world, completely human, observed with penetrating awareness of reality and absolute honesty and directness."[19]

Without repeating herself over a twenty-year period (1880–1900), Cassatt explored the intimate accord of two human beings in closest relationship to each other. In *Mother About to Wash Her Sleepy Child* (1880) the mother has all the time she needs to accomplish her task without distressing the child, who might, without such gentle firmness, begin to struggle.[20] In *Baby's First Caress* (1891) the mother remains completely relaxed, her hand holding the baby's foot even as her body cradles his, while he awkwardly explores her face with his hand and eyes.[21] In *Baby Reaching for an Apple* (1893) the standing mother gently pulls the branch toward her baby's hand.[22] The intensity of the child's desire, rendered in his eyes and in his pose, and the degree of concentration in the mother's gaze, also fixed on the apple, give this painting mythic significance. The mother's role here, as elsewhere in Cassatt's work, is to foster independence. In a different view *Breakfast In Bed* (1897) shows Cassatt's capacity to consider the mother in a less authoritative role.[23] Here the child, seated upright beside her mother, is wide awake and ready to eat, while the mother's eyes are barely open and her arms encircling the child are nearly limp as she continues to doze.

In each of these cases the child is so secure in the mother's love that there is no question of rebellion; the mother is so absorbed in the child that there is no strain. Nor is there any excess of emotion or unjustified idealism in these works. They are, like Cassatt's portraits of her own mother, expressions of respect the artist felt for persons (often peasant women) who presided over the intimate spheres of life.[24]

By contrast, another younger and shorter-lived contemporary of Cassatt's, Paula Modersohn-Becker (1876–1907), painted an extraordinary set of works just before her own experience of motherhood. In those works, as Linda Nochlin says, Modersohn-Becker "transforms the mother into a being entirely transcending time or place, a dark anonymous goddess of nourishment, paradoxically animal like, bound to the earth and utterly remote from the contingencies of history or the social order."[25] In her vision epitomized in *Mother and Child* (c1903), the mother's authority derives not so much from her sensitivity to the nuances of other lives as from her oneness with nature.[26] Cassatt and Modersohn-Becker, for all their differences, however, both express a turn-of-the-century preoccupation with feminine power in its maternal form,[27] which no doubt also fired the imaginations of C.G. Jung and Erich Neumann. This preoccupation has continued, in the wake of anthropological and religious studies of the goddesses, and changed in works by women who are more free than were either Cassatt or Modersohn-Becker to explore the internal stresses of mothering in the modern world. Although I know of no serious artist since their time who has devoted herself exclusively to the image of the mother, in many cases an artist's exploration of this theme is among her most compelling works.

Niki de Saint Phalle's massive sculpture *hon/a cathedral* is a case in point, even though it was the result of collaborative work between de Saint Phalle (b1930) and two men, Jean Tingueley and Per Ultvedt.[28] *Hon* was exhibited in Stockholm from June to August 1966 and then destroyed, despite its impressive dimensions (82' x 20' x 30'), weight (6 tons), and sturdy construction (steel and papier-mâché). It was a statement about the impermanence of art, a pot shot at the art world's insistence on capturing art and holding it in the museums. This intention was shared among the three artists, but the image was de Saint Phalle's. For several years she had been making giant Nanas or Venuses—lighthearted sculptures of fat, voluptuous, black figures who were more icon than woman. The brilliantly painted figure *hon* was positioned on her back with legs spread and bent, her vaginal canal open to serve as the entrance for her visitors, the museum audience. The entire structure resembled a cathedral, the tiny head representing the apse. Visitors (worshippers?) found inside a goldfish pond in her womb, a bar near her breasts, and a planetarium with a lookout atop her belly. The experience of re-entering the mother's womb, taking nourishment, and partaking in her power was unmistakable. But this experience was undercut by the presence of an exhibit of forged art in one of the figure's legs, a bottle crusher near the bar, and a machine of bonelike parts that made scraping noises near her head. In fact, both sets of religious images, the maternal and the Christian, were forcefully qualified by the feats of technology contained within the sacred space. The event was at once a celebration of Neumann's Great Mother and a demonstration of how she is defiled in modern life. The image of the mother was positive in the sense that it became the ground against which technology was negatively evaluated. But her prone position and ridiculously small head called attention to the least pleasant aspects of the archetype—the mother's assumed passivity, her supposedly slight intelligence, her acceptance of all who enter her without regard for her own feelings.

According to the newsprint catalogue distributed at the exhibit, the work was intended to be critical of both the society that defiles the mother and the image itself.[29] The artists freed the participants to enter the mother's sacred space, to return, and to celebrate her presence without being overcome by her mythic power. They also merged the images of the good mother and the seductress in a way that Neumann didn't foresee, showing graphically how the desire to enter the woman is linked to the desire to return to the mother. Thus, *hon* effectively revealed the biases in our sexual arrangements at the same time that it acknowledged the importance of the image it perpetuated.

This doubleness of perspective is a feature of many women's works. Certainly it is one of Frida Kahlo's hallmarks. Kahlo (1907–1954) lived in Mexico all her life but felt the split between her father's German and her mother's Mexican ancestry. *My Nurse and I* (1937) is both a dramatization of this split and a striking manifestation of the archetypal mother.[30] Instead of showing her infant self at her own mother's breast, Kahlo shows a child's body with her own adult-sized head at the breast of a masked figure who represents mother Mexico. The child is rigid, while the nurse, apart from her face, is relaxed; the milk flows easily from her breasts. The artist has removed the skin from one of them to show the lacy structure of the ducts that provide the miraculous sustenance. The contradiction between the immobile mask and the flowing milk is repeated in the setting, where an oversized leaf is veined like the breast but dessicated, and the sky is full of drops of milk. Mask, leaf, breast, and the artist's face, registering her adult consciousness of the relationship, dominate the painting. The traditional image of the mother as nurturer is undeniably present, as is her association with mother country and a less familiar image of mother sky. But the nurse is prevented by her mask from conveying any but physical warmth, and the "child" is prevented by her consciousness from taking any but physical sustenance.

The image seems to record ritual care on the part of the mother and qualified acceptance on the part of the child. Literature by women is full of such impasses. I think that Kahlo's intent is not to criticize but to acknowledge painful realities of the mother-daughter relationship.[31] Our interpretation of the painting is complicated by the fact that the artist's own desire to nurture an infant was thwarted by a nearly fatal accident in her teens that made it impossible for her to carry a baby to term.[32] Her work casts the issues of mother-child relationships differently than either Neumann or Wolff do, in terms of the inevitable gap between two persons who must be separate from each other no matter how much they desire union. Perhaps this is the central meaning of the Demeter-Persephone story, obscured for so long by the business with Hades. The issue addressed in both is not the adequacy of nurturance or its continuation beyond its appropriate time, but a complex range of needs and desires of both parties that cannot be met in this relationship.

While Kahlo's painting may have come from her struggle to make a viable relationship with the "failed" mother in herself, the sculpture called *Mother with Twins* (1937) by Käthe Kollwitz (1867–1945) came from her effort to objectify the grieving mother within herself so as not to be overwhelmed by it.[33] In 1914 she lost her younger son in World War I. By 1937 she had expressed her grief in many woodcuts and sculptures, creating in the process a series of extraordinarily strong women. *Mother with Twins* is one of these. It shows a naked mother holding two children with her entire body, sheltering and enclosing them in her strong arms. Neumann's concern for the child who is restrained would be misplaced here, overriden by the mother's assertion of her will to protect, even though she may lack the power to do so. Such an assertion becomes cultural rather than merely personal in this work and two others, *Tower of Mothers* and *Seed Corn Must Be Ground*, from the same period. Perhaps for the first time in the Christian era, we see protectiveness from the point of view of the mother (or the artist who is fully sympathetic with the mother), whose vulnerability to the child's death makes her body strong. In Kollwitz's late works the body is not a vessel but an instrument of defense, whose inadequacy in the face of attack gives the works their special poignance. The paradox of strength in vulnerability is repeated in the physical presence of *Mother with Twins:* the massive image is embodied in a small (30-inch) format.

The mother may be stronger than Jungians have thought without being "terrible," and also more vulnerable, not just in her relationship to children whom she must lose one way or another, but in her own body, particularly in the so-called "mysteries" of menstruation, parturition, and lactation. Camille Billops (b1933), a black American who teaches at Rutgers University, gives us insight into such matters in her tiny (16½-inch-high) sculpture *Mother* (1971), a ceramic chair in the form of a woman's body.[34] The figure is coal black with white hands and a white saclike shape extending from under her black breasts to where her crotch would be if she had one, and a white tear shape at the front edge of the chair's seat, where her dress would end if it were kneelength. Both white shapes have black lines in them, as if to suggest puddles, and the womblike sac has red blotches in it. The head, with a hole instead of a face, is detached, suspended on a pole that rests on her shoulders and separated from the body by an empty space in place of her upper chest. From her jaw hang two small white fetishes. The feet are merely sculptural supports.

The piece is full of paradoxes: it is frightening in its suggestion of death, its stark contrasts, its emptiness. Yet it is inviting; it is a chair, maybe even a magic chair. But it is too small and, judging from the red blotches, too frail to hold us. The only possible relationship we can have with it is distant and unreciprocal. We may feel what we wish, but we cannot know what the mother feels. Yet our knowledge of her wound prevents our judging her as terrible; it allows us to respond to her from the inside, however forbidding or perplexing her exterior may be.

Perhaps the most striking externalization of maternal feeling is Audrey Flack's *Macerena Esperanza* (1971), a photo-realist painting of a seventeenth-century polychromed wood sculpture by Louisa Roldan.[35] The Macerena is the patron saint of Seville, and Flack (b1931) discovered on a trip to Spain in 1970 that the sculpture is still carried through the streets during Holy Week each year to be newly covered with lace, emeralds, pins, rings, and pearls. Flack was overwhelmed by its beauty and by the love the people showed it. She was so influenced by Roldan's work that when she painted her own skin in her *Self-Portrait*, she "eliminated the scars and imperfections on [her] cheeks and replaced them with that buttery smooth surface of La Roldana's *Macerena*."[36]

The painting shows only the Macerena's head, as it is after centuries of adornment, nearly enveloped in bejeweled lace. Clearly the beautiful face, with its full lips, long straight nose, large eyes, and dark thick brows, was the most important feature of the sculpture from Flack's point of view. Comparable to El Greco's more famous *Mater Dolorosa*, both the painting and the sculpture differ from it in three telling ways: in the tears on the Macerena's cheeks, in her deeply furrowed brow, and in the depth of sorrow expressed in her eyes. The tension between these elements and the silky skin and heavy adornment is breathtaking. Instead of the Virgin known to us in high art—the one who overcomes her own desires and feelings to obey God's will—we have a passionate woman who is none the less a queen for her identification with human pain. This, of course, is why she symbolizes hope rather than sorrow; because she has experienced these depths, she can intercede for others. The image makes us aware that passion has been missing from our descriptions of the mother.

Militance has been missing as well. In Betye Saar's mixed-media box, *The Liberation of Aunt Jemima* (1972), we see militance of a sort that is relegated by Toni Wolff to the type of the amazon. Saar's work focuses on a large, dark, smiling Aunt Jemima shown in relief, a smaller painted Jemima holding a screaming white child in a mock photograph that covers the larger woman's skirt, and a three-dimensional black fist that covers the skirt of the smaller woman. In the background are multiple images from the well-known pancake-mix box. As Saar (b1926) herself says, "I take the figure that classifies all black women and make her into one of the leaders of the revolution."[37] The large Jemima has a revolver in one hand and a rifle in the other. Clearly, Saar sees the loving family-woman as a source of unexpected power. She continues to smile as she gets ready to battle. This too is part of the archetype.

A mixed-media sculpture *The Family* (c1969) by Escobar Marisol provides still another dimension of insight.[38] Marisol (b1930) shows Mary, Joseph, and Jesus in their customary colors and arrangement—but there tradition stops. The standing Mary is black-skinned, perhaps reflecting Marisol's consciousness of dark goddess icons from South America (she is from a Venezuelan family and lived there as a child). Furthermore, the full moon is shown behind Mary's head, an allusion to her goddess lineage. In the middle of her body is a large protruding bejeweled egg, despite the fact that the baby lies before her on the floor. On closer inspection, the viewer finds that the egg slides to one side and reveals an empty cavity lined with mirrors. Since the viewer's image is reflected in the mirrors, she or he seems to have entered the Virgin. Instead of taking everyone into herself physically as did *hon*, Marisol's mother reflects everyone's image.

Lest we think of this mother as too powerful, however, Marisol makes Mary's wooden cloak act as a straitjacket for her two left hands. Joseph is a straightforward red rectangle with a moderately realistic head, unremarkable in every way save one: his hands, closed in an attitude of prayer, are positioned so that the thumbs face outward. The baby is likewise conventional except that he sleeps on a bed of neon lights. On one level, the work is a brilliant commentary on how commercialism has eroded religious significance. On a more profound level, it makes Mary the central figure in the Holy Family. She is a goddess, capable of revealing us to ourselves; that is her creative power. But she is bound by whatever her immovable cloak symbolizes in various periods of history. She is unable to come to us; we must go to her.

As we move through these images, a pattern emerges—not the pattern of the good and terrible mother who either cares for or restrains her child, but of the vulnerable mother whose great capacities for sheltering, nurturing, protecting, supporting, caring, liberating, and reflecting the other (child or adult) cannot ensure her success. Remedios Varo's *Celestial Pabulum* (1958) expresses this pattern in an unforgettable way.[39] The female protagonist is shown inside a multisided structure among the clouds in a dark sky. She is feeding a caged waning moon spoonfuls of stars, which she grinds in a conventional food mill. The object of her nurturance literally has cosmic importance, and yet her attitude is one of dejection. She cannot escape her task. The stairs from her house lead only into thin air.

But what bearing do these images have on the archetype of the mother? The archetype is, presumably, nothing more than the tendency to form images in response to recurrent or shared experiences of mothering or being mothered. Undeniable images of the mother exist in every possible medium of expression from prehistoric times to the present. The pattern of images presented here enriches our knowledge of human experiences of the mother by differing from previously articulated patterns. In fact, it suggests a whole new line of historical inquiry into the mother's own feelings of power and vulnerability.

Perhaps a more difficult question, from a feminist perspective, concerns what we gain by calling the mother an archetype. Would we not be better off to discard the term,[40] since "mother" is only an imperfect metaphor (like "God") for something unseen? What do we gain from acknowledging a tendency to form a certain kind of image? Presumably we come to know and respect the deepest patterns of our experience. As long as we acknowledge many archetypes (tendencies to form many different kinds of images), as long as we do not freeze the images or arrange them in a hierarchy, as long as we remember that we are creating a metaphor for a phenomenon that no one can measure—we have nothing to lose by accepting the term. These are, of course, radical qualifications of current practice that will require considerable discipline.

Even if a more Platonic notion of the archetype were to prevail, I would not want to deny the archetype of the mother in a society that regards the father as divine. But we need not reify any one set of manifestations of an archetype (ancient Greek, European, Renaissance, twentieth-century), particularly if that set comes mainly from members of one sex, one race, one culture. It is the reification of Renaissance, Romantic, and Victorian ideologies of the mother that we need to protest, not the archetype of the mother.

Since all human beings have mothers (and since many men are now partaking in child-rearing from the point of a baby's delivery until its adulthood), we cannot argue that images of the mother by women give us the only true access to the archetype, but we can claim that descriptions which neglect images by women are faulty. Centuries of experience in mothering, or in identifying with the mother, have produced insights we cannot afford to neglect. (According to the same principle, linguists examine the habits of native speakers in formulating the grammar of a language.) Rather than turn our backs on the archetype of the mother, let us insist on the validity of our history. By using the concept of the archetype as a means of organizing that history, we can make available to theorists and therapists the images that will allow a new perspective on women to emerge. By so doing, we validate the importance of the primary figure in our lives with whom women must identify in part in order to mature. If, as Nancy Chodorow argues, the central developmental task of women is to separate ourselves from our mothers *without rejecting them* (because then we reject part of ourselves), we need to keep before us the full range of images that will allow us to complete the task successfully. The concept of the archetype allows us to collect and compare these images.

Now let us look again at what the images of the mother by twentieth-century women artists reveal. First, the doubleness of perspective I have documented, which yokes strength with vulnerability, has little or nothing to do with Neumann's axes of

nurturance and inspiration and still less to do with his evalua-
tions of good and terrible mothering. One could argue that the
figures I have cited are all nurturant, inspirational, good, and also
terrible or frightening because of the ways that they are bound—
either by the degree of their caring (as in *Mother with Twins,
Macerena Esperanza,* or *Celestial Pabulum*) or by their role in or
relationship to society (as in the other works). The sense of great
power or strength without sufficient scope to exercise or realize it
is the dominant impression one gains from seeing these works
together. Of the strengths revealed, only the beauty of the
Macerena and the plenitude of the nurse are traditionally ascribed
to the mother. Sexual openness, protectiveness of the sort Kollwitz represents, the power over life and death implied in Billops'
fetishes, passion, militance, the power to show the viewer who
she is, the power to save the moon—these are unfamiliar attributes of the mother in the cultures reflected by the European
Masters of art. Without having done a statistical study, I suggest
that these images emerge frequently in works by women. And
the "binding" forces revealed here are also common: the
machine, the mask, the vulnerability to violence, the internal
wound, the inability to act directly, the stereotype, the straitjacket, the stairs that lead nowhere. The image that emerges is both
less ideal than Neumann's good mother and less reprehensible
than his terrible one. His terms are simply insufficient.

The works I have described, for the most part, give us only the
illusion of being close to the mother. Although several of them
(hon, My Nurse and I, Mother, and *Family)* actually allow us to be
inside or to see inside the mother, only one *(Macerena Esperanza)*
allows us direct access to her feelings. Nor does the feeling of
authenticity in these works come necessarily from the artist's
experience of mothering. To my knowledge, only Kollwitz, Billops, Flack, and Saar were mothers themselves at the time these
works were completed. Still, each work contains within it an
element that allows us to identify with the mother, even when
she is masked or has a severed head. In Kahlo's work the presence of the fully conscious child in the pictorial space helps us to
see that the maternal (death) mask is not all that separates the
two. In Billops' case, the wound humanizes what might otherwise be a purely ritual presence. These points of access make all
the difference in the feeling elicited by the image. And until all

such feelings are known, we will not have described the archetype of the mother.

To refuse to see these images together as an archetypal pattern, one of many yet to be seen or described, would be to insist on the integrity of the individual's expression at the expense of collective vision. Yet to take one pattern or one image as ideal, or even as normal, would be to confuse the image with the tendency to form it. Thus the concept of the archetype could, in feminist hands, function as a force against the reification of any one cultural construction of reality. It is the never-to-be-exhausted tendency to imagine that is the ultimate justification of cultural pluralism.

II   THE ANIMUS OR THE CASE OF
THE DISAPPEARING ARCHETYPE

In the case of the mother we are dealing with a widely acknowledged pattern that is clearly present in works by both men and women in many eras and cultures. The case of the animus is quite different. The concept is neither clear nor clearly manifested in works by women.

Our troubles begin with the word itself. "Animus" means "spirit" or "mind" in Latin, whereas in English it has come to mean, according to the *Oxford English Dictionary*, "actuating feeling, bias, animating temper; hence animosity." In contemporary usage, shades of both meanings are retained without being reconciled, and a third is added. According to the *American Heritage Dictionary* (1980), "animus" is first "an animating motive; intention or purpose"; second, "a feeling of animosity; bitter hostility or hatred"; and third, in Jungian psychology, "the masculine inner personality, as present in women. Compare *anima*." From these various meanings we might deduce that women experience the masculine within themselves as an animating motive that arouses their hostility. Indeed, the phenomenon of the animus is often described by Jungians in negative terms, as a voice within the woman that issues prohibitions, gives commands, and makes pronouncements, as if a woman could not express her mind without animosity. This formulation has several curious features. It is not clear, especially in a culture that values masculinity so highly, why the presence of the masculine in women should be negative; the feminine within the male is not primarily negative.

Nor is it clear why there should be only one archetype for the multiple and diverse behaviors women perform that might be called masculine. It is even less clear why a woman's intentionality or purposiveness would be called masculine. Before we even begin to look for manifestations of the archetype, then, we must confront the illogic of conventional usage.

In the fullest Jungian treatment of the subject, Emma Jung restored to the term "animus" its Latin connotation of "directed spiritual power."[41] Acknowledging that many women had successfully integrated the active masculine virtues into consciousness, she thought that they still lacked adequate awareness of "spiritual functioning." If such awareness remained undeveloped, she said, women would fall prey to the negative animus, and would begin to behave with animosity. She hypothesized that women become aware of the positive animus first in the outside world, projecting it onto family members, who then serve as the woman's guide to "the objective documents of the human spirit"—to which the woman does not otherwise have direct access. Emma Jung argued that women cannot afford to be permanently satisfied with this state of affairs where their spiritual values are projected onto men. Her essay was designed to help women get past the point of being possessed by an archetype or caught with men in an endless cycle of animus-anima projections.

The problems with Emma Jung's formulation are still serious. Why, for example, would women not have access to documents in public institutions? Such problems, however, concern me less than the difficulties that arise when we ask how the animus appears to a woman. While the archetypal mother may be recognized by references to her physical relationship to childbearing or child care, or by a restricted range of symbols and attitudes related to these functions, the animus, according to Emma Jung, can be virtually any male, related or unrelated to the female, who serves to give "flashes of knowledge" (already formulated in words) to the female.[42] Emma Jung lists the forms in which he may appear: father, lover, brother, teacher, sage, sorcerer, artist, philosopher, scholar, builder, monk, trader, aviator, or chauffeur; indeed he may be any man "distinguished by his masculine qualities."[43] The animus emerges as a "lightning-change artist who can assume any form and makes extensive use of this ability"; he is the ancient Hermes, whose most characteristic modern guise is the stranger. The animus can also appear as a "plurality of men—a group of fathers, a court, a gathering of wise men." How, then, is it possible to recognize these multifarious figures as manifestations of the animus?

Our task is further complicated by Emma Jung's idea that the phenomenon need not appear as an image at all, in the way all other archetypes do, but may instead appear as a voice.[44] This assertion seems even more strange than all the others. Why would this archetype differ from the others in its manifestations? And how does one perceive transpersonal, transcultural patterns as establishing the presence of an archetype if its manifestations occur mainly in the form of internal voices? Where is the catalogue of those internal appearances? How does one identify a Hermes figure by voice?

Logically speaking, the concept of the animus is far too broad to be useful in therapy or anywhere else; or, alternatively, it is broad enough to be used in any way a therapist likes. Emma Jung, for example, in citing animus images from therapy, identifies a bird-monster, a chthonic fire spirit, and a dragon as masculine—all images that might also be interpreted as feminine in the light of current research on the mythology surrounding the goddesses. Clearly the theory must be rethought. In saying so, I am merely joining a chorus of female voices.[45] But before we conclude that the concept of the animus must be abandoned completely, I want to show what happens when we try to use it to locate images in visual works by women.

In looking for possible appearances of the animus in women's works, I have supposed that the animus can be any man, men or masculine figures (however abstract) who function as spiritual guides for the artist and appear as protagonists in her work. I have been particularly attentive to signs that indicate the relationship of those figures to the self in question, since the animus is supposed to be the embodiment of the masculine within the woman's self. I have searched in particular for spiritual guides, Hermes figures, or strangers. But in keeping with Emma Jung's own examples of the animus from therapy and with the manifestations of the mother archetype already examined, I have looked for images of the masculine within the woman portrayed with psychological or spiritual intensity.

In combing through all the available historical sources on visual art by women, I found that men have not been so important to women as subjects for art as women have been to men. To be sure, images of men exist in works by women, but they are not very revealing. They tend, before the twentieth century, to be religious images, portraits or genre paintings rather than the equivalents of Leonardo's *Mona Lisa* or Dante Gabriel Rossetti's *Beatrice*. Among the most interesting of this small group is a religious painting of *St. Anthony of Padua* (1662) by Elisabetta Sirani (1638–1665), whose fame so rivaled her father's that she became the sole support of her household until her early death by poisoning. Sirani shows the young saint stroking the foot of a celestial cherub who is supported on a cloud above his table. Elsa Fine remarks, "Rarely before have celestial children been portrayed with such earthly delight."[46] But the painting seems more likely to represent Sirani's insight into a man's capacity to feel love for an idealized child than to reveal her own desires; other far more direct opportunities for such self-expression were open to her within the artistic conventions surrounding the Madonna and the female saints.

Similarly, women do not seem to have seized upon portraits of men as a means of representing their own inner lives. The young Italian painter Lucia Anguissola (1540–c1565) created in her *Portrait of Pietro Maria* (c1560) what Ann Sutherland Harris has called "an impressive, sober image of a distinguished elderly man," which conveys in its color and composition "an impression of conservative caution."[47] One raised eyebrow indicating the sitter's quizzical sense of humor marks the work as an attempt to capture his particular character. The presence of a snake wound around his walking stick is less an emblem of archetypal significance than it is a conventional sign of his profession. About another painting, *Portrait of Paolo Morigia* (1596) by the Italian artist Fede Galizia (1578–1630), Harris comments that the result was "effective precisely because Galizia seems to have recorded [her patron, a Jesuit scholar] just as he presented himself to her, unfiltered by either idealizing conventions or the artist's own personality."[48] Despite, or maybe because of, the wrinkles, squint, and drawn mouth shown in the painting, Morigia liked it very much. Later depictions (Ellen Sharples' *George Washington*, Sarah Goodridge's *Portrait of Gilbert Stuart*, Harriet Hosmer's full-length sculpture of Thomas Hart Benton) show the same devotion to realism rather than to self-expression, perhaps because they were executed for public purposes.[49]

In the area of genre painting, the same tendency toward realism prevailed. Two paintings by the American Lilly Martin Spencer are the most telling examples. In *The Young Husband: First Marketing* (1856), the beleaguered man is shown walking home in the rain clutching his closed umbrella and struggling to keep the contents of an overfull basket of groceries from spilling into the street.[50] Another man passes him with umbrella held high and a derisive grin on his face. In *Fi! Fo! Fum!* (1858) the man is shown with a daughter on each knee telling the story of Jack and the Beanstalk.[51] The lamp casts a soft light in the dark room, the cat licks its paw in the foreground, and the mother plays a supportive role. It is an image of family solidarity.

The lack of content reflecting the female psyche in such works is evident by the fact that they were often attributed to male artists. Thus the moving *Portrait of an Old Man and Boy* by the Venetian Maria Robusti Tintoretto (1560–1590) was considered to be a masterpiece by her father until 1920.[52] And *The Jolly Toper* (1629) by the Dutch artist Judith Leyster was long attributed to Frans Hals.[53]

The history of visual art by women does not document the existence of the animus. There are several possible explanations for this. One is that men, as patrons, may not have wanted to own paintings that were reflective of a woman's animus.[54] Paintings with these psychological dimensions may have existed but passed into oblivion, as many other works have done.[55] Another possibility is that such paintings exist but are not yet known. Many works by women remain unseen in museum storage rooms around the world, and still others are in private collections or in attics or in studios. Another is that such images existed in women's dreams but were inhibited by convention from ever being realized in paint or sculpture. Only a few women, such as Artemesia Gentileschi (1593–1652/53), managed to defy convention successfully.

By the twentieth century these potential difficulties were somewhat diminished as women became more active in the art world and as the conventions of art loosened to allow a broader range of subject matter. But when psychological works involving men did appear, only a tiny handful could by any stretch of the imagination be described as animus images. Of these, Betye Saar's *Wizard* (1972) stands alone as an example of an attribution of spiritual wisdom to the masculine in the female self.[56] The wizard is clearly a psychopomp, a guide, or at least a gatekeeper to the layers of inner mystery. He kneels in the foreground of an image that is composed of a series of smaller and smaller rectangles (doors) leading back to a tiny altar. The symbols repeated through the space are the eye, the crescent moon, and the keyhole, all potentially feminine in their association and all present in many works by women. The piece is related to Saar's own mystical search for meaning in the Moslem tradition, and it reveals a profound desire for integration of the outer and inner layers of the self. It does not belong, however, to a pattern of visual images portraying the wizard in the woman as a masculine presence. Nor does this lone image justify the hypothesis that the impulse toward wholeness is masculine in origin; the feminine imagery in the work is equally important.

Another psychological work that seems to represent the masculine within the female and to credit it with spiritual power is the *Self-Portrait as a Tehuana* (1943) by Frida Kahlo (1907–1954), where a miniature portrait of the artist's husband, Diego Rivera, appears in her forehead in the position of the third eye.[57] Painted in the fourteenth year of the couple's marriage, three years after they had divorced and remarried, it shows Kahlo in a white native Mexican headdress surrounding her face and upper body, with a floral hairpiece from which tendrils grow up, out, and down into the painting to create the effect of a web. Far from being an homage to Rivera or an assimilation of his spiritual power, however, Kahlo's biographer argues, it represents one of a long series of episodes in the Riveras' stormy marriage: "Frida's obsessive love for her unpossessable husband has made her trap his image in her forehead in the form of a thought."[58] Earlier in their relationship Rivera was a guide for Kahlo, who learned a great deal from him about painting and benefited from his contacts with the art world. But his value to her as a spiritual guide is debatable. Although Kahlo adored him and even credited him with wisdom, she also found his effect on her painful. In an unguarded moment she said, "I suffered two grave accidents in my life. One in which a streetcar knocked me down. . . . The other accident is Diego."[59]

The accident that crushed her spine and saddled her with a life of physical suffering gave her an awareness of death which was at least as important a facilitator of spiritual growth as was Rivera. Indeed, a parallel painting called *Thinking About Death*, also done in 1943, places a skull and crossbones in the position of the third eye.[60] And other paintings from the same period show that her relationship with nature was a similarly powerful force in her spiritual life. In fact, in *Sun and Life* (1947) the sun, shown surrounded by plants close to the earth's surface, seems to have Kahlo's features.[61] In her final painting of Rivera, *The Love Embrace of the Universe, the Earth (Mexico), Diego, Me and Señor Xolotl* (1949), Kahlo shows herself holding a naked Rivera on her lap as if he were a baby, while she in turn is seated on the lap of a great mountain-like idol of a goddess. All of them, including Kahlo's dog Xolotl, are cradled in the light and dark (night and day, earth and sky) arms of an even greater goddess.[62] It is doubtful that Rivera was the primary facilitator of this vision, although it is surely one of the most compelling figures of the "world anima" ever created. If we choose to think of Rivera as Kahlo's animus, we will be forced to redefine the archetype as a much more limited force than Emma Jung supposed.

A third potential image of the animus that also proves to be a dead end is a *Self-Portrait* (1923) by the expatriate American Romaine Brooks (1874–1970).[63] Here the artist is austerely dressed in a black coat with a man's top hat drawn over her penetrating dark eyes. Only the redness of her lips belies the passion of this ramrod straight figure who presides over a ruined city in the background. But instead of being a portrait of the masculine elements within her, this painting shows the way Brooks used a masculine exterior to protect herself. It was a strategy to make a living in a world that was still unreceptive to women artists, and perhaps a ploy to gain acceptance by the Parisian artistic elite. Brooks's surrealist drawings of the 1930s show that her inner life had little to do with her masculine exterior. Instead of being a guide to the woman's soul, these masculine trappings belong only to her persona; they are a social mask.

As for Hermes figures, the best example comes from Remedios Varo. Her *Vegetarian Vampires* (1962) shows three human-bird-ghost figures whose disintegrating garments recall Hermes. They are seated on stools around a small table greedily sipping in turn a watermelon slice, a rose, and a tomato through long straws. Two collared and leashed animals with rooster heads, four legs, fur, and plumes as tails are pictured under and beside the stools.[64] Such images are scarce in art by women. But this painting raises still another issue: whether all images with psychological resonance are necessarily self-images. Varo's paintings of men in the period of the *Vegetarian Vampires* are sharply differentiated from her self-images, not only in appearance but also in activity and attitude. Rather than portraying the masculine within the painter, they portray the effects of the masculine on the world. They are psychological critiques.

The entire force of Varo's work from 1960 to 1963 is directed against the kind of science she associates with the males she portrays. Earlier in her career there was a painting of a Dr. Chavez who held a key to unlock men's hearts; by 1959, however, Varo had envisioned a female Minotaur to hold the key—not to other people's hearts but to the cosmos, in the form of the night sky. Her visionary "science" was pitted against that of the botanist, the geologist, and the physicist, whom she understood as being to some extent in opposition to nature. Her own energy was spent in efforts to regenerate nature. Her vegetarian vampires, then, do not represent Hermes the psychopomp (though they may criticize Hermes the thief). They do not give spiritual meaning to the artist's own quest.

In fact, Varo's painting *Woman Coming Out of the Psycho-analyst's Office* (1961) suggests, as Sylvia Brinton Perera does later in this book, that a woman's health may require her to discard whatever masculine guide she has internalized. Varo's protagonist, who looks something like the artist, leaves an office labeled Dr. F.J.A. (Freud, Jung, Adler) holding her father's disembodied head by its white beard as she prepares to drop it into a well in the center of the plaza. The woman carries a basket containing a clock, a key, a pacifier, which Varo's notes identify as additional "psychological waste." Art historian Janet Kaplan sees the painting as symbolic of Varo's necessary dissociation from her domineering father.[65] Indeed, the spiritual dimensions of the

painting are strongly feminine in their associations. The protagonist's hair may have turned white like her father's, but it has
begun to take the shape of the crescent moon, a thoroughly
feminine image in Varo's imaginative world. Her choice of the well
as the appropriate depository for the masculine element may also
be seen as an affirmation of feminine regenerative capacity. The
veils that previously masked the woman's face have dropped
away; only one layer remains over her mouth preventing her
from fully revealing the self that had been obscured by the
father's presence. If the father is an animus figure here, his effect
is neither spiritual nor positive.

Emma Jung also suggested that the animus might appear as a
stranger. Varo's work is full of strangers, or "characters" as she
calls them, but they are female as often as male. Similarly, in a
work by Léonor Fini (b. 1918), the "stranger who gives all the
orders" has the artist's own face.[66] If the idea of the stranger can
include familiar men who become one's judges, executioners or
captors, however, then there is a small pattern of such images
dating back to the Renaissance. *Noli Me Tangere* (1581) by Lavinia
Fontana (1552–1614) is the most positive of these.[67] Fontana depicts the moments after Christ's order not to touch him, when he
instructs Mary Magdalene and gives her his blessing; but the
firmness of her stance (noted by Harris) and the seductiveness of
Christ's makes the image less spiritual than erotic despite its title.
Christ is a spiritual guide by tradition, but here the human drama
of Magdalene's strength and his ambiguous rejection is the subject of the painting (not his virtue and her need of reform as in
other versions). *The Martyrdom of St. Eurosia* by Giulia Lama
(1685–c1753) shows the brutal beheading of a virgin from Bay-
onne who refused to marry a Moorish chieftain.[68] The execution-
er is sure of his rights and dares us to differ with him. *The Fugitive*
(after 1874) by Lucy Maddox Brown Rossetti (1821–1893) places a
desperate young woman in a primeval forest where she rests for a
moment; behind the tree on which she leans there lurks a bearded
old man who holds a potion for her in a glass.[69] The men in these
pictures may think they are spiritually superior to the female
protagonists, but the artists who painted them do not agree. Nor
do the artists portray these figures as symbolic of the masculine
within the woman.

In our search for the animus in visual art by women, we are

defeated at every turn. First, there is the problem of scarcity. Men do not appear as subjects in art by women as frequently as do other subjects, and they appear even less frequently as psychological subjects. Women do not often present images of the self as masculine. Thus, the concept of the animus does not serve to identify any substantial pattern of images. Second, and even more disconcerting, is the fact that when psychological images of the masculine do appear, they are not well explained by the concept of the animus. If we accept Emma Jung's formulation of it as an internal spiritual guide comparable to the anima in the male, we must conclude that it is virtually nonexistent in women's art.

If we were desperate to prove the existence of the animus as an archetype, we might consider the fairly widespread expression of anger toward men in art by women as its manifestation. Take, for example, the kind of attitude that shows up in works by May Stevens. Her "portraits" of her father wrapped in an American flag with an army helmet on his head and a bulldog in his lap are commentaries on a kind of masculinity from which Stevens wishes to dissociate herself.[70] A man would not wrap himself in a flag and become, in his military persona, a human watchdog without drastically misunderstanding his human place, and Stevens' satire makes us aware that such an attitude is inappropriate. Similarly, Nancy Grossman's black zippered helmets are moving statements about the ugliness, emptiness, and degradation of the embattled human being. Most of her images are decidedly masculine, and her point of view is not at all sympathetic.[71] But why would anger toward men derive from a masculine source in the woman's self? Once again we are caught in an illogical tangle.

If we were to derive an archetype from such images, assuming that sufficient data exists to establish a pattern of negative representations, we might describe the archetype as a tendency to form images of men as oppressive and dangerous. If we labeled this the animus, however, in keeping with the word's second meaning of animosity, we would be altering the concept to refer to female experiences of men and not to the masculine within the female self.

As soon as we cut ourselves free of the concept of the animus, however, and begin to look without preconception at the images of men created by women, we find other patterns that are potentially just as pervasive and charged with feeling. One of these concerns male frailty. For example, Alice Neel's famous nude portrait of *Joe Gould* (1933) with three penises, ostensibly a portrait of male virility, turns out to be a statement about the fragility of his ego. Her *T.B. Case, Harlem* (1940) has been understood as a Christ image, and it may be, but if so, Christ is badly in need of care.[72] Neel (b1900) does not satirize or denigrate the human beings she paints, but she does reveal what lies beneath their personae. She discriminates, understands, abstracts without animosity. Other images of male frailty include such different works as Käthe Kollwitz's woodcut of the communist leader Karl Liebknecht in death and Lois Mailou Jones's painting, *Mob Victim* (1944), of a black man about to be lynched.[73] These are numinous images in their knowledge of impotence and death, and they may document a tendency to form images of men based on empathy as well as on anger.

Instead of struggling with the ill-fitting concept of the animus, would it not be more productive to examine all the images of men and the masculine in works by women to see whether any substantial patterns exist? Our results might yield a complex redefinition of the masculine as well as a reformulation of the idea of the masculine within the woman. We may find that men do not play so crucial a role in women's spiritual development as Emma Jung thought. It is even possible that men are not often numinous for women, instrumental as they may be in women's entry into society. This hypothesis would corroborate Nancy Chodorow's idea that women are the primary love objects for women as well as for men,[74] and it might explain the preponderance of images that assign social rather than spiritual significance to the masculine.

III   THE INDEPENDENT WOMAN: IMAGE OR ARCHETYPE?

Thus far, I have argued that, in the case of the archetype of the mother, we need to revise our descriptions of the archetype to accord with images created by women. In the case of the animus, we need to suspend the notion that such an archetype exists until we can see more clearly what patterns emerge as we examine women's images of men and which patterns have archetypal significance. Now I want to examine an extensive pattern of images that could be indicative of an archetype of the independent woman.

One of the most striking facts about the new books on visual art by women (see note 5) is that they show so many images of women engaged in productive tasks, usually alone or with subordinates. In the medieval period the woman depicted is often a scribe, visionary, weaver, or warrior. In the Renaissance we find a saint reading, Judith beheading Holofernes, Mary Magdalene meditating. From then on we find self-portraits of the artists in the act of painting; Gentileschi, Van Hemessen, Leyster, Kaufmann, Vigée-Lebrun, Labille-Guiard are only the most famous women artists to leave such records of their attitude and skill. In the nineteenth century, portraits of other strong women begin to appear. Susan Sedgewick's *Mum Bett* honors Elizabeth Freeman, a black who took the institution of slavery to court in 1781. Anna Klumke's *Rosa Bonheur* and Adelaide Johnson's *Susan B. Anthony* likewise celebrate heroic women. Symbolic works showing wronged women, such as Harriet Hosmer's *Zenobia in Chains* or Edmonia Lewis' *Hagar* mark the beginning of the contemporary process of recovering women's mythic heritage.[75]

Self-portraits in the late nineteenth and early twentieth centuries also became declarations of psychological strength rather than more convention-bound statements of accomplishment.[76] Again, those by Suzanne Valadon, Gwen John, Romaine Brooks, Marianne Werefkin, Gabriele Münter, Paula Modersohn-Becker, Käthe Kollwitz, Frida Kahlo, Charley Toorop, Frances Gillespie, Audrey Flack, and Léonor Fini are merely the most accessible and striking examples. Similarly, Romaine Brooks's portraits of upper-class European women, Kollwitz's images of Berlin working-class women, Léonor Fini's imaginary priestesses, Remedios Varo's female questers, Faith Ringgold's *Family of Women*, Germaine Richier's symbolic identifications of women and nature, and Barbara Chase-Riboud's abstract assertions of female power are only the most obvious examples of a large class of images showing strength in other women. Before we examine several representative works, however, let us recall the descriptions of the feminine available in archetypal theory to explain such images.

Neumann would have us subsume all aspects of the feminine under the archetype of the Great Mother. As we have seen, this schema cannot even encompass the diverse images of the mother, and it surely does not take into account images of women with no apparent relationship to men or to children. One axis of Toni Wolff's description of the feminine psyche also deals only with the woman who is defined by her intimate relationship to men and children. The other axis of "impersonal" relationship offers us the concepts of the medium and the amazon. Let us see whether or not they can be useful in interpreting representative figures of strength from art by women.

The medial woman (or medium) is the figure Wolff intends to be relevant to the woman artist. She is the means, agent, mediator, or conveyor of the "psychic atmosphere of her environment and the spirit of her period."[77] She can exert a positive influence on her environment only when she becomes a "mediatrix" who possesses the "faculty of discrimination" or understands the limits of the conscious and the unconscious, the personal and the impersonal. In that case, as Wolff says, "she consecrates herself to the service of a new, maybe yet concealed, spirit of her age, like the early Christian martyrs, the female mystics of the Middle Ages, or, within a smaller sphere, she devotes herself to the life-work of an individual man."[78] It is the medial woman's task to find "an objective language" to express the meaning of the collective unconscious. I do not doubt that such a figure exists, but it still correlates better with well-known images of the muse who inspires others than with the images of women who are themselves inspired or otherwise empowered to act.

The figure of the amazon is more relevant to the present inquiry. According to Wolff, the amazon is

> characterized by the emphasis placed upon the individual's own personality and its development *within the limits of the objective cultural values of our time,* quite independent of other persons and of instinctive or other psychic factors. In as far as our present time offers widest scope to the amazon structure, it is this form which, beside the "mother," can most frequently be found in the lime-light of public life, or which is perhaps chosen as the outer way of life whenever it corresponds to a necessity or an ideal, *even though it may not be fully consistent with the natural structure.*[79] [Italics mine]

The amazon is independent and self-contained; her development is not based on a psychological relationship with a man. Her interest is directed toward "objective" achievements of her own. Wolff includes in her list of examples great sportswomen and travelers, women in civil service or business, secretaries, dedicated volunteers, and women who keep their households under military discipline. This catholicity would be very promising if we could forget that the word "amazon" already carries the meanings of "female warrior" and "masculine woman" in common usage. Indeed, the term best fits Wolff's description of the negative amazon, whose independence shows itself in "masculine protest," in her desire "to be equal to her brother," in her unwillingness to recognize any authority or superiority, and in fighting by "using exclusively male arms."[80] Wolff's negative amazon deals with personal complications in a masculine way or represses them, and she lacks "patience or comprehension for anything still undeveloped."[81] She is in danger of misusing her relationships for the sake of her career. In other words, as soon as the female's independence threatens her personal relationships, it becomes negative.

Wolff's description of the "positive" amazon, however, is also problematic. The phrases I have emphasized in the Wolff citation suggest that she sees "objective" culture as, by rights, a male-defined sphere and female leadership in it as unnatural for most women. Her range of examples is too broad to be useful and includes roles that are not noted for independence. Neither her qualifiers nor her list of roles corresponds to the realities presented in works of art by women. Not much can be saved from this formulation except Wolff's assertion that an archetype exists in relation to a certain kind of woman whose development is not based on a psychological relationship with a man and whose interest is directed toward objective achievements of her own. Perhaps this is enough for anyone to have contributed to psychological theory about women. It is up to others now to clarify the evidence for the archetype and to revise the description of it so as to alleviate the fear that women may abandon relationships.

A third approach to the description of feminine independence is suggested by the new (post-1960) developments in archetypal psychology, wherein the goddesses of ancient civilization are used to provide clues to the enduring aspects of the feminine. Mary Esther Harding's essay on the "Virgin Goddess" in *Women's Mysteries: Ancient and Modern* is a precursor of this approach; in describing the goddess who is "one-in-herself," Harding suggests a model of independence.[82] Following more recent leads offered by James Hillman and Christine Downing,[83] we might look for goddesses who are to some degree independent of children and men and then focus on the parts of their stories that show them acting independently: Artemis or Daphne in their rejection of lovers, Athena in her role as judge of Orestes, Demeter in her decision to counter Hades' power by making the earth barren, Inanna in her descent into Ereshkigal's realm, Isis in her restoration of Osiris and her self-fertilization, Psyche in her successful use of natural resources. All these actions might contribute to a new understanding of women's capacities for independence. Perhaps these are parts of a whole image of female power that was fractured into parts when the goddesses went through various transformations as they were assimilated by patriarchal religions. One danger of this approach is its potential to suggest that human nature is unchanging, or that the separate contexts of these figures have no bearing on their value as models. Still, the presence of such episodes in our cultural mythology suggests that post-medieval images of female independence are not aberrations in the course of female evolution.

Keeping such definitional spadework in mind, let us examine several modern visual works to discover what they can tell us about women's experience of independence. Again, as with the images of the mother and the masculine, I will restrict my discussion to images that have a numinous quality and that can be seen in available sources.

Germaine Richier's sculpture *Hurricane* is perhaps as close as we can come in our era to an image with the force of an ancient nature goddess.[84] A massive bronze standing figure completed in 1948/49, *Hurricane* is a naked female whose assertive stance, scarred and pitted skin, and headstrong attitude defy the tradition of the nude in art. Her knees are slightly bent to suggest flexibility and mobility; her muscles are tense, arms ready to grasp or ward off whatever comes her way. Her face is described by Elsa Fine as "filled with the terror of the battle-scarred," and her eyes do express fear, but her head is held high, even thrown back a little; her gaze is direct, her jaw firm.[85] She partakes of the collected force of the hurricane at the same time that she serves as its metaphor, and she stands alone. Her male counterpart, *Storm,* who has excrescences and hollows in place of facial features, presents a more menacing image. By contrast, the integrity of the female figure is preserved. *Hurricane* stands for assertion, not protest; for strength even in the face of fear, not instrumental power over others; for readiness to act, not belligerence. Normal human relationships are not in question here; the image stands outside their scope altogether. We can consider her in relation to Demeter's power to lay waste to the landscape, but *Hurricane's* power is not directed against anyone, as Demeter's was directed against Hades.

As if to draw on another venerable tradition of female power, Barbara Chase-Riboud's *Confessions for Myself* (1972) shows a female figure whose outline corresponds to that of a nun in the old habit with arms folded inward.[86] The upper body to the mid-thigh is covered with copper strips; underneath, extending to and even dragging on the floor, are coils and knots of black rope. The life-sized figure is both enigmatic and imposing, her abstract face to be revered. Chase-Riboud (b1940) intended "to salute that power that exists in all beings in the form of illusion." She declares, "Reverence to Her. All reverence to Her."[87] She is both hard and soft, bright and dark, strong and vulnerable.

Elizabeth Catlett's wood sculpture *Homage to My Young Black Sisters* (1969), showing a single figure with her face and one arm lifted, is ostensibly a militant image because of the symbol of the raised fist.[88] In Chase-Riboud's similar work, *She Number One*, (1972) a freestanding arm and fist made of rope and copper does seem to be an ego-centered image of power. But on closer inspection, Catlett's work reveals a different spirit. The abstract features of the upturned face are calm and determined, not avenging. The large womblike opening in the front and the smaller one in the lower back of the sculpture call attention to the woman's permeability. (They do not bring to mind the idea that she is empty, as Henry Moore's sculptures of women in the late 1940s do.[89]) Despite the holes, Catlett's image is one of solidity, confidence, pride, idealism. The fact that Catlett made it to honor the struggle for liberation by black women clarifies its nature as a symbol of freedom rather than a harbinger of destruction.

Likewise, Käthe Kollwitz's *Outbreak* (1903) shows a woman as a leader without embracing the idea of individual recognition that has colored our image of male independence for centuries. Here the central figure is the historical leader of a justifiable peasant rebellion; her back is to us and we see only the image of her gathered energy and its effect upon the peasants in battle.[90] It is as if she were lifting them up to spur them on.

Kollwitz is also famous for her many images of "Woman Reflecting," apparently the opposite of the active leader, yet no less independent for her reflective posture. In a lithograph from 1920, for example, the woman is shown with closed eyes, drawn cheeks, and turned-down mouth, bracing her creased forehead against her broad open hand. The hand is used almost defensively, to protect her thoughts from our gaze, and yet we are drawn into her anguish; we are asked to value her struggle.[91]

Léonor Fini also provides us with an image of the female thinker. In *La Pensierosa* (1954) she shows one of her bald priestesses with her head buried in her hands, elbows braced on her knees, deep in thought. Her irridescent cloak resembles insect's wings, and her leotard-clad limbs resemble an insect's legs.[92] By implication, her activity puts her in touch with the natural order. The interpretation is justified by other Fini images from the 1950s that show the priestess as the *Guardian of the Red Egg* or the *Guardian of the Phoenixes*, in other words, as the one who presides over birth and regeneration in nature. After a journey that resembled Inanna's descent into the underworld, Fini emerged in a more judgmental frame of mind, but her paintings of the 1960s and 1970s continue to develop the notion of female responsibility for life and death.[93]

Remedios Varo's images of the woman on her own independent quest also suggest that the female is more attuned to natural processes than is the male. Varo makes her protagonist responsible not only for righting the balance of civilization and nature, particularly in *Journey to the Sources of the Orinoco River* (1959),[94] but also for recovering the spiritual elixir of civilization itself, notably in *To Be Born Again* (1960), *The Calling* (1961), and *Emerging Light* (1962).[95] Psyche's journey for personal happiness is transformed by Varo into a spiritual journey on behalf of life itself.

Other images of independent women include some who have been sacrificed, like Harriet Hosmer's *Zenobia in Chains*, who nonetheless remain faithful to their ideals. And they do also include historical female heroes. A female hero par excellence is represented in May Stevens' painting *Artemesia Gentileschi* (1976).[96]

Stevens' painting is a huge work (108 x 60 inches) completed for the Sister Chapel, a collaborative traveling exhibit in honor of women. It shows a large-boned, hefty woman in seventeenth-century garb, holding a paintbrush delicately with her right hand as she gestures emphatically with the left. Her head is held high, chin set, mouth firm, eyes gazing over our heads. Her stance is solid, not unlike the figure in *Hurricane*. The painting offers a striking image of strength even if one knows nothing of Gentileschi's life. But Stevens makes history a part of the painting by printing the names and dates associated with Gentileschi's life on the wall behind the figure. Thus her history becomes part of our responsibility in viewing the image.

Artemesia Gentileschi (1593-1652/3) was a native of Rome who managed to survive being raped by her father's colleague in her father's studio, to withstand cross-examination under torture and win her case against the disreputable man, and to become a member of the Accademia del Disegno in Florence at twenty-three.[97] She married at nineteen and had at least one daughter, but apparently these events did not interfere with her development as an artist. Her painting *Self-Portrait as "La Pittura"* reveals that she saw herself as part of the continuous tradition of her art, as an equal and not as a freak.[98] She encouraged her daughter to follow in her footsteps. Her favorite subjects were heroic women of the Old Testament: Judith, Esther, and even Bathsheba and Susanna. She was active until the time of her death, having earned her living by her art in Rome, Florence, Genoa, Naples, and London, and having influenced a generation of painters in Naples. Gentileschi's best-known and probably her best painting, *Judith and Maidservant with the Head of Holofernes* (1625), done in her thirties, shows a Judith who can perform the military offices of a man when necessary, with vigor and efficiency, and a servant who is a capable and loyal assistant.[99] Her *Susanna and the Elders* (1610), done when she was only seventeen, is a clear denunciation of lascivious old men.[100] Her Mary Magdalene is heroic even in penitence.[101] Her *Fame* (1623) is far more than a routine execution of a conventional subject.[102] In it Gentileschi departs from the traditional iconography of fame: her protagonist has no olive branch, wings, gold chain, or heart, only a trumpet and laurel leaves. Beyond that, her body type and features are close enough to Gentileschi's to suggest that the work may have been informed in part by the artist's experience of fame. In any case, it is another image of strength in woman. Fame here is not capricious, but steady, clear-eyed, and commanding in her presence. By implication the women who experience her grace will partake of her attributes.

Stevens' painting, then, is symbolic of many strengths united in one person: independence, leadership, commitment to a profession, refusal to be demeaned, clear-sightedness. These qualities have little to do with the supposed masculinity of the amazon, although the image does involve a capacity for militance. Instead of acting within the limits of "objective" culture, the independent woman rises above them. She cannot pause to think whether or not her activities are "natural"; she simply uses her talent and energy as best she can. She is neither the mythological amazon who protests male power nor the virgin goddess who ultimately serves the "higher" principle of Eros. She marshalls her creative energy with passion, intelligence, and responsibility on her own behalf and on behalf of others. Her presence in modern works helps us to identify her in earlier works.

But is there cause to identify this pattern as the manifestation of an archetype? I think so. Again, to do so helps to clarify women's place in history. Women have not always lived in dependence on men, nor has our independence always been regarded as negative. In times of war throughout the centuries, for instance, women have run businesses, cities, even states, drawing on substantial resources of mind and spirit. The acknowledgment of women's tendency to create an image of independence helps us to connect modern expressions with earlier ones and to forge a link with our future. Just as the image of the mother seems to have dominated for centuries as the human species established its place on the earth, so the image of the independent woman seems likely to become increasingly important in a world restricted to zero population growth. Women whose energies are freed from child-rearing will need richer models for female accomplishment. I am suggesting here that we turn to our arts, as well as our poems, diaries, and dreams, to identify our most enduring resources. But let us not think that our description of the past and the present determines the future. We must leave room for the emergence of other Gentileschis who will reveal to us other images of the human in its female forms.

IV   IMPLICATIONS FOR FEMINIST ARCHETYPAL THEORY

In this essay I have examined three archetypes that were posited by Jung and his followers, accepting one with revisions, rejecting a second, and positing an alternative to a third—all on the basis of evidence from works of visual art by females. Of course, my conclusions must be tested against other female sources. But other investigators might wish to ♦tart with a pattern of archetypal images in the dreams or poems of one person. For example, several images of women together in the work of Léonor Fini seem to reach back into Greek mythology. There is no precedent for calling them manifestations of an archetype, but they may be. Others might wish to start with a hypothetical phenomenon such as penis envy, which would surely appear in women's images if it is not simply a product of the theorist's imagination. Whatever the starting point, it will be important to cross disciplinary lines—to check research into images in religion, psychology, literature, art—and to correlate the results. Such studies will help us to avoid setting up new governing absolutes by enriching our understanding of the image. The concept of the archetype could be, in the hands of feminists, a way of recovering and revaluing women's experiences, of discovering nodal points in women's history.

As for the usefulness of Jungian theory regarding female development, that is a different story. We have already seen how uneven the results were of using three archetypes (mother, animus, and amazon) to probe one body of experimental data from women. Only the archetype of the mother proved sound, and that only in part because Jungian theory has not accounted for the special problems the female faces in separating herself from the mother without destroying the possibility of identifying with her. Nancy Chodorow's theory offers a better explanation of images of the mother in works of art by women. Still, the other archetypes Jungians have posited as central to human development—the persona, the shadow, the Self, the wise old woman, and so on—deserve our scrutiny. As maps that can be redrawn depending on what we learn about the territory, they may take us further than we could go without their guidance. Whether a new map of archetypes would support the most important point of Jungian theory regarding women, the identification of the feminine with Eros, I do not know. I suspect not. The domination of woman by Eros may have been a fantasy that served well while survival of the species was at issue and that will be kept alive in some form in case we need to repopulate the world, but I think it is not the cornerstone of female psychology.

As for why we find different patterns in works by women than have been described in works by men, I also do not know. We do not yet know enough about women to write a comprehensive theory of sex differences, cultural or innate. Many of the early Jungian statements about the animus should have been laid to rest by recent research into differences in mental functioning which indicates no deficiencies in females.[103] But subtle shadings of psychological difference will be harder to discern, and it will be harder still to know if they are individual or collective, current or timeless. Again, I suspect that we will discover collective differences (which can be overcome by individuals) and that they will be related to our biology—not to the presence or absence of a penis, which is irrelevant in an era of free sexual expression and progress toward equal opportunity, but to the fact that women experience the body as permeable.[104] The boundaries between self and other, upon which Western civilization rests, are not so firm for women as for men. Precisely at this point the archetypal approach to images produced by women becomes crucial. For how else will we find out how women regard the body except by examining women's images? How else will we find out which images are most important except by examining their patterns? And how will we determine which patterns are limited to one time or culture except by examining them in the context of history?

Granted that Jungian theory is an imperfect basis for feminist theory of female development and that archetypal theory is in its fledgling stages, there are two other reasons for expanding rather than abandoning these frameworks. The first is institutional. Jung established a powerful network of therapists and theorists, among them many strong and intelligent women. If these people were to look to female sources outside the theory-bound clinical interview for models, the practical effect on hundreds of women each year could be substantial and the indirect effects far more pervasive than a less organized approach to our images would allow. Second, in an era where economic values seem to dominate all others, archetypal theory restores dignity to psychological, religious, and aesthetic values. Feminist archetypal theory insists on the reciprocity of behavior and image and can restore images created by women to their rightful position in human history.

Camille Billops, *The Mother*, 1971, ceramic sculpture, 12 x 16½ x 9 in. Photograph of the artist with the sculpture taken c. 1973. Courtesy of Camille Billops.

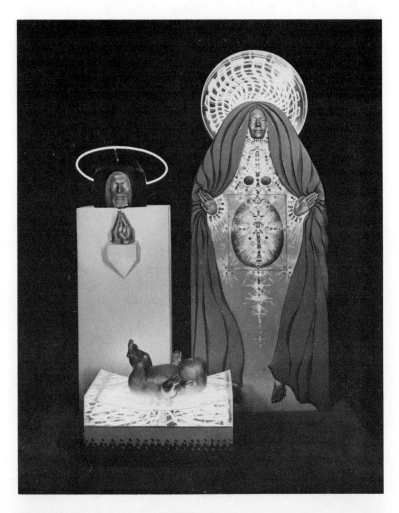

Escobar Marisol, *The Family*, 1969, wood, plastic, terracotta, and neon, 88 x 56 x 65 in. Courtesy of the Memphis Brooks Museum of Art. Commissioned for Brooks Memorial Art Gallery, Memphis, Tennessee.

Remedios Varo, *Celestial Pabulum (Papilla estelar)*, 1958, oil on masonite, 36¼ x 24⅜ in. Courtesy of Walter Gruen.

Betye Saar, *Wizard*, 1972, mixed media assemblage box, 13¼ x 11 x 1 in. Courtesy of Betye Saar.

Frida Kahlo, *Self-Portrait as a Tehuana*, 1943, oil on masonite, 24¾ x 24 in. Courtesy of Mr. and Mrs. Jacques Gelman, Mexico City.

Remedios Varo, *Woman Coming Out of the Psychoanalyst's Office (Mujer saliendo
del psicoanalista)*, 1961, oil, 28 x 16⅛ in. Courtesy of Walter Gruen.

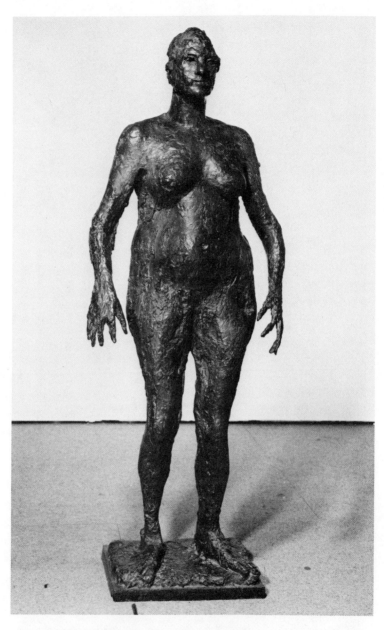

Germaine Richier, *Hurricane (L'Ouragan)*, 1948–49, bronze. (c) by ADAGP, Paris 1984. (c) VAGA, New York/SPADEM, Paris, 1984. Courtesy of the Musée National d'Art Moderne, Paris.

Elizabeth Catlett, *Homage to My Young Black Sisters*, 1969, cedar, 71 in. high. Courtesy of Elizabeth Catlett.

May Stevens, *Artemesia Gentileschi*, 1976, acrylic, 108 x 60 in. Courtesy of May Stevens.

iv | Spinning Among Fields: Jung, Frye, Lévi-Strauss and Feminist Archetypal Theory

ANNIS V. PRATT

I ON THEORY

The word "theory" derives from a Greek term meaning a speculation, a beholding; we can think of theory as a contemplation of data resulting in a system of ideas that describe the phenomena under scrutiny. An alternative connotation in Greek antiquity derives from the association of theory with a group of "Theors," or celebrants, hired by the state to perform a religious ritual. The first definition describes an open-ended, inductive process; the second a traditional, unreflective activity based on a set of deductive assumptions. As theoreticians, we often assume that data can be arranged according to traditionally agreed upon patterns or *a priori* formulations. For example, we tend to assume that all items can be sorted into one of two categories, and we set the categories up as poles in a dualistic, either/or formulation. We frequently go on to identify one category as superior and the other as inferior. Likewise, we find it difficult to entertain two contradictory ideas in the mind simultaneously, and we shy away from both/and reasoning. This tendency to think about ideas in dualistic, hierarchical terms makes us uncomfortable with fields of inquiry that bring a variety of theories and methods to bear upon a problem. When we put more emphasis on an *a priori* set of ideas than on our data, and when we insist on one method of categorizing data as the single appropriate scholarly approach, then we fall into the trap of "methodolatry." As Mary Daly writes, "One of the false gods of theologians, philosophers, and other academics is called Method. It commonly happens that the choice of a problem is determined by method, instead of method being determined by the problem."[1] The result is that the intellectual process becomes atrophied and any new discoveries become impossible.

As Women's Studies has grown up as an academic discipline, theoretical absolutism has been in ascendancy, and thus women scholars have been under pressure to adhere to one theory or method rather than another. Feminist thinkers, however, have been wary of either/or reasoning, positing instead a both/and mode which comprehends phenomena holistically. Implicit in both/and thinking is the willingness to "spin among fields," as Mary Daly puts it, "leaping over the walls that separate the halls in which academics have incarcerated the 'bodies of knowledge.' "[2] The separation of knowledge into discrete fields walled off from each other so that interchange is discouraged has been an unfortunate intellectual development in recent years. A delight in leaping from one field to another, circling each one to gather the best fleece and then spinning out and interweaving our gatherings into an interdisciplinary fabric, has been one of the characteristics of women's studies scholarship.

Such spinning among fields often involves taking what we need from an existing theory, even one that is not amicable to feminism. I once watched with puzzlement as a group of French feminists happily debated the uses of Freudian thought for feminist literary criticism. I wondered how could they justify themselves as feminists? "We just play upon the two meanings of the verb *voler*," they reassured me. "In French it means both to steal—as in rob, fleece, plunder—and to fly away, take wing, to soar. We intend to fly away with those Freudian methods useful to our feminist purposes, and to leave the rest behind."

Implicit in this interdisciplinary approach is the notion of theory as a perspective based not on universals or absolutes or on the mind of the beholder but on things as they are. Because theory not only arises from the world of particulars but also changes as those particulars change, our hypotheses can only be tentative. This flexible empiricism contrasts sharply with the kind of theoretics that places more value on a set of formulations than on the data from which they derive. Even the staunchest inductive thinkers, however, have a tendency to universalize their findings. Aristotle disputed Plato's concept that particulars derive from abstract universals but still universalized the patterns he had induced. Moreover, neither the inductive nor the deductive approach guarantees a humanistic ethos. The idealistic Plato envisioned a state in which male and female were potentially equal, while Aristotle concluded that men and women were inherently unequal. Feminist scholarship needs to be idealistic, capable of imagining better modes of being without solidifying them into immutable principles. It also needs to be pragmatic, to observe things as they are and have been without despair. There is room in feminist thinking for both vision and realism.

Literature is a particularly apt field for the joining of the ideal and empirical approaches because it brings together both the ideal and the real in a relationship of tension and conflict. This tension was present in many British and American novels written by women between 1700 and 1978. In searching more than three hundred such works for recurrent patterns of plot symbolism, characterization, and theme, I was struck by the conservatism of even purportedly feminist writers, whose women characters showed a kind of mindless, tacit accommodation to gender norms. Patriarchal values proved to be far heavier a burden for these women authors than I had expected. At the same time, though, they wove into their texts strands of a more fully human potential self that contradicted gender norms. These two conflicting tendencies produced an ambivalence of tone, irony in characterization, and strange disjunction in plotting which indeed mirror women's social experience.

In spite of the rigid patriarchal ideology that has prevailed in much of women's literature over the past three centuries, portrayals of more ideal possibilities for women characters—images of total feminine selfhood in which sexuality, intellect, and creativity have developed in the same person—have occurred quite frequently. When women heroes explored their unconscious, they came up against ancient archetypes, often encoded, frequently hieroglyphic, but nevertheless present as possibilities to be assimilated and emulated. There seems to be some kind of forgotten code or buried script underlying the normative plots which women authors in a patriarchal culture internalize. If in the early years of the new feminist movement, consciousness-raising, or becoming aware of gender roles, was the primary task, in recent years "unconsciousness-raising" has assumed equal importance. Whether or not they derive from some golden age of women in our actual past, the archetypes we find in our literature represent vital psychological possibilities. The feminist archetypal critic seeks to elucidate these feminine counterstructures, to show how gender norms affect tone, attitude, imagery, characterization, and plotting, to trace the counterstructures through the total work of an author and then throughout the field of women's literature as a whole.

Here I will not criticize specific literary works but rather explain how the methods that emerged in the course of my inductive study differ from traditional archetypal approaches. I will explore ways that feminist theorists can "woolgather" in the rich fields explored by Jung, Frye, and Lévi-Strauss and offer some guidelines for using what we gather in our own rich weavings.

II   JUNG

I have always enjoyed the story of Jung's attempt to break away from Freud in order to develop his own theory because it offers a valuable lesson. Coming up against all sorts of emotional resistances and mental impediments, Jung took to playing with stones, building cottages and castles and whole villages down by the lakeshore. New theories do not necessarily spring like Athena from Zeus's frontal lobes. They depend as much on intuitions that arise while fooling about with ideas, building up and knocking over hypotheses, as on sophisticated thought processes. Lewis Thomas has argued that new ideas are discovered by making mistakes, erring by being errant, wandering from idea to idea, "being flung off into blind alleys, up trees, down dead ends, out into blue sky, along wrong turnings, around bends," leaping "across mountains of information to land lightly on the wrong side."[3]

Jung developed a definition of the unconscious which he differentiated from Freud's subconscious as less subordinate to than in balance with consciousness and less inferior to reason than valuable to the personality as a whole. Although both Freud and Jung saw the purpose of psychoanalysis as a balance between the Ego and the subterranean realms of the self, Jung emphasized the destructive capacity of too much Ego, on the one hand, and, on the other, insisted on the positive, beneficial qualities of the unconscious.

One would think that, in valuing the unconscious, Jung would have transcended the dualistic sexism that pervades Freudian theory. But Jung's association of emotion and illogic with women and logical rationality with men led him to a similar dichotomy. "Although man and woman unite," wrote Jung, "they nevertheless represent irreconcilable opposites which, when activated, degenerate into deadly hostility. This primordial pair of opposites symbolizes every conceivable pair of opposites that may occur: hot and cold, light and dark, north and south, dry and damp, good and bad, conscious and unconscious."[4] Although his theory valued the feminine and the unconscious, Jung placed these ideas on one side of a dualistic value system along with things "cold," "dark," "south," "damp," and "bad," and this categorizing undermined his integrative goals.

Jung admitted that he and his colleagues had little perspective on the feminine personality: "The elementary fact that a man always presupposes another's psychology as being identical with his own aggravates the difficulty and hinders the correct understanding of the feminine psyche."[5] Jung himself fell into difficulties when he tried to analyze women's dreams as if they were identical in configuration to men's. He once had a woman patient whose dreams and fantasies featured very powerful feminine archetypes, including sphinxes, Egyptian queens, and an Aztec god-lover.[6] Ironically, Jung derived his theory of the heroic quest from this single female patient who was diagnosed as schizophrenic. Later in his career, however, Jung recognized that there were specifically feminine archetypes like the Demeter-Kore narrative that were probably only accessible to and definitive of women.

Jungian psychoanalysis tends to assume that archetypal patterns derived from male experience are applicable to women's as well. As a consequence, female archetypes are interpreted according to male patterns, and the male patterns may be allowed to eclipse women's experience altogether. The feminine may be reduced to an attribute of the masculine personality rather than seen as an archetype deriving from women's experience that is a source of power for the self.

I once tried to explain to a Jungian therapist what I faced as a woman employed in a largely male academic world. "I wish that *you* could be a woman for just one day!" I finally burst out. "I don't have to do that," he replied smugly. "I come to terms with my anima every day." Even though femininity in the form of the anima, an assimilated attribute, must be experienced quite differently from being a woman oneself, the therapist felt that experiencing his anima was equivalent to understanding the experience of a real woman in the real world. He also regarded it as a secret internal source of power. Once one has decided that the internal experience of a quality is more valuable than the external phenomena from which the quality derives, one is open to an extremely dangerous kind of conceptual narcissism. The idea that men and women are inherently androgynous, each containing masculine and feminine qualities, is transformed into an assumption that if one has come to terms with these qualities internally, the problems associated with being a man or a woman in the social world will handle themselves.

The focus on internal integration of masculinity and feminity assumes that what goes on inside of the human mind is of more importance than what goes on in the world of other humans and the world of nature. Although Jung thought that society would benefit as individuals became more attuned to their psyches, he demonstrated an idealistic valuation of mind over matter. From the dualistic assumption that mind is ontologically other than and superior to matter, it is a short step to the notion that matter is derived from mind. Since men have been associated with mind and women with nature, or matter, there has been a tendency, given this idealistic bias, to see women as extensions or even creations of male imagination. If women are taken as attributes of the male psyche, or if women as representations of nature, the body, and the chthonic are understood only as others in relation to male questers, then women cannot be analyzed as creators and questers in their own right.

So easily does Jungian theory fall into this posture toward women that some feminist scholars have been wary of adapting Jung's ideas on the unconcious for feminist purposes.[7] But just as I am not willing to deny the richness and depth of women's dreams (which individual women, and not Jung or Jungians, create from within themselves), I am not willing to discard useful archetypes because Jung happened to formulate them. When I use the word "archetype" to describe images, symbols, and narrative patterns recurrent in women's literature, however, I am not defining myself as a Jungian. Some feminist scholars, assuming that the use of the term "archetype" constitutes a pledge of allegiance to Jung's system, prefer the term "archetypal" or even "prototypical" because it suggests a more fluid description of unconscious configurations. Naomi Goldenberg, in *Changing of the Gods*, prefers the word "archetypal" because "archetype" seems infected with the Jungian assumption that archetypes contain absolute and transcendent power: "While we must recover lost history and buried images of women, we ought not to set up these images as archetypes. If we do, we run the risk of setting bounds to experience by defining what the proper experience of women is. This could become a new version of the ideology of the Eternal Feminine and it could result in structures just as limiting as those prescribed by the old Eternal Feminine."[8] The new "Eternal Feminine" would consist of feminist scholars' descriptions of recurrent archetypes of feminine power, but it is not inevitable that the concepts we arrive at become as rigid as Jungian formulations. Archetypes, to take the dreaded example of the swastika, are value-free in themselves, though they can have a considerable destructive impact when used as cultural weapons.

Two further tendencies among women Jungians may account for Goldenberg's hesitation about promulgating the feminine as an eternal archetype. First is the tendency, best exemplified in Ann Bedford Ulanov's work, to posit a polarized model of the human psyche, with the feminine as one pole complementary to the masculine pole. Second is the insistence as in June Singer's work, that archetypes remain absolutes, separated from experience in a psychic realm of their own.

Ulanov, in *The Feminine in Jungian Psychology and in Christian Theology*, affirms the polar Jungian concept of the feminine as a "matrix," "container," "anima," a "central resource of the human spirit."[9] Ulanov's books, however, do contain other descriptions of women's experience that are recognizable and worth exploring for typical or recurrent patterns, such as the development of intuitive cognition, a nonlinear sense of time, and an adaptation to natural cycles. The works of women such as Mary Esther Harding, Toni Wolff, Emma Jung, and Marie Louise von Franz, all of whom Jung encouraged to undertake research on women's archetypes, similarly fascinate us with their descriptions of triply powerful moon goddesses, magic cauldrons, golden bowls filled with generative power, and magical feminine landscapes. But at the same time they repel us with statements that these archetypes make up half of a transcendent dualistic system in which men belong to the realm of light and logic while women, to quote Harding, derive from "the primordial slime."[10] We need to spin among these writings as among masculine fields, taking those ideas that can best elucidate our lives, dreams, art, and literature.

When feminist archetypal critics adapt Jung's system to their own purposes, they come up against Jungians who insist that they are in error. Thus June Singer, an American Jungian who has explicitly abjured Jung's gender bias, contends that we should not confuse the word "archetype," in the literary sense of a recurrent image, symbol, or narrative pattern, with Jung's definition of an acultural, wordless, and transcendent essence. In her view, the patterns I describe in my study of women's literature are not archetypes but archetypal images derived from inchoate and indescribable forms. "When we speak of images as if they were the archetypes," she writes, "they lose the quality of numinosity and the sense of power that characterizes them."[11] It is this belief in the absolute transcendence of archetypes that both Goldenberg and I find disquieting.

Goldenberg prefers to abandon the idea of fixed sets of archetypes along with the separation of the archetype from its expression in images which Singer posits. For Goldenberg it is "the separation of the absolute from experience which lies at the base of all patriarchal experience."[12] I, likewise, am not willing to separate the archetype from its expression in images, to divorce concepts from life. In concentrating on women's experience as expressed in literature, I have taken care that my descriptions fit rather than distort the text. Freed of the conceptual absolutism that grips both Jungians and the "theoretically sophisticated," feminist scholars can redefine Jung's concepts in accord with women's experiences. With the knowledge that not only men but also women undertake quests, encounter shadows, and deal with figures of the same and the opposite sex, we can adapt Jung's formulations to our own purposes.

The literary critic rarely encounters feminine archetypes in their purely feminist form in women's texts. Because gender norms are often unconsciously internalized by women authors, their writings are adulterated to a great degree with patriarchal cultural material. Symbols and narratives of feminine power are secrets kept hidden not only from men but from women as well. For thousands of years women have been forced to disguise and deny the heady mixture of intellectual, sexual, inventive, political, and procreative powers embodied in the ancient goddesses. When archetypal figures appear in works by women, one author may dread and another admire the same figure.[13] Moreover, a single author may take different attitudes toward such a figure within a single text, creating an ambivalence in tone and ambiguity in attitude that literary critics need to scrutinize. As we reconsider existing criticism which deals only with male heroes as questers and excludes consideration of texts dealing with women's quests for selfhood, we must be careful not to dismiss women heroes who are less than absolutely authentic in transcending gender norms. Feminine aspirations, existing in dialectical relationship to societal prescriptions against women's development, create textual mixtures of rebellion and repression which can be discerned by careful textual critics.

We can see how men's and women's archetypal experiences diverge by examining a typical narrative pattern, described by Jung, which often structures women's fiction: the rebirth quest or journey. (This pattern was most thoroughly described by Jung in *Symbols of Transformation*.) Many feminist critics would agree with Jung that patterns found in myths and stories, in fables and in more formal literary productions reflect the psychological development of the individual. In Jung's archetypal rebirth journey, the male hero crosses the threshold from the conscious to the unconscious world in an attempt to come to terms with his internal nature, seen not only as his own individual inner state but as part of a collective unconscious whose archetypes correspond to known cultural patterns. The male hero journeys from the day-to-day world of society into a different realm that is nevertheless translatable in cultural terms. One of the figures he encounters is his "shadow," which represents a collection of antisocial tendencies, his opposite or wicked self, himself as a self-hater and social rebel. The attributes that gather around the shadow at the first stage of the journey are social in the inverted sense, deriving from feelings repressed by the hero's good-citizen persona. As the male hero moves from the realm of the

personal unconscious down into the collective unconscious, the
shadow changes sex, merging alarmingly with his buried feminine self. The shadow and anima together form a powerful
"autonomous complex" which Jung calls the "dual mother" or
"terrible mother." The crux of the adventure is the hero's struggle
with this powerful feminine component of himself; his goal is to
absorb her import, master her autonomous control over his impulses, and then return, a reborn psyche, to everyday life.

Jung does not suggest that the hero is easily reintegrated into
society. In fact, the hero can expect suspicion and ostracism for
assimilating the anima figure, that is, for becoming androgynous.
His rebirth journey is nonetheless socially beneficial. Even if he
remains less than fully acceptable, his story becomes, as in the
case of Jesus and Virgil in Dante's *Divine Comedy*, the stuff of
legend and religion. Both figures are prototypical, and worthy of
ritual emulation. When women heroes emerge from such quests,
the least suggestion of androgyny makes them fearfully odd creatures, and they become social outcasts. Demeter, to use a classical
example, effected the rescue of her daughter Persephone without
ever being admitted to Olympus; and in American local color
fiction, strong autonomous country women are often under
suspicion of being witches. Thus when feminist archetypal critics
interpret women's literature with this pattern in mind, warps and
distortions arise.

When I began my research on women's novels, my initial
hypothesis was that women's literature would reveal patterns
parallel to the male rebirth quest with only incidental variations. I
expected, for example, a dual god, or powerful male figure,
where Jung found the dual mother. Maud Bodkin had suggested
that Heathcliff is to Catherine in *Wuthering Heights*, as Beatrice is
to Dante,[14] and Heathcliff, like the Aztec god of Jung's female
patient, at first seems to exemplify a blend of shadow and animus
at the core of feminine consciousness. In accepting Bodkin's
suggestion, I overlooked the fact that Beatrice, acting as inspiration and guide, leads Dante straight up to heaven, whereas
Heathcliff acting as demon lover, drives Catherine to a socially
correct marriage and later to her death. The sublimated love of
Dante for Beatrice gave him a vision of paradise and allowed him
to pen a masterpiece understandable to his reading public; the
Eros Heathcliff calls up in Catherine ruined her for life in society

and allowed Emily Brontë to produce a "freakish" book whose unfavorable reception may have contributed to her death. The difference is not merely between medieval spiritual love and romantic libido. Whenever women encounter erotic, godlike figures in literature, the encounters are often natural, antisocial, and above all antimarital; the women end up mad, dead, or socially outcast. An integrated feminine self, particularly when it includes full-fledged Eros, is frightening to society. Thus women's rebirth literature casts its heroes *out of* the social community rather than, as in men's rebirth literature, elevating them to the status of hero.

Very few women heroes are so fortunate as to encounter a Heathcliff, or "green world lover" who represents a natural Eros. This combination of the shadow and animus figure corresponds to Pan, Dionysius, and the horned god of the Celts and is always antimarital and antisocial. More often in women's literature, the male figure has only social content; he represents not the animus but the shadow, which plays quite a different role in female than in male experience. Jung's male shadow, or antiself, is antisocial, for man's dark impulses spring from rebellion against cultural norms and mores. Women's shadows are socially conformist, incorporating women's self-loathing for their deviations from social norms, specifically the norms of femininity. Women heroes in the novels of Edna O'Brien, Mary McCarthy, Olivia Manning, and Joyce Carol Oates, as in nineteenth-century fiction such as George Eliot's, punish themselves for violating gender norms. Their shadows are swollen with self-administered opprobrium for rebelling against what society wants them to be. For example, they punish themselves for any erotic feelings that spring from authentic, self-ish, desire. Should the female hero fail to reproach herself, the author accomplishes the task for her in a disproportionately punitive denouement. We do not find men punishing themselves for their libido (or other normal human desires); quite the contrary, they celebrate their sexuality. Women's shadows, rigidly social in content, fill them with self-hate for the very forces that should carry them toward greater development.

Whereas Jung's male hero encounters the dread figure of the dual mother, giving birth to himself in relationship to a loathed and revered femininity, the woman hero often encounters a "horrible husband" who stops her dead in her tracks. In women's experience, the gynophobic shadow and the animus are often fused in a masculine character who loathes the woman character every bit as much as she loathes herself, reinforcing her self-blame and dragging her into masochistic compliance with social standards. Examples of such male characters are Harald in Mary McCarthy's *The Group*, Sam Pollit in Christina Stead's *The Man Who Loved Children*, Jonathan in Sue Kaufman's *Diary of a Mad Housewife*, and husbands and lovers in novels by Fay Weldon, Doris Lessing, Katherine Anne Porter, Edna O'Brien, and Joan Didion. Confronting the horrible husband, the female character falls into madness, determines to commit suicide, or lapses into a zombielike state that precludes further development.

These novels describe partial, truncated, or failed rebirth journeys. The women heroes are unable to go beyond the personal realm of the unconscious because of the destructive messages communicated to women in everyday social experience. Male characters more easily get past the internalized social messages because social norms do not restrict men to the extent they do women. Because men are considered to be primary beings in our culture, and their physical and sexual development is regarded as a valuable part of their identity, men more easily overcome self-hate. Women, by contrast, tend to devalue their own bodies. A significant number of women's novels (Olive Schreiner's *The Story of an African Farm*, Sylvia Plath's *The Bell Jar*) feature characters blocked in growth by a hatred of their bodies as well as an emotional self-hate projected onto dismal lovers and horrible husbands. Such portrayals suggest that the journey through personal to unconscious experience is far more perilous for women than men. Women heroes are seldom able to assimilate these animus-shadow constellations which embody proscriptions against women's maturation. The green world lover, who embodies a powerful and amarital feminine eroticism, and the anima, often represented in the strong mother or goddess archetype, remain inaccessible. Thus novels in which women go mad or die at the hands of "perfectly nice" husbands outnumber by far novels in which women achieve rebirth and transformation.[15]

In some novels by women authors, the characters do overcome the animus-shadow block and reach a deeper and more holistic sense of the feminine. Examples are Lily Briscoe in Virginia Woolf's *To the Lighthouse*, the narrator in Margaret Atwood's *Surfacing*, and Martha in Doris Lessing's *The Four-Gated City*. Characters who do get past sadistic lovers, horrible husbands, and their own self-hate often do so in a journey of rebirth structured along the lines of the archetypal narrative of Demeter and her daughter Kore. In broad outline, Demeter's daughter Persephone is seized by Pluto, god of the underworld, while gathering flowers; he takes her away to his underground kingdom where she is forced to marry him. Grieving deeply, Demeter wanders the earth in search of her daughter until she meets Hecate, who has heard Persephone's cry. In fury, Demeter goes to Olympus to complain to Zeus, who refuses to help her. She then refuses to allow vegetation to grow upon the earth until her daughter shall be restored to her. After various adventures Demeter is finally able to effect the raising of Persephone from the land of the dead although, as a compromise, she will only spend the spring and summer months with her mother and return to Pluto for a third of the year. Jung found this narrative so specifically feminine that he felt it held no import for the masculine personality.[16] That Jung was able to recognize an archetypal pattern of primary concern to women shows that he realized the feminine psyche has different characteristics from those of the masculine psyche.

Whereas Jung's male heroes often confront the terrible mother at the nadir of their journey, women characters at the core of their quest often encounter a powerful integrative mother figure who offers regeneration. Like Martha at the end of Lessing's *The Four-Gated City*, the hero herself sometimes becomes such a mother or generative being. And often, as in Esther Broner's *Her Mothers* and Margaret Laurence's *The Diviners*, the daughter questing for a mother achieves transcendence in reconciling herself to her own daughter. The hero of Laurence's novel, Morag, is typical in that her journey does not lead her back into society but leaves her on its perimeter, writing in an isolated country house about her life's experiences. Woman's incursion into the unconscious is much more tinged with the personal and the social. For Jung's male questor the socially rebellious shadow leads the way to adventure; for the woman hero the shadow in the unconscious *is* society, the marital norms and sexual prohibitions that impede her full development. In the male version the ultimate encounter is with an "other" and takes the form of a struggle with and taking over of the feminine within the male psyche. The woman's encounter with a feminine figure at the depths of her psyche, when it occurs, is more a fusion than an agon; the woman encounters a being similar to herself which empowers even as it exiles her from the social community. Although women's journeys to a core of being where a holistic goddess provides beneficence and strength do not reconcile them to a society dominated by men, the journey itself continues to provide the structure of novels, poems, and dramas.

III   FRYE

The body of works which literary critics have most consistently studied for patterns of meaning is a selection of books which J. Hillis Miller has called "privileged texts."[17] Annette Kolodny has noted that the designation of these texts as authoritative is based on a "canonical sense of a shared and coherent literary tradition" that is not necessarily shared by women.[18] I studied this "canonical" body throughout my entire undergraduate and graduate career without ever (with the exception of one short story by Katherine Mansfield in freshman English) being assigned a single work by a woman author.

In my bachelor's thesis and doctoral dissertation, I applied Jung's archetypal patterns to William Blake's *Jerusalem* and Dylan Thomas's early prose, respectively. The Canadian critic Northrop Frye had previously applied these patterns successfully to what he called the "total verbal order," a body of literature corresponding closely to Miller's "privileged texts." Frye's *Anatomy of Criticism* (1957) is a systematic exposition of categories derived from a study of a wide sample of classical and European literature. Since the body of literature I had studied corresponded to the verbal order Frye assumed was "total," I did not question its perimeters; indeed, his manner of looking at literature and arriving at descriptive categories helped me immensely in my explication of Blake's and Thomas's recondite texts. In *Anatomy of Criticism* and later in *The Secular Scripture* (1976), Frye did refer to a few women authors in passing, but he did not distinguish women writers such as Jane Austen, Virginia Woolf, and Charlotte Brontë from male writers in discussing his general literary categories. Following Frye's lead, I assumed that women's literature would follow patterns not structurally distinct from those in men's literature, and that the variations in literary convention and narrative archetype found in women's texts would be interesting but incidental. In his theory of myths, for example, Frye arranged the seasons and the genres into a cycle of categories—summer/romance, autumn/tragedy, winter/irony and satire, and spring/comedy. As we shall see, his distinction between comedy, which he defines as inevitably social, and romance, which he associates with dreams and fantasies and wish-fulfillment, is useful in my study of the way women authors subvert traditional literary genres. Both comedy and romance initiate the hero into society, an acceptance most often symbolized by marriage.

As I undertook my survey of what looked to be a quite unexplored field, several aspects of Frye's approach appealed to me. I was impressed by his purportedly pragmatic and inductive approach to literature, his distaste for critical absolutes, and his common-sense assumption that literature differs from philosophy in being constructed of "images rather than abstractions" and dependent on metaphor rather than logic.[19] Frye defines archetypes as recurrent images, symbols, and narrative patterns rather than as transcendent absolutes in the Jungian sense. "I mean by archetype," he writes, "a symbol which connects one poem with another and thereby helps to unify and integrate our literary experience. . . . Archetypes are associative clusters, and differ from signs in being complex variables."[20]

Frye finds Jung's concept of an *a priori* collective unconscious useless to the inductive critic, calling it a wholly "unnecessary hypothesis."[21] "The first thing the literary critic can do is read literature, to make an inductive survey of his own field and let his critical principles shape themselves solely out of his knowledge of that field. . . . Critical principles cannot be taken over ready-made from theology, philosophy, politics, science, or any combination of these."[22] Though there might be a danger that this critical method would lead to an aesthetic ("art for art's sake") view of the relationship between literature and society, Frye explains that "seeing literature as a unity in itself does not withdraw it from a social context. On the contrary, it becomes far easier to see what its place in civilization is."[23] It seemed that I had found a practical, inductive critical method based on the assumption that literature affects society, albeit on its own rather than in theological, philosophical, or political terms.

For five years, with increasing frustration, I tried to make women's images and narrative archetypes correspond to Frye's categories. At last I realized what should have been obvious from the outset: men's and women's literature were sufficiently different that the same critical principles could not be applied to both. It is extremely hard for scholars trained in the study of a limited canon or "verbal order" to admit that the critical principles they have depended on do not necessarily apply to works outside of the canon. To be sure, these latter works are created within the culture and hence employ traditional literary conventions. It was precisely because women's texts in part conformed to general Western literary trends that I continued for such a long time to try to force feminine literature into the existing critical categories.

My first temptation was to make my material conform to Frye's categories or alter Frye's categories to fit my material, but Frye's own inductive method precluded either course. My second temptation was to declare there was no fit at all and conclude that women's fiction was a wholly self-defined body of texts. Frye's structures, however, are not entirely unconfirmed by women's literature. Women's fiction seems to be in a state of tension, for it exhibits standard literary conventions as well as contrary patterns deriving from women's long-standing exclusion from culture. Frye himself noted a perennial tension in Western literature between received tradition and revolutionary desire, between aristocratic and bourgeois conformity to things as they are and a recurrent proletarian attempt to destroy the existing system and build a world more consonant with human needs and desires. In my study, this opposition between what human beings desire and what society prescribes emerged as the formative structural characteristic of women's novels over the last three hundred years.

Although Frye purportedly limits his sample to literature, he includes the Bible. He treats it, however, not as another text but as a kind of metanarrative, a structural sourcebook for many other individual works. While this treatment is perfectly appropriate for examining a body of literature largely Christian in derivation, the weight Frye assigns to the Judeo-Christian story leads him to assume that there is a natural split between reason and emotion, logos and chthonos, the world of spirit and the world of matter. Frye's attention to Christianity leads him (as dualism did Jung) to take spirit as representing heaven and matter as potentially demonic, belonging to the lower reaches of hell. This split divides men from women, the latter being associated with nature. Men perceive women as closer to nature, the body, and the material world than themselves and hence see them as threatening sources of spiritual peril.

The archetype of Frye's that is most applicable to plots in women's fiction is the romance quest, a recurrent narrative pattern parallelling Jung's rebirth journey. Frye illustrates this pattern using literary plots rather than drawing on a broader field of clinical, religious, occult, and artistic evidence as Jung did. The romance quest is an adventure story, consisting of a series of forays that culminate in a major adventure, "the completion of which rounds off the story."[24]

The relationship between the hero of Frye's romantic quest adventures and the world of nature (although he mentions heroines, he presumes a masculine identity for his protagonist) is one of ego and other, of consciousness and a realm alien to it. Frye's hero starts out in a green world of innocent nature, a "pastoral and Arcadian world, generally a pleasant wooded landscape, full of glades, shaded valleys, murmuring brooks, the moon, and other images closely linked with the female or maternal aspect of sexual imagery."[25] Though nature is feminine, the hero is still described as "virgin." This figure Frye understands as "a vision of human integrity imprisoned in a world it is in but not of . . . always managing to avoid the one fate which really is worse than death, the annihilation of one's identity." Perceiving nature as other, the male hero fears for his selfhood should he lose his virginity, or ability to avoid sexuality.[26] When Frye describes the virginity of a feminine archetype, the goddess Diana, he intends something quite different. Diana's virginity expresses "the elusiveness of a nature that remains unreconciled to man" and involves identity with, rather than a holding back from, nature. The Diana figure is the natural trap that the virgin hero tries to avoid. In women's fiction, in contrast, the young woman hero accepts rather than fears her connection with nature; she is happy in a green world and feels threatened only by incursions from culture. Women's novels confirm Frye's apparently stereotypical statements about women's affinity with nature, but their perspective on the relationship between women and the green world is altogether different.

Scholars such as Joseph Campbell, M. Esther Harding, Jane Ellen Harrison, Sarah Pomeroy, and, more recently, Nor Hall, Merlin Stone, and several feminist theologians have researched the ancient concept of virginity. They argue that the figure of Diana/Artemis antedates Hebrews, Greeks, Romans, and Christians alike. This figure belongs to a period of time stretching back to about 7000 B.C. when goddesses were revered for a complex of qualities including generation, intellect, political power, and creativity. The virginity of the priestesses who served these goddesses, and the virginity of the goddesses themselves, was the virginity suggested by the word itself—"a woman (*gyn*) like a man (*vir*)." Such a virgin retained at all times the right to choose what to do with her own body, whether to roam at will or stay home, whether to practice celibacy or engage in sexual activity. Sarah Pomeroy has documented that, in temples dedicated to goddesses, celebrations of amarital feminine sexuality continued down to the last years of the Roman Empire. Here married women freely engaged in sexual intercourse to express allegiance to the female divinity. "To be virginal," writes Nor Hall, "does not mean to be chaste, but rather to be true to nature and instinct. . . . The virgin forest is not barren or unfertilized but rather a place that is especially fruitful and has multiplied because it has taken life into itself and transformed it, giving birth naturally and taking dead things back to be recycled. It is virgin because it is unexploited, not in man's control."[27]

Nature, out of man's control, may serve to enrich women's psychological self-sufficiency, but as anthropologist Sherry Ortner has suggested, men perceive such natural women as a fundamental threat to culture. "Culture (still equated relatively unambiguously with men) recognizes that women are active participants in its special processes, but at the same time sees them as being more rooted in, or having more direct affinity with, nature."[28] Ortner assumes that this vision of women as being closer to nature, playing the role of mediator between mind and matter, is itself a cultural construct, a "devaluation" of women.

Feminist archetypal theorists, encountering the powerful archetype of the nature goddess at home in her green world and answerable to no man, wonder if the construct is entirely a male invention. Feminist theory veers between decrying the male assumption that women are natural and hence culturally devalued, and affirming our allegiance to the natural world and the psychological strength we gain from it. Since women anthropologists and archetypal critics alike work within the academic establishment, receiving our training and permission to teach and conduct research from a culture that is male, we risk internalizing our culture's distaste for the delights of being a woman.

Ortner's anthropological conclusion that men see nature as an alien and alienating realm is certainly borne out in Frye's description of the hero's adventures in the myth of romance. Leaving behind the edenic realm of innocence, the hero must suffer the middle world of human action and choice, but he is only allowed full (heroic) leadership in that world after he has journeyed into a lower, dreadfully natural realm, "an environment of alienation, a sub-moral and sub-human world."[29] In order to become authentically cultural, the hero must enter the "dark and labyrinthine world of caves and shadows which is either the bowels and belly of an earth-monster, or the womb of the earth-mother, or both."[30] To most women, the womb is hardly an alien or a dreadful place, but Frye's findings clearly echo Jung's archetype of the dual mother. Not surprisingly, feminist critics have shied away from Frye's gynophobic definition of women as the inhabitants of hell.

The hero not only ventures down through the dreadful feminine, he tries to seize some of its power as a boon or elixir for culture. In *Creation and Recreation* (1980) Frye notes that "the cultural aura, or whatever it is, that insulates us from nature consists among other things of words, and the verbal part of it is what I call a mythology, or the total structure of human creation, conveyed by words. Such a mythology belongs to the mirror, not the window. It is designed to draw a circumference around human society and reflect its concerns, not to look directly at nature outside."[31] Like the mirror that the hero Perseus used to see Medusa's face without looking at her directly and being turned to stone, representations of women in male literature

become deflections of feminine power; beholding them indirect-
ly, men can harness women's natural wildness and assimilate
their energies into culture.

For Frye, literature is a conduit for natural power, and language
is a means of controlling and appropriating that power, which
vitalizes but is potentially disruptive to culture. The world of
nature eagerly sought by women is alien to Frye's heroes: "Man is
born into physical nature, the world of animals and plants . . .
and this world is theologically 'fallen.' It was not the home originally destined for man, and man cannot adjust to it as the animals
do. There is a higher order of nature which God intends man to
live in, and everything helps to raise him towards his own proper
level of human nature."[32] One of the aspects of nature that Frye's
hero must transcend is women.

Although women write their literature within culture, and
frequently display overt agreement with culture's devaluation
both of themselves and nature, a study of their fiction reveals a
positive and recurrent archetype of feminine identification with
nature explicitly at odds with the norms of culture. To the young
hero of women's fiction, nature is a home from which she is
forced into society. Nature is therefore less of a staging ground for
initiation into culture than a world in itself where she, like the
ancient virgins, can freely enjoy her own body. The distinction
between archetypal nature imagery in woman's mythology and
male culture's view of nature and women as ladders to heaven
becomes clear when we compare the Demeter-Kore narrative to
the rebirth journey as described by Frye. Whereas the male story
offers a view of human beings as alienated from nature, the
female archetype presents a picture of human beings at one with
the organic world.

The most important type of rebirth journey depicted in
women's literature parallels the story of Demeter's rescue of her
daughter Persephone (also known as "Kore," or maiden) from
the rapist Pluto, who abducted her while she was gathering
flowers in the fields of Rhia. Jung recognized the Demeter-Kore
rebirth journey as a distinctly feminine archetype unrelated to the
masculine psyche; in it men figure only as obstructions in the
quest of mother for daughter. Frye, however, merges the Demeter-Kore archetype with Christ's harrowing of hell and the
marriage plot in courtship fiction:

In Christianity the archetype of the completed romance is Christ rising from the dragon of death and hell with his redeemed captives; but the central figure need not take on such portentous overtones. The heroine who is saved from rape or sacrifice, even if she merely avoids Mr. Wrong and marries Mr. Right, is reenacting the ancient ritual which in Greek religion is called the Anabasis of Kore, the rising of a maiden, Psyche or Cindrella or Richardson's Pamela or Aristophanes' Peace, from lower to a higher world.[33]

It is the task of the feminist archetypal critic to disentangle the feminine archetypal woof from the masculine warp, to show the presence of the Demeter-Kore archetype, which expresses the deeply rooted quest for mother-daughter unity, in courtship fiction as women have conceived it.

The way in which Christians view heaven, earth, and hell differs from the way worshippers of Demeter and Persephone understood it. To Christians, heaven is "above," completely spiritual and antimaterial; the middle earth of trial and tribulation stands below heaven; and hell, a dread realm of retribution for wrong behavior, lies "below." In Frye's description of romance, hell is the place into which the hero plunges in order to overcome the feminine. (Jesus, apparently, is an especially divine questor.) In Frye's schema, life in the middle realm becomes an instrumental and transitory affair. The idea of the hereafter disrupts the natural balance. Nature, one's body, the seasons are seen as less real than heaven and so become sources of trial, means of ascent or descent rather than sources of being in and of themselves.

To the Demeter-Kore initiates, in contrast, the earth was all that there was. The seasons were of ultimate importance, and their cycles were embodied in the Demeter-Persephone story. Winter was a punishment by the goddess for the rape of her daughter. The cycle of initial unity of mother and daughter, Pluto's rupture of that unity, and its restoration in Persephone's anabasis represents psychologically "an internal conjunction of woman and woman, a woman's integration of her own parts, or, in Nor Hall's words, "a re-membering or a putting back together of the mother-daughter body."[34]

This kind of feminine self-sufficiency and integrity, upsetting to patriarchy, seems to have evoked tales of rape and usurpation committed by the Olympian divinities. In some accounts Demeter is raped by Poseidon; when she turns herself into a mare to repel him, he changes into a stallion. In other accounts Demeter is raped by Zeus when she appeals to him against Poseidon; she turns herself into a cow, but he subdues her by changing himself into a bull.

These transformations of Olympian divinities into animals remind us that preclassical goddesses were associated with powerful animals.[35] In Europe before 3000 B.C., for example, animals appear as consorts or companions to female divinities. The fact that the raping divinities so often take the form of animals familiar to goddesses may imply an archetypal rape narrative in which male beings employ disguise and trickery to usurp the power of the feminine divinity. Scholars such as Joseph Campbell, Marija Gimbutas, and others have suggested that the hordes invading early Europe replaced cultures in which women were not subordinate to men (at least in religious observance.). "In Old Europe," writes Gimbutas, "the world of myth was not polarized into male and female as it was among the Indo-Europeans and many other nomadic and pastoral peoples of the steppes. Both principles were manifest side by side."[36] It would be important to the Greeks, therefore, to illustrate the dominance of male gods over powerful and androgynous local goddesses through new narratives.

Demeter's rescue of Persephone, then, is the raped mother's attempt to save her raped daughter from the hands of her own rapist's brother. When Demeter goes to Olympus to appeal to Zeus, who has already raped her, Pluto, down below, is busily raping her daughter. The archetypal narrative thus encloses mother and daughter in patriarchal violence. With rapists above and rapists below, the hierarchy offers these feminine divinities no hope of redress or restoration. They have been torn from their proper place in the middle world of nature, which in its generative, life-giving, cyclical powers is world enough for them. In Greek accounts, and in European redactions, Persephone, not Pluto, becomes "Queen of the Underworld." She is a dread chthonic power luring men to their doom, an inhabitant of the feminine labyrinths so dreaded by Jung and the heroes of the romance quest. That myth should replace a king of hell with his own victim, and derogate femininity rather than rapacious and usurping masculinity, was wholly in accord with the historical shift from reverence of goddesses and the cycling seasons to worship of male gods associated with the sky, and with spirit, and logic. Considering all this, the two-thirds of a year that Persephone gets to spend with her mother represents a considerable triumph.

Persephone's return to life by no means parallels that of Jesus or the hero of Frye's romance. She is rescued from the demonic masculine and returned to earth to be reunited with her mother; after rape she regains her feminine integrity. Pluto, abducting the young girl into marriage, is surely the opposite of Frye's "Mr. Right." In Frye's archetypes of the romance quest and the happy comedy, marriage for the hero signifies "a return to the idyllic world," or a symbol of this return, and a cause for rejoicing. But in women's novels of development (Olive Schreiner's *The Story of an African Farm* provides a classic example) the young heroes, like Persephone, are pulled away from a green world of feminine integrity and enter, often against their wills or in a state of self-hypnosis, the airless and stultifying enclosure of marriage. In courtship novels by authors such as Jane Austen, Charlotte Brontë, and George Eliot, which Frye seems to be referring to in his "Mr. Wrong/Mr. Right" model, the female heroes work out a compromise. They reject the Plutos among their suitors and choose, with a modicum of self-will, seemingly more pleasant fiancés. Since traditional courtship fiction rarely depicts the outcome of these better marriages, the happy ending of the festive romance, that is, marriage, comprehended as the way membership in society is granted, remains problematical. In novels of marriage, however, even in the most conservative novels of manners, the laughter and ridicule characteristic of the comic genre is sometimes so ironic as to suggest that women's perennial desire to return to Demeter is at war with the strictures of Pluto; that is, allegiance to self and the commitment to marriage are at odds.

Frye traces the comic genre back to the classical period and defines it as an essentially social form designed to purge the "abnormal" or antisocial tendencies of the audience by laughter and ridicule of exaggerated behaviors. As in the rebirth journey and the romance quest, the male heroes are restored at the end to membership in the cultural community. Because women are not full-fledged members of society, the dénouements in women's fiction, no matter how purportedly normative the genre, are often full of wry discontent and forced accommodation. The structure of the comic genre does not leave room for women's aspirations; the freedoms women truly desire are denied or limited in such narrow confines. Women writers do employ the comic genre and the other conventional forms of literature, but the discrepancy between what women desire and what society prescribes is reflected (perhaps unconsciously) in strangely acerbic tones, ironic overtones, ambivalent attitudes, and uncomfortable endings. Marriage belongs to culture, and culture is male. To the Demeters and Persephones in the world, who revel when they can in the green world, both marriage and culture seem destructive.

From the perspective of feminine archetypes, Frye's association of the Demeter-Kore quest with Christ's harrowing of hell and the structure of courtship fiction appears misguided. On the one hand, women's literature tends to undermine the comic resolution of marriage through an ironic ridicule of social norms and mores. On the other hand, much of women's fiction and, also, poetry, rejects culture in favor of a marginality closer to nature.

Women mediate between nature and culture. As mediators or translators, women can be approached by men as they try to create poetry. Frye recognizes woman's closeness to nature as a useful vehicle for male poets who wish to approach the "primitive" well-springs of inspiration, a way to get at the roots of creativity. In a rather peculiar statement, he differentiates between the "discursive writer," whose conscious will places him "over and against the body of things he is describing" (and hence on the side of culture as removed from or alienated from nature) and the poet, "who writes creatively rather than deliberately" and who is "not the father of his poem [but] at best a midwife, or, more accurately still, womb of Mother Nature herself: her privates he, so to speak."[37] Here conscious, discursive writing is viewed as fatherly, patriarchal, but poetry requires of the male writer a kind of metaphoric transvestism; he must acquire women's organ of generation. Male poets must assume women's identity if they are to find a closeness with nature that will allow them to write poetry. Woman thus becomes the vehicle for creativity, or a genitalic muse.

The male writer usurps the power of giving birth as Zeus did by swallowing Metis, the goddess of wisdom, and then giving birth to her daughter Athena through his forehead. Athena had ruled Athens before the arrival of the Greeks, and the story illustrates Zeus's supplanting of local divinities. Once swallowed, goddesses can be regurgitated and made to speak in the voice of the new gods. The fabric of culture, which Frye says insulates us from nature, is woven of natural material which has been transformed for the purposes of patriarchy. For Frye, one can only arrive at words, which are the tokens of culture, by approaching nature and ravishing her for her generativity. The result is Frye's "total verbal order," the established canon of literary critics.

Actually, Frye in some ways shows himself to be as alienated from the verbal order as women are from culture. When he turns his attention to his own literature, in his collection of essays on Canadian literature, *The Bush Garden,* he comes up with archetypes quite different from those found in the received European canon. This collection includes significant numbers of women's texts and considers the animistic and totemistic attitudes of tribal Canadians. It also describes the tendency in Canadian male literature to regard the male hero as victim rather than victor. Frye, in this collection, recognizes the "Cartesian egocentric consciousness" of European literature as a dangerous and spiritually limiting tendency, for it underlies "a turning away from nature so completely that it becomes an idolatry in the reverse." This excessive attention to reason compromises the heroes' psychological integrity and leads them to ecologically disastrous practices. Missing in Frye's Canadian criticism is the foul and fetid belly of the terrible female, "Diana of the triple will, the white goddess who always kills, and whose rebirth is only for herself."[38] In her place we find, in addition to plenty of men and women for whom self-sufficiency is a goal and ideal, a "poetic consciousness formed within the leviathan of Canadian nature, feeling that it belongs there and can no longer think of itself as a swallowed outsider."[39]

When Frye extends the "canon" to include women and noncanonical male writers, he must adjust his inductive findings in accord with his new data. It is as though Canadians, in their own way as alienated from "privileged texts" as women, look beyond standard European cultural norms for their own modes of expression. When they do, they find their marginality far closer to nature, more humanistically whole, than the culture which they never felt comfortable with in the first place. The sexism so noticeable in Frye's archetypal categories apparently derives from the Classical, Christian, and European literature he surveys rather than from some *a priori* theoretical principle. When he turns his attention to different writings, his categories shift inductively.

Feminist critics can be grateful that Frye pursues the facts wherever they may lead him, unafraid to alter his hypotheses in accordance with new data. Feminist scholars must be wary of becoming so alarmed by masculine scholarship's lack of perspective on women that they reject all of its methods as useless in describing our own experience. The muses men seek were originally singers in their own right, innocent of heaven and hell, celebrators of the seasons and the earth. That men have swallowed them should not deter us from looking for them again, re-visioning them for our own purposes. To ignore the patterns Frye has identified because the works he analyzes offer gynophobic stereotypes would be to reject the rich stores of expression which we have generated during our prolonged marginality. Frye's method, principally the description of archetypal categories as they structure literary form, is a tool that feminist critics can appropriate profitably and use for our own purposes.

IV   LÉVI-STRAUSS

Like Jung and Frye, anthropologist Claude Lévi-Strauss considers himself an inductive, empirical scholar who wants to describe recurrent patterns in his data and who does not want the patterns he describes to be taken as absolutes. Lévi-Strauss does not expect that other researchers will necessarily reach his same conclusions. He says that he tends to forget his postulations as soon as he has written them down and that nobody, least of all himself, should take his observations as categorical absolutes.[40] We have seen how both Jung and Frye, despite similar disclaimers of theoretical absolutism, are limited by their masculine perspective on feminine experience and by their exclusion of much feminine experience from consideration as relevant data. Their perspective on their data is further skewed by the assumption that ideas can be classified into dualistic categories which can be arranged in a hierarchy, and that this kind of categorizing is in the nature of the intellectual process itself. This frame of mind arises from the unconscious equating of patriarchal values with the normal or the real.

Anthropologists arrive at conceptualizations about societies by categorizing data from field work and observation. Lévi-Strauss's contribution to anthropological theory has been the discovery that various activities in a given culture—barter, for example, or cooking, or marriage—are organized in similar ways, deriving from a structure or basic code underlying all of the activities in that society. By figuring out the mode of organization common to a variety of activities in a given culture, he arrives at a model or basic pattern of organization. Lévi-Strauss calls invariant elements in a culture's activities "bundles of relations" and says that they are not incidentally recurrent but reflect the substructure of the group's behavior. A study of several "bundles of relations" thus yields a hypothesis that can be used to elucidate other aspects of the same culture. Furthermore, by comparing one culture to another, a remarkable similarity in cultural models emerges, suggesting an ultimate basic model, or deep structure, underlying human societies in general. Lévi-Strauss thus arrives at an "ultimate code," a hypothesis applicable to the whole range of human behavior based on certain invariant elements in a wide variety of cultures. This deep structure is analogous to the collective unconscious in Jung's system and the total verbal order in Frye's. The concept of a deep structure in human behavior is important not only in anthropological research, in describing human life on a cross-cultural basis, but also in linguistic and literary studies. Structuralism was especially fashionable in literary criticism during the 1970s.

Feminist archetypal critics have found Lévi-Strauss's methods quite interesting although they have questioned his basic assumptions as well as the range of data that structuralists have used to arrive at their conclusions. Like Lévi-Strauss, I have assumed, in applying my archetypal descriptions to women's needlework and crafts as well as literature, that all aspects of a culture can be analyzed in a similar manner (See note 13). Whereas Frye's data was strictly literary, Lévi-Strauss, like Jung, ranges through a variety of cultural areas, seeking analogies between them.

When I first came across Lévi-Strauss's idea that "the true constituent units of a myth are not isolated relations but bundles of such relations combined to produce a meaning," I was teaching a course on mythology in which the students' first assignment was to report on various gods, goddesses, and heroes such as Apollo, Zeus, Demeter, Aphrodite, Helen, Athena, and so on. Students invariably droned off dull summaries lifted wholesale from Larousse and the various dictionaries of classical mythology. When I asked them instead to report on "bundles of relations" in the stories about these figures, the results were stunning. They furnished analyses of invariant activities among the standard accounts: "Apollo tended to attack people, frequently women"; "Zeus was 'the god of' a lot of things, like weather, war, etc."; Hera "was mostly jealous, and spent a lot of time nagging Zeus for playing around"; "Aphrodite was promiscuous in a deceitful way" and "a real floozy." As the students reported on these recurrent patterns in Olympian relations, I listed them on the board, thus creating an overview of typical behaviors in Greek mythological narratives. One of the most recurrent activities among the heroes' and divinities', we discovered, was rape. Another invariant characteristic of the gods and goddesses was that they were said to be 'gods or goddesses of' this or that activity, implying an original invention and mastery over weather, the sun, poetry, and the like, and a lot of tugging and hauling was going on over who was god or goddess of what.

Lévi-Strauss talks of reading myths like an orchestral score, from top to bottom, so that all of the elements can be sorted out. Using this approach, the students could see that Greek mythology was typically structured around a conflict, often between a god or male hero and something considered hostile, which was to be conquered and its powers taken over. The fact that so many myths turned on these conflicts, that gods and heroes battled animals and bizarre beings, goddesses and mortal women, over and over suggested that whatever it was they were fighting was never completely conquered. The question arises, then, whether this perpetual dualism, or arrested dialectic, is based on a universal pattern of conflict. Structuralists would be likely to see the conflicts in Greek mythology as evidence of a deep structure of antagonism underlying all of Greek life and thought. If similar conflictive patterns were discovered in archetypes from other mythologies, the structuralists might conclude further that attacks on women and animals by men and the struggle against formidable natural powers are invariant patterns describing human society in general. Greek culture, however, was not a static phenomenon whose manifestations were fixed over time; rather, it was one among many cultures in a common area that clashed with each other in a historical sequence. The research of Harrison, Campbell, Gimbutas, and others suggests that the Greeks in the Mediterranean gradually replaced various peoples whose societies were quite differently organized. Thus the conflictive pattern typifying Greek mythology was more likely the result of an evolutionary process by which a dominant culture usurped other cultures, partially rejecting and partially assimilating those cultures' norms in the process.

Lévi-Strauss, however, tends to see each culture he describes as nonevolutionary, frozen in historical time. He describes the primitive, mainly non-Western societies from which he gathers his data as being structured according to dualistic patterns. So frequently do the cultures he studies seem to fall into two groups, each with its own set of symbols and activities antithetically related to the symbols and activities of the other, that he concludes that dualistic, or "binary," patterning is the most typical attribute of all cultures. "Mythical thought," he concludes, "always works from the awareness of oppositions toward their progressive mediation."[41] Rituals, mythic narratives, and cultural practices mediate by combining opposites, but the balance achieved is only temporary and the sets of opposites recur eternally.

Thus, like Frye and Jung, Lévi-Strauss posits a static set of contraries as a constant not only in human experience but in the ultimate code or deep structure of thought by which that experience is shaped. But what of the deep structure of these contraries themselves? What is the reason for the head-on clash between one thing and another? This line of questioning leads us to look at who was god or goddess of what before the Greeks arrived, what Hera was up to before she met Zeus and how this affected their marriage, and what the original powers of the goddesses were from whom the Greek Aphrodite, Artemis, Athena, and Hera were derived. In spinning out answers to these questions, we will not be surprised to find that Lévi-Strauss's ahistorical bundles of relations derive some of their rigidity from *a priori* assumptions about men, women, and nature, assumptions which derive as much from Western European thought processes as from the data he studied.

One of Lévi-Strauss's *a priori* assumptions is that the normal relationship between human beings and nature is a dominant-submissive pattern. He asserts that the purpose of "scientific thinking is to achieve mastery over nature—I don't need to elaborate that point, it is obvious enough."[42] Just as scientists strive to control the natural world, structural anthropologists, and the literary critics who derive their methods from them, assume that the purpose of the intellect is to transcend nature, to use its powers to construct something unnatural, namely, culture. The goal of this process is to create abstract or conceptual patterns which will be useful in further analyzing data, the end product being a primary symbolic structure rather than a reciprocal relationship with nature. The purpose of the thinker is to act upon nature in order to translate its powers into language and culture, which exists in opposition to the natural world it feeds upon.

In Lévi-Strauss's writings, dualistic and hierarchical thinking is taken for granted as the natural way the human mind works. But such a deep code seems doubtful given that the peoples whom Lévi-Strauss studies take a far different attitude toward nature than Europeans do. It is surprising that for all his admiration of the "pensée sauvage" of his primitive subjects, Lévi-Strauss's perspective contrasts so sharply with their totemistic and animistic belief systems, which are based on a holistic view of nature. Animism involves a sense of reciprocal interchange with rocks, trees, and animals, while totemism (from an Algonquin word denoting a family or clan's association with some natural item) is a kind of animism in which a tribe traces its origins to some object and maintains a right relationship with the nonhuman, intrinsic essence of that object. To the totemist an owl, sycamore, or fox is valued for its owlness, sycamoricity, or foxhood. To the structuralist the owl, sycamore, or fox valued by the totemist is "a *sign* which explains a natural event or phenomenon by means of an already existent cultural construct."[43] While the natural item is important to the totemist in and of itself, to the structuralist it is a secondary item, an auxiliary or proxy for an abstract concept belonging to the realm of culture which transcends objects. Lévi-Strauss's goal of creating a "science of the concrete" and "logic of totemic classifications" out of totemistic belief systems means that logic overwhelms nature, imperialistically subsuming phenomena by translating them into abstract essences.

A group of British anthropologists have taken issue with the deep structure of Lévi-Strauss's descriptions of nature and culture. Carol MacCormack points out in *Nature, Culture and Gender* that

> although Lévi-Strauss has attempted to cast the nature-culture contrast in a timeless, value-free model concerned with the working of the human mind, ideas about nature and culture are not value free . . . . The opposed categories of nature and culture (or society) arose as part of a historically particular ideological polemic in eighteenth-century Europe; a polemic which created further contradictions by defining women as natural (superior), but instruments of a society of men.[44]

In the eighteenth century, although nature was regarded as a source of wisdom and women were associated with nature, women were disassociated from wisdom. Throughout this crucial period in Western intellectual history, women continued to be associated with nature in a pejorative sense, despite the high valuation given by the Enlightenment community to nature as a source of truth and even social contract. Examining Lévi-Strauss's concepts of women, nature, and culture in depth, these anthropologists have discovered that even when he admits that the idea of bundles of relations is merely a methodological tool, and not necessarily an absolute, he continues to examine the behavior of primitive peoples with a patriarchal mind.

Not surprisingly, women fare just about as well as nature under Lévi-Strauss's analysis. Just as natural items are less important than the signs for them, women in masculine culture become vehicles or useable objects in culture rather than agents in their own right. In Lévi-Strauss's view, women derive from nature (they are closer to natural processes) and men from women, but culture is born when men master both women and nature. His conceptual imperialism leads him to reduce the concrete reality of nature to empty forms or concepts and, similarly, to posit women as vehicles for male use in culture. As with Jung and Frye, what seems to give rise to this model of nature, women, and culture is first, a fear of women and their natural powers; second, and equally fearsome, an association of language or the origin of words with women; and third, a theoretical rigidity stemming from the valuing of concepts over reality.

Lévi-Strauss's attitude toward women and the birth process resembles, in some striking ways, Frye's awe of the goddess of "triple will" and Jung's fear of the dual mother who can as easily devour as create. Commenting on the dragons and sphinxes in Greek mythology, Lévi-Strauss remarks that a dragon is a "chthonian being which has to be killed in order for mankind to be born from the earth" and that "the sphinx is a monster unwilling to permit man to live." Like Jung, he associates these powerful primordial beings with a dreaded birth process and the concept of the "autochthonous origin of mankind."[45] Autochthonous birth means being born only from the earth, that is, having a parthenogenetic origin in the feminine rather than a transcendent (male) divinity. Although animistic and totemistic cultures often celebrate such origins, re-enacting emergence from the belly of the mother through rituals such as the dancing in and out of the seasons, the Greeks, and Lévi-Strauss, find such an earthy origin abhorrent.

However loathsome the earth may be, nature remains the source of life and nourishment. Culture, comprehended as male, can hardly remove itself from nature entirely but must remain in close symbiosis with it for both bodily and intellectual nourishment:

> Men by cultural means exchange women who perpetuate these same men by natural means and they claim to perpetuate species by cultural means and exchange them *sub specie naturae;* in the form of foodstuffs which are substitutable for each other since they all provide nourishment and since, as with women also, a man can satisfy himself by means of some foods and go without others in so far as any women or any foods are equally suitable to achieve the ends of procreation and subsistence.[46]

Lévi-Strauss's conflation of women and words as items of exchange in culture derives from this observation of marriage practices in which women are exchanged for bride prices. Since women are tokens of exchange in these customs they are, in his strange logic, analogous to the words exchanged in linguistic communication. Like words and food women are items of barter rather than subjects in their own right: as in eating, so in language. However coyly Lévi-Strauss may answer feminist protests at his association of women with words as common items of exchange ("words do not speak, but women do; as producers of signs, they can never be reduced to the status of symbols or tokens"), he insists on an analogy between the exchange of women in marriage and words in language: "The position of women . . . may afford us a workable image of the type of relationships that could have existed at a very early period in the development of language, between human beings and their words."[47]

Women may be the source of men, in birth, but in society they must submit to them; they may provide food and sustenance, but they must be assigned a minor position in male culture. And by corollary, since both women and words are exchanged in the process of communication, women and language can both be subsumed as items of use in culture. This concept of women being like words becomes less bizarre when we recall certain stories from Greek mythology: Apollo's destruction of the pythoness at Delphi and his assuming of her oracular powers; Perseus' stealing of winged horse Pegasus, the source of poetry, born from the body of Medusa after he murders her; and the seizing of Athena's powers by the Greeks when they conquered a city she had ruled for thousands of years. The connection between women and language is also made by Jung and Frye. The generative feminine, assimilated to male uses, becomes a potent source of poetic and spiritual inspiration.

Once the word has been split from its source in nature, the sign from its object, nature and natural objects can be cast aside in favor of the abstract representations. Although Lévi-Strauss's models are supposed to derive from descriptions of concrete data, they become the building blocks for an ultimate code that supersedes the phenomena from which they derive. Frederic Jameson deplores this shift from data to models because "the basic conceptual units are given from the outset and organize the data. . . . At this point the mind/body opposition is transformed into a structural or conceptual distinction on the one hand and the meaningless physical substratum or hylé by which that significance is vested."[48] If meaning derives only from concepts, rather than concepts from data, then intellectuals give themselves permission to do whatever their ideas suggest with matter, women, and the earth itself. Commenting on a particularly virulent structuralist fracas that took place at Cambridge University in Great Britain in the winter of 1981, Richard Webster wrote: "In the whole of our cultural history there has perhaps never been an intellectual movement claiming to belong to the humanities which has carried the cult of precision and purity, and the habit of reducing human nature to pseudo-mathematical formulae, to such an improbably cruel extreme as has structuralism in recent years."[49] The particular cruelty to which Webster referred has to do with the brutal competition among British academics. The greater cruelty is that the adherence to concepts at the expense of data, the belief in the human mind as not only superior to but the source of the external world, endangers not only intellectual life but the earth itself.

The assumption that ideas have a life of their own, or reach us from some suprahuman source, whether it be a collective unconscious, total verbal order, or ultimate structuralist code, separates mind from environment, spirit from body, perception from things as they are. In recent years academics have been plagued by a craving for absolutes. We long for a set of terms and hypotheses which we can cling to in mutually bonded groups. But this craving could make us prey to some of the worst excesses of the Enlightenment mind. It was during the Age of Reason, after all, that the greatest numbers of heretics and witches were burned, their offense in many cases being an insistence on integration of mind and body, spirit and nature. Holy wars, crusades, and fascist nation states have emerged out of mutually agreed upon belief systems that savagely attack all outsiders. In the academy, one would hope, the commitment to inductive and collective scholarship would give rise to a greater openness, a greater willingness to experiment with hypotheses while respecting material data. Logic *can* be employed for the sake of nature, mind for the sake of psyche, without alienating scholars from nature and their own bodies.

Jung, Frye, and Lévi-Strauss are quite open to shifts in method and new hypotheses. All three take a broad field of human experience and apply painstakingly descriptive methods to elucidate the complex productions of the human brain, whether in the form of manifestations of the unconscious, in the case of Jung, the literary forms these sometimes assume, in the case of Frye, or deep structures of social behavior as in Lévi-Strauss. Jung's concept of androgyny as a synthesis transcending polarities, Frye's admission of a more balanced relationship between human beings and nature in Canadian literature, and Lévi-Strauss's belief that many societal activities mediate between nature and culture suggest that these theorists are willing to take a process approach to intellectual inquiry. Feminist archetypal critics, exploring women's productions in dreams, art, literature, and social behavior, can abjure their limited perspectives while adapting as many methods as necessary in constructing our own hypotheses on the nature of the feminine and the nature of the human mind.

V   FEMINIST HYPOTHESES AND ARCHETYPAL CRITICISM

One of the principal feminist hypotheses put forward in recent years is that the forms of behavior regarded as proper for women and men are not absolutes handed down from above but rather human inventions. They are sexual paradigms, as Elizabeth Janeway says, which we have taken as "part of the seamless web of cultural connections and directives" but which in fact "force contradictions upon one's sense of self."[50] Culture's seamless web appears seamless only to fully empowered (male) members of the culture. In women's experience the web is less seamless, just as Frye's total verbal order and Jung's collective unconscious are less total and less collective, than in men's experience. In fact, from women's marginal position in culture, this web seems to be ripping apart at the seams; it is an "obsolescent disciplinary matrix" (in Janeway's words) disintegrating under the "good new questions" feminists are asking.

"Feminism," writes Adrienne Rich, "means finally that we renounce our obedience to the fathers and recognize that the world they have described is not the whole world."[51] Pointing out that the emperor has no clothes can be dangerous, however, psychologically as well as professionally. When academic women challenge authority, we may come to wonder whether we are insane or hallucinating. We begin by trying to conform to

traditional thinking precisely because, as outsiders, we fear re-
prisal if we bring in new data or, even worse, shift from either/or
to both/and reasoning and begin to argue in circles and spirals
rather than in straight logical lines. As Rich admits, renunciation
is not a one-step process. It involves many years of struggling to
transcend one's educational conditioning, a conditioning as likely to operate from within one's own head as from without.

"Female *a priori* knowledge," notes Janeway, "cannot be taken
as valid by the female self who is required by the laws of otherness to live as a displaced person not only in man's world but
within herself. As a result, her primary impulses to act are always
caught and held on a frustrating brink. Even if the delay is only
momentary, the need to overcome it by an act of conscious will
changes the quality of female activity by robbing it of the full,
playful freedom of spontaneity."[52] Feminist archetypal scholarship must tread a careful path between acceptance of the "laws
of otherness," or masculine culture's definitions of women as
other, and affirmation of "female *a priori* knowledge," or those
things it seems we have known from a time long before the laws
of otherness closed in upon us like the spikes of iron maidens.

The characterization of women as other comes from culture
rather than our intrinsic sense of ourselves. Simone de Beauvoir,
in her influential book *The Second Sex*, becomes so caught up in
describing women's alienation that she sounds as if she were not
a woman but some gender-free commentator dwelling above
womanhood itself. In writing about the female reproductive cycle, she is particularly dismissive, as if describing someone else's
body rather than her own. (Her mentor Sartre likewise tended to
define all flesh, including his own, as nonself.) Scholars who, like
de Beauvoir, concentrate too singlemindedly on cultural definitions of women, tend to think of women in wholly negative
terms. Such scholars work under the patriarchy's laws of otherness and turn away from *a priori* wisdom and experience. For
example, L.J. Jordanova has noted in de Beauvoir's critique of the
myths of feminine subordination a tendency to accept these
myths as validated hypotheses:

> Simone de Beauvoir (1972) was right to emphasize the importance
> of myths in the ways women are seen. She takes for granted,
> however, that the polarities they contain are basic to the way the

human mind works. Thus, for her, it is inevitable that woman has been taken as other by man, and so seen only in relation to him.[53]

In their rejection of women's otherness, however, feminist scholars tend to take not only norms prescribing subordination for women but all descriptions of femininity as myth, or untruth. Because some stories and symbols describing feminine experience have proven sexist, they dismiss all of them and thus they throw out the crucial archetypes along with the stereotypical images. This tendency to consider as tainted by patriarchy everything found in cultural repositories leads, paradoxically, to assumptions like de Beauvoir's that women are to be defined wholly in terms of their otherness and not in terms of their intrinsic being.

Just as Jordanova, MacCormack, and the anthropologists who contributed to *Nature, Culture and Gender* insist on asking questions of women not previously asked by male and masculine anthropologists, feminists using archetypal theory insist on asking questions not previously asked by archetypal theorists. We need to get behind the mirror of womanhood, with its false and sometimes glittering patriarchal images or stereotypes, into the zinc, the deep background of women's lived experience. Judith Plaskow and Carol Christ make an important distinction between the activity of deconstructing patriarchal axioms and the equally vital task of examining our traditional experience as women:

> Thinkers who focus on traditional experience believe that whatever sexist culture has rejected or denigrated must be revalued in a holistic feminist vision. Whatever is considered "feminine" may be reappropriated from a feminist perspective. While some would argue that women's traditional experiences are simply a product of alienation, others believe that women's values are less alienated than men's. Women's body experiences—such as menstruation, pregnancy, lactation, and menopause, and the traditional association of women with nature that is based on these experiences—are also part of women's traditional experiences that many feminists wish to affirm.[54]

It is possible to reappropriate women's responses to our experience and reaffirm feminine *a priori* knowledge. Those responses are available in women's writings, folklore, and artifacts. These materials exist within the patriarchal enclosure, buried in each feminine self (and also in the psyches of humanistic men), and they survive from women's historic and prehistoric past in spite of the overarching masculine culture. Some feminist critics have studied the interaction between women's historic (and often unconscious) knowledge and the culture's prescriptions, and the ways in which this interaction affects the conventional structures of literary texts. Nancy K. Miller, for example, points out a discrepancy between women's fantasies of power and the "approved maxims" or "grid of concordance" through which society forbids power to women.[55] In my study of women's novels, I saw how traditional modes of characterization differ from what women heroes seek for an identity. In my future studies of poetry I will be undertaking a close reading of individual poetic texts to discover whether the same interaction between society's norms and women's desires affects imagery, tone, and poetic structure.

In describing a dialectic between women's personhood and society's rules, I do not mean to suggest a static dualism like the binary paradigm that structuralists posit as the ultimate code within the human brain. Archetypal theory must understand the feminine as more than a negative or positive pole in a masculine-feminine duality. It must transcend what men have projected from within their own psyches as ultimate feminine archetypes, and it must be based on a re-evaluation of long-held beliefs and practices which characterize women as outsiders in culture.

The tension between Lévi-Strauss's ultimate code and the feminine experience of self is not static and unhistorical but dynamic and changing through time. If one accepts the melioristic doctrine that human life has been getting better and better, it is hard to grasp the idea that for half the human race conditions in the past might have been better, psychologically if not physically, than they are now. In cultures which valued femininity and celebrated women's bodily experiences in ritual and religious practicies, girls would develop greater psychological well-being and sense of self than girls conditioned by a society which throughout its "seamless web" devalues women. "Where the Goddess had been venerated as the giver and supporter of life as well as the consumer of the dead," writes Joseph Campbell, "women as her representatives had been accorded a paramount position in society as well as in cult."[56] Campbell bases his hypotheses that a world-wide system of goddess worship, accompanied by matriarchal culture, antedated patriarchy on the theories of Jane Ellen Harrison and others of "The Cambridge School." As we shall see, more recent researchers like archaeologist Marija Gimbutas have suggested a less monolithic and monotheist but nonetheless widespread system of folk beliefs in goddesses, worshipped with gods in polytheistic religions.

Thus, although the Harrison/Campbell theory of a goddess-worshipping system representing a diametrically opposite, though similarly dominant, culture antedating the patriarchy is oversimplified, recent scholarship has nonetheless established that the veneration of women and women's cyclical physiology formed the basis of many prehistoric and historic religions around the world. Eventually, however, cyclical, natural and goddess-oriented world views were overcome by one that emphasized dualism, conquest, and gynophobia. Jane Ellen Harrison analyzes literary texts to elucidate this epic struggle. Examining specific texts which describe myths and rituals and making her own translations of historical documents, this Oxford classicist identifies a complex feminine substructure that reacted against classical religious practices. She documents classical and preclassical strata:

> The southern and earlier stratum, which is Anatolian as well as Cretan . . . has the dominant Mother-God, while the northern stratum which is Indo-European has the Father-God, head of a patriarchal family. . . . The northern religion of course reflects a patrilinear, the southern a matrilinear social structure. It is not a little remarkable and shows how deep-seated was the sense of difference that the Mother was never admitted to the Olympus of Homer. Even Demeter, honored though she was through the length and breadth of Greece, had never in Olympus any but the most precarious footing.[57]

Relying on Harrison, Campbell describes the process by which the northern stratum in Europe and the Semitic tribes in the Middle East ravaged with their god-oriented absolutism an "essentially organic, vegetal, non-heroic view of nature" underlying "older mother myths."[58] Gimbutas' research on Old

Europe (7000–3500 B.C.) reveals a similar tension between masculine and feminine world views:

> This masculine world is that of the Indo-Europeans, which did not develop in Old Europe but was superimposed upon it. Two entirely different sets of mythical images met. Symbols of the masculine group replaced the images of Old Europe. Some of the old elements were fused together as a subsidiary of the new symbolic imagery, thus losing their original meaning. Some images persisted side by side, creating chaos in the former harmony. Through losses and additions new complexes of symbols developed which are best reflected in Greek mythology. . . . The study of mythical images provides one of the best proofs that the Old European world was not the proto-Indo-European world and that there was no direct and unobstructed line of development to the modern Europeans. The earliest European civilization was savagely destroyed by the patriarchal element and never recovered, but its legacy lingered in the substratum which nourished further European cultural developments. The Old European creations were not lost; transformed, they enormously enriched the European psyche.[59]

The masculine world-view of the Indo-Europeans supplanted a variety of pre-Indo-European cultures and assimilated along with the Old European images a variety of symbols and myths from Minoan, Phoenician, and Middle Eastern cultures. The interplay of imageries within Greek mythology thus becomes a complex interaction of many ways of looking at men and women and of revering gods and goddesses. This dynamic interplay would account for what my students have noticed as a constant rivalry and wrangling among the Greek divinities, as well as a perennial struggle between mortal heroes and (often feminine) chthonic monsters.

Ever since women writers began to circulate their productions on a wide scale after the European renaissance they have used mythological archetypes in poems and stories. A task for feminist archetypal critics is to analyze these texts for the interplay of images. Puzzlingly, what we often find is a combination of attitudes toward goddesses in a single text, similar to the ambivalence which I noted in women's novels. Again, the patriarchal overlayer of gender prescription seems to come into conflict with an underlayer of women's desire for authenticity as human beings. For example, a sampling of poems about Medusa by male and female poets reveals attitudes ranging from horror (Robert Lowell's "Near the Ocean," Sylvia Plath's "Medusa") to affirmation (May Sarton's "The Muse as Medusa"), with the majority of poems falling between the two poles. From a preliminary study of these poems, however, I have found that although both men and women poets express ambivalence about her—combinations of awe, reverence, and loathing—the poems by women move to an identification with Medusa while the men, however hypnotized into complicity, remain separate from her, at a distance. We need to explore the psychoanalytic theories about male and female development in relation to the mother in order to comprehend these distinctly different quests; our knowledge of the divergence between the romance quest of Frye's male hero and the development of the woman hero in women's novels should provide us initial hypotheses.

Although there are thus noticeable distinctions between male and female poets writing on the same archetypal figure, the relationship between reverence for goddesses and fear and loathing of their powers cannot be reduced to simple dualism, with masculine literature viewed as gynophobic and feminine literature as affirmative. The archetypal perspectives are not as gender-rigid as one might believe. Feminine archetypes are depicted according to the respect for authentic feminine being by a particular writer at a particular time in history, and it thus becomes necessary to pay close attention to how both personal and historical elements influence an individual poet's writing.

My research in Canadian literature and in the folklore of native peoples suggests that archetypal descriptions of feminine images, symbols, and narratives can be found not only in women's literature but in western male literature as well as in native American and Canadian works. I am thus moving beyond a study of women's literature in isolation to an exploration of male as well as female writing. Since such an undertaking is unmanageably vast, I have developed a method of focusing on one symbol or archetype at a time. Thus my analysis of poems and other artifacts concerning Medusa, and an exploration of a variety of texts which focus on the archetype of the bear. Since the symbol of the bear appears in a large sample of masculine, feminine, and native texts I have found it useful and feasible to examine it as a single recurring element. The crucial question left hanging in the air by my analysis of specific texts, on the one hand, and my exploration of prehistoric religious practices, on the other, is the link between (in this instance) Old European bear worship and recent poetry about bears. Am I positing a specific historical link between prehistory and the present? This question cannot be answered without much further study into the transmission of symbols; however, it is an interesting question which might lead us at least to posit the hypothesis that some link exists, whether in the unconscious or through recurrent instances of the same image producing similar responses, between prehistoric archetypes and modern writers' fascination with them. Since only a limited number of animals—crows, owls, frogs, toads, turtles, snakes, bears, and deer, for example—were associated with Old European religions, these animals could serve as the focus of continued archetypal study.

"Good Lord!" I can hear some skeptical feminist scholars exclaiming. "How can one take the study of recurrent images of snakes and toads seriously in a world where the ERA is in jeopardy, the lust for war rises afresh, and men are devising ever more subtle ways to defeat women at the polls and abhorrent ways to rape us on our streets?" The academic study of archetypes, I propose, empowers women both personally and politically, since the ancient worship of goddesses suggests truths vital for the survival of the human race today. In discussing the contributions that psychoanalytic thought can make to feminism, Jean Elshtain calls for "the articulation of a philosophy of mind that repudiates the old dualism with which we are still saddled in favor of an account that unites mind and body, reason and passion, into a compelling account of human subjectivity and identity, and the creation of a feminist account of human subjectivity and identity, and the creation of a feminist theory of action that, complicatedly, invokes both inner and outer realities."[60] Elshtain's philosophy of mind is already available to feminist scholars, not only in the figurines and paintings unearthed by our archaeologists and in the habits and customs described by our anthropologists, but in rich archetypal images and themes embedded in our literature.

Archetypes are value-free. Like deeply buried stores of uranium, they can be exploited by whoever gets to them first and has the power to employ them most broadly. In 1982 a television presentation by an articulate and clearly powerful woman advertising researcher illustrated the potential for the amoral and unethical use of archetypes.[61] The researcher made a persuasive case that advertisers should employ feminine archetypes in order to sell products. Her research had proven that a compelling feminine archetype or archetypal story produced a galvanic response on the surface of the target's skin, a change in temperature signifying the impact of the archetype upon the body. She suggested using the archetypes of the willful woman, the hetaira, the mother, and even the rebirth narrative implicit in the family reunion, since her research had proven conclusively that these figures and themes elicited strong galvanic reactions. Her research went beyond her readings in Jung to analyses of data derived from a broad sample of American women. She was spinning among fields for her own profit and that of commercial advertisers. As damaging as the use of such mass-media images can be, the same sorts of archetypes could be employed by propagandists to produce even more harmful social effects inimical to women and humanity as a whole. In light of such uses, feminist scholars can hardly afford not to study archetypes.

Archetypal criticism is neither a solitary nor a short-term task, and spinning among fields turns out to be a not so lightfooted activity. There are unconscious blocks against trespassing. Self-doubt holds one back like the bogs that immobilize one's legs in nightmares; and once one has seized the sought-after fleece, there is always somebody following along after trying to reclaim it or deny its importance. More than these obstacles, however, the problem of time looms largest for feminist scholars. Women themselves and women's experience have been excluded from academe for so many years that we are impatient for results that cannot be garnered as quickly as we want. As Carol Christ writes:

> The discovery and recovery of women's experience will not be accomplished overnight. The alienation of ourselves from our own experience is deep; the resources that can aid our journey of self-discovery are slim. To ask for definitive conclusions prematurely is to misjudge the depth of the problem. We are in a time for ripening. . . . We must discover a mode of thinking about the ultimate which can be modulated by a sense of timing, a mode which will not require the definitive word in a time when soundings are more appropriate.[62]

In universities where young women are overworked and then pushed out of revolving doors without time to publish, where tenured women are alone on so many committees that they either succumb to or are driven crazy by masculine standards and behaviors, where all of us swing between a false masculine self and authentic feminine being, we keep right on setting deadlines for ourselves that are impossible to meet. Significant scholarly research requires thirty or forty years to complete; we need time to test and discard various hypotheses, and time to sit back and muse. These activities, in turn, require freedom from attack, fewer committee duties, lighter teaching loads, and the ability to sit quietly alone in our studies doing the intellectual work so vital to our future. That we have constructed in the midst of hostile or apathetic academies viable women's studies programs engaged in a multiplicity of interdisciplinary projects is a tribute to our individual endurance and collective strength.

$\mathcal{V}$ The Descent of Inanna: Myth and Therapy

SYLVIA BRINTON PERERA

I   THE STORY

Many myths and tales exist about the descent of and to the goddess. Among them are the stories of the Japanese Izanami, the Greek Persephone-Kore, the Roman Psyche, and the fairytale heroines who go to Mother Hulda, Baba Yaga, or the gingerbread house witch. The oldest known myth that states this motif was written on clay tablets in the third millenium B.C. (though it is probably much older, reaching into preliterate times). It is usually known as "The Descent of Inanna," the Sumerian queen of heaven and earth.[1] There are two later Akkadian versions based on this source, but with variations that we know as "Ishtar's Descent."[2]

In the Sumerian poem Inanna decides to go into the underworld; she "set her heart from highest heaven on earth's deepest ground,"[3] "abandoned heaven, abandoned earth—to the Netherworld she descended."[4] As a precaution, she instructs Ninshubur, her trusted female executive, to appeal to the father gods for help in securing her release if she does not return within three days.

At the first gate to the Netherworld, Inanna is stopped and asked to declare herself. The gatekeeper informs Ereshkigal, queen of the Great Below, that Inanna, "Queen of Heaven, of the place where the sun rises,"[5] asks for admission to the "land of no return" to witness the funeral of Gugalanna, husband of Ereshkigal. Ereshkigal becomes furious, and insists that the upperworld goddess be treated according to the laws and rites that apply to anyone entering her kingdom; she must be brought "naked and bowed low."

The gatekeeper follows orders. He removes one piece of Inanna's magnificent regalia at each of the seven gates. "Crouched and stripped bare," as the Sumerians were customarily laid in the grave, Inanna is judged by the seven judges. Ereshkigal kills her. Her corpse is hung on a peg, where it turns into a side of green, rotting meat. After three days, when Inanna fails to return, her assistant Ninshubur sets in motion her instructions to rouse the people and gods with dirge drum and lamenting.

Ninshubur goes to Enlil, the highest god of sky and earth, and to Nanna, the moon god and Inanna's father. Both refuse to meddle in the exacting ways of the underworld. Finally Enki, the god of waters and wisdom, hears Ninshubur's plea and rescues Inanna, using two little mourners he creates from the dirt under his fingernail. They slip unnoticed into the Netherworld, carrying the food and water of life given to them by Enki, and they secure Inanna's release by commiserating with Ereshkigal, who is now groaning over the dead, or with her own birth pangs. She is so grateful for their empathy that she finally hands over Inanna's corpse. Restored to life, Inanna is reminded that she will need to send a substitute to take her place. Demons assigned to seize this scapegoat surround her as she returns through the seven gates and reclaims her vestments.

The last part of the myth involves the search for her substitute. Inanna does not hand over anyone who mourned for her. But finally she comes upon her primary consort, Dumuzi (later called Tammuz), who sits enjoying himself on his throne. Inanna looks on him with the same eyes of death Ereshkigal had set on her, and the demons seize him. Dumuzi flees with the help of Utu, the sun god and Inanna's brother, who transforms him into a snake to permit his escape. In a related poem, Dumuzi dreams of his downfall. He goes to his sister, Geshtinanna, who helps him to interpret his dream and urges him to flee. When flight proves useless, she shelters him and finally offers to sacrifice herself in his stead. Inanna decrees that they shall divide the fate and spend half a year each in the underworld. The final poem ends with the words:

> Inanna placed Dumuzi in the hands of the eternal.
> *Holy Ereshkigal! Great is your renown!*[6]

II INTRODUCTION

This myth of descent and its goddesses Inanna, Ereshkigal,

and Geshtianna have moved and oriented me since I discovered the Kramer translations in 1973. I have found that by relating to this very early material from an age when the Great Goddess was still vital, I have been able to reclaim some of my own relation to the archetypal feminine instinct and spirit patterns. We cannot know precisely what these stories meant to the Sumerians, but they hold a cosmic pattern, one that is astronomical, seasonal, transformational, and psychological. And they have served as a projection screen on which I have tried to see a way of healing some of the psychological wounds in myself, in my women friends and colleagues, and in the unmothered women with whom I work in therapy. We all have grown up under the patriarchy and struggle with similar problems. The clinical material I will be citing in this essay comes from dreams and experiences of myself, my friends, and my analysands.

The return to the goddess for renewal in a feminine source and spirit is a vitally important aspect of modern woman's quest for wholeness. We women who have succeeded in the world are usually "daughters of the father"; that is, we are well adapted to a masculine-oriented society and have repudiated our own full feminine instincts and energy patterns, just as the culture has maimed or derogated most of them. We need to return to and redeem what the patriarchy has often seen only as a dangerous threat and called terrible mother, dragon, or witch.[7]

The patriarchal ego of both men and women, to earn its instinct-disciplining, striving, progressive, and heroic stance, has fled from the goddess, or tried to slay her, or at least dismember and thus depotentiate her. But it is toward her, and especially toward her culturally repressed aspects—those chthonic and chaotic, ineluctable depths—that the new individuating, yin-yang balanced ego must return to find its matrix and the flexible strength to be both active and vulnerable, assertive and empathic.

This return is often seen as part of the developmental pattern of women—what Erich Neumann calls a reconnection to the Self (the archetype of wholeness and the regulating center of the personality) after the wrenching away from the mother by the patriarchal uroboros and the patriarchal marriage partner.[8] But Adrienne Rich speaks for many of us when she writes, "The woman I needed to call my mother was silenced before I was born."[9] Unfortunately, all too many modern women have not been nurtured by the mother in the first place. Instead, they have grown up in the difficult home ruled by abstract, collective authority. "Cut off at the ankles from earth," as one woman in therapy put it, they have been guided by superego shoulds and oughts. Or they have identified with the father and their patriarchal culture, thus alienating themselves from their own feminine ground and the personal mother, whom they have often seen as weak or irrelevant.[10] Such women have the greatest need to meet the goddess in her primal reality.

This inner connection is an initiation essential for most modern women in the Western world; without it we are not whole. The process requires both a sacrifice of our identity as spiritual daughters of the patriarchy and a descent into the spirit of the goddess because so much of the power and passion of the feminine has been dormant in the underworld—in exile for five thousand years.

It is precisely the woman who has a poor relation to the mother, the one through whom the Self archetype first constellates, who tends to find her fulfillment through the father or the male beloved. She may be a woman who can find no relation to the Demeter-Kore myth because she "cannot believe," as one put it, that "any mother would be there to mourn or to receive" her again if she vanished into a crevasse. She may have an intense experience in the contrasexual sphere, but she lacks the ballast of a solid ego-Self connection. One patient expressed this early in her analysis almost as a manifesto:

> I insist on caring coming from a man. A female source enrages me. A male is in charge of the universe. Females are second best. I hate tunnels and Kali and my mother and this female body. A man is what I want.

The speaker was a young woman who had come into therapy because, although she was considered an excellent student, she was having difficulty writing her Ph.D. thesis.

The problem is that we who are badly wounded in our relation to the feminine usually have a fairly successful persona, a good public image. We have grown up as docile, often intellectual, daughters of the patriarchy, with what I call "animus-egos." We strive to uphold the virtues and aesthetic ideals which the patriarchal superego has presented to us. But we are filled with self-loathing and a deep sense of personal ugliness and failure when we can neither meet nor mitigate the superego's standards of perfection.

Often identity is based on persona adaptations to what the animus tells us should be, so we adapt to or rebel against the projections hooked onto us; thus we have almost no sense of our own personal core identity, our feminine value and standpoint. In the West, women have too often been defined only in relation to the masculine as the good, nurturant mother and wife, the sweet, docile, agreeable daughter, the gently supportive or bright, achieving partner. As many feminist writers have stated through the ages, this collective model (and the behavior it leads to) is inadequate for life; we multilate, depotentiate, silence, and enrage ourselves trying to compress our souls into it, just as surely as our grandmothers deformed their fully breathing bodies with corsets for the sake of an ideal.[11]

We also feel unseen because there are no images alive to reflect our wholeness and variety. But where shall we look for symbols to suggest the full mystery and potency of the feminine and to provide images as models for personal life? The later Greek goddesses and Mary, Virgin Mother and Mediator, have not struck me to the core as have Inanna-Ereshkigal, Kali, and Isis.[12] An image for the goddess as Self needs to have a full-bodied coherence. So I have had to see the female Greek deities as partial aspects of one wholeness pattern and to look always for the darker powers hidden in their stories—the Gorgon aspect of Athena, the underworld Aphrodite/Urania, the Black Demeter.

Historically, the original creatress deity was differentiated or broken up into different aspects, including upper and lower world forms. Thus it became necessary to traverse both regions in order to restore a sense of creative wholeness and to comprehend the rhythmic interplay of life. Inanna, Queen of Heaven, was perhaps the first initiate described in writing to suffer this journey.

Inanna's descent to and return from Ereshkigal can be seen from at least four perspectives. First, it depicts the rhythmic order of nature: the seasonal changes in vegetation, the dwindling and replenishing of the storehouse,[13] the transformation of grain and grape by fermentation, and the alternations of the planet Inanna (our Venus). This planet stays in the sky as evening or morning star for 250 and 236 days respectively; then it seems to descend below the horizon as it disappears in front of or behind the sun for a period of time before it rises on the other side of night.

Second, it is a story of initiation into the mysteries of nature and the unconscious. A gate at the boundary of the underworld was called Inanna's or Ishtar's door. Through it others who wished to make the journey to become conscious of the underworld were advised to pass.[14] Thus Inanna's path and its stages may present a paradigm for the life-enhancing descent into the abyss of the dark goddess and out again. Inanna shows us the way, and she is the first to sacrifice herself for a deep feminine wisdom and for atonement. She descends, submits, and dies. This openness to being acted upon is the essence of the experience of the human soul faced with the transpersonal.[15] It is not based on passivity, but on an active willingness to receive.

In the West the process of initiation into the esoteric and mystical traditions involves exploring different modes of consciousness and rediscovering the experience of unity with nature and the cosmos that is inevitably lost through goal-directed development. This necessity—for those destined to it—forces us to go deep to reclaim modes of consciousness which are different from the intellectual, "secondary process" levels the West has so well refined. It forces us to the affect-laden, magic dimension and archaic depths that are embodied, ecstatic, and transformative; these depths are preverbal, often pre-image, capable of taking us over and shaking us to the core.

In those depths we are given a sense of the one cosmic power; there we are moved, and taught through the intensity of our affects that there is a living process of balancing. The conscious ego is overwhelmed by passion and by numinous images. And, though shaken, even destroyed as we knew ourselves, we are recoalesced in a new pattern and spewed back into ordinary life. That journey is the goal of the initiation mysteries and of work on the astral plane in magic, even as it is the goal of therapeutic regression (for both men and women). The need for this journey fuels the current interest in the psychology of creativity and the early, pre-oedipal stages of human development and their pathologies.

Connecting to these levels of consciousness involves a sacrifice of the upper-world aspects of the Self to and for the sake of the dark, different, or altered-state aspects. It means sacrifice to and for the repressed, undifferentiated ground of being with the hope of gaining rebirth with a deeper, resonant awareness. And it means returning with those resonances, adding them to mental-cerebral, ordinary Western consciousness, in order to forge what Jean Gebser calls "integral consciousness."[16] From this perspective the story of Inanna's descent is the revelation of an initiation ritual, and it is directly relevant to feminine experience today.

Third, the myth also describes a pattern of psychological health for the feminine, both in women and in men. It provides a model of the incarnation-ascension rhythm of the healthy soul, and also of a process to promote healing. "The soul comes 'from the stars' and returns to the stellar regions," writes Jung.[17] Inanna's descent, as we shall see, may be viewed as the incarnation of cosmic, uncontained powers into time-bound, corrupting flesh, but it is also a descent for the purpose of retrieving values long repressed and of uniting above and below into a new pattern.

I have often found myself oriented in deep analytic processes by this myth, for it shows, by analogy, how the conscious ideal of the personality—what we could call the ego-ideal, or the hypertrophic, superego-ridden animus-ego—when it has been wounded by being cut off from its roots by the devaluation of matter and the feminine, can approach the dark forces of earthly reality and the unconscious. By slowly peeling away defenses and persona-identifications, the analysand regresses gradually to those primary-process, beginning levels where the death of inadequate patterns and the birth of the authentic, validated, balanced ego awaits. This myth shows us also how those dark, repressed levels may be raised, and how they may enter conscious life, through emotional upheavals and grief, to radically change conscious energy patterns.

Fourth and last, the tale of Inanna may suggest some orientation in our own perilous age as the powers of the goddess return to Western culture. The return of Inanna from the underworld was at first demonic (even though it restored fruitfulness to the earth, which was barren when the goddess was absent); yet finally, as I read it, engendered a new model of equal and comradely relationship between woman and man.

Our planet is passing through a phase—the return of the goddess—presaged at the beginning of the patriarchy in this myth.

Its emphasis then was on the descent of the goddess, the loss to culture of her energies and symbols, and the subsequent retrieval of the powers symbolized in Ereshkigal. Our age can appreciate the full *circulatio*, for more and more of the feminine was repressed, and it has been too long in the underworld.

III   INANNA

The goddess Inanna (her Semitic name is Ishtar) provides a many-faceted symbolic image, a wholeness pattern, of the feminine beyond the merely maternal. Other goddesses in Sumer were great sea and earth mothers. And while Inanna took the double-axe symbol of the ancient goddesses into her cult, she combined earth and sky, matter and spirit, vessel and light, earthly bounty and heavenly guidance. Originally, perhaps, she was associated with grain and the communal storehouse as vessel or the container of dates and grain and livestock. Among her oldest emblems were this storehouse and a looped cloth or bundle, perhaps of reeds, as the closure to her storehouse, and the date god was one of her earliest divine bridegrooms.[18] She is thus, like Demeter and the Celtic goddess Ceriddwen, a numen of impersonal fertility.[19] In one song, she is said to pour forth grains and legumes from her womb.[20]

She is also, from the beginning, a goddess of the heavens and appears on ancient seals and vases as a star. As goddess of gentle rains, terrible storms, floods, and of the overcast sky (the clouds of which were likened to her breasts), she is called Queen of Heaven and said to be the spouse of An, the ancient heaven god. She is also from very early times goddess of the radiant, erratic morning and evening star, awakening life and setting it to rest, ruling the borderlands, ushering in or out her brother the sun god and her father the moon god. She represents the liminal, intermediate regions, and energies that cannot be contained or made certain and secure. She is not the feminine as night, but rather she symbolizes consciousness of transition and borders, places of intersection and crossing over that imply creativity and change and all the joys and doubts that go with a human consciousness that is flexible, playful, never certain for long.

As evening star she holds court at the time of the new moon to hear the gods' petitions and to be celebrated with music, feasting,

and staged, bloody battles. She claims the *me*, the ordering principles, potencies, talents and rites, of the civilized, upper world,
and as judge she holds court to "decree fate" and "trample the
disobedient." She symbolizes the feeling capacity to evaluate,
periodically and afresh, that goes with the sense of life as a
changing process.

As queen of the land and its fertility, she bestows kingship on
the mortal chosen to be shepherd of the people and welcomes
him to her bed and throne (made of a world tree which Gilgamesh
cut down from her garden).[21] To her consort she gives throne,
scepter, staff, crook, and crown, as well as the promise of a good
harvest and the joys of her bed.

But she is also goddess of war. Battle is "the dance of Inanna";
giving victory, she is "the quiver ready at hand," "the heart of the
battle," "the arm of the warriors."[22] More passionate than Athena (with the energies of wild instinct which were later in Greece
assigned to Artemis), she is described in one hymn as "all-
devouring," "attacking like the attacking storm," and having an
"awesome face" and "angry heart."[23] She sings with delighted
abandon of her own glory and prowess: "Heaven is mine, earth is
mine,—I, a warrior am I. Is there a god who can vie with me?"[24]
"The gods are sparrows—I am a falcon; the Anunnaki (the gods)
trundle along—I am a splendid wild cow."[25] In one myth she is
described as battling the dragon of *kur* and slaying it. Her companion animal is the lion, and seven of them pull her chariot.
Sometimes on ancient seals she is accompanied by a scorpion.

With equal passion, Inanna is the goddess of sexual love. She
sings ecstatic songs of self-adornment, desire and of the delights
of love-making. She calls her beloved consort, her "honey-man"
who "sweetens me ever,"[26] and invites him to her "holy lap" to
savor her life-giving caresses and the sweetness of sex with her on
the sacred marriage bed. More extroverted than Aphrodite, she
craves and takes, desires and destroys, and then grieves and
composes songs of grief. She generally does not arouse desire
from within but claims her need assertively and celebrates her
body in song. Her receptivity is active. She calls out to have her
body filled, singing praises to her vulva and bidding Dumuzi
come to her bed to "Plow my vulva, man of my heart."[27] She is
thus goddess of courtesans, the harlot "hailing men from the
alehouse" as she rises in the form of the evening star. And in

heaven she is called bridesmaid and hierodule (high priestess and ritual prostitute) of the gods.

Inanna is also healer, lifegiver, composer of songs (to which she is said to give birth); she is creative in all realms. And the behavior of the emotions is considered to be in her keeping:

To pester, insult, deride, desecrate—and to venerate—
is your domain, Inanna.
Downheartedness, calamity, heartache—and joy and good
cheer—is your domain, Inanna.
Tremble, afright, terror—and dazzling and glory—is your
domain, Inanna.[28]

The many poems about her portray her as loving, jealous, grieving, joyful, timid, exhibitionistic, thieving, passionate, ambitious, generous, and so on. The whole range of affects belongs to the goddess.

Often Inanna is described as "daughter" of the gods and "maid." And indeed, by the time the later hymns to her were written, she, like Athena, is often seen as "conditioned by bondedness to the father,"[29] although some poems suggest a close, joyful, personal relationship to her own mother. Though she has two sons and the kings and people of Sumer are called her progeny, she is not motherly in the usual sense. Like the goddess Artemis, she is at the "border-region midway between motherhood and maidenhood, joie de vivre and lust for murder, fecundity and animality."[30] She is a quintessential, positive puella, an eternally youthful, dynamic, fierce, sensuous, harlot-virgin (in Esther Harding's term, "one-in-her-self"). She is never a settled and domestic wife or mother under the patriarchy. She keeps her independence and magnetism as lover, young bride, and widow. And she is not a mother-lover to sons. That role and concept seems to be an invention of patriarchal culture and times when women were depotentiated, living their potential in projection on envied and beloved male offspring.[31]

Yet, in spite of her power as goddess of fertility, order, war, love, the heavens, healing, emotions, and song, and in spite of having the titles Lady of Myriad Offices and Queen, Inanna is a wanderer. Like Ereshkigal, she was dispossessed by Enlil, the second generation sky god. Her roots lie deep in prepatriarchal time, but from the perspective of the patriarchy, with Gilgamesh

as its spokesman, Inanna/Ishtar is fickle and unreliable, the certain cause of grief to her beloved consorts.[32] Thus Gilgamesh,
who originally lent her his human strength to build the bed and
throne of kingship, turns against her and derogates and insults
the goddess of the land in order to claim her power. In one
plaintive song Inanna laments to Enlil the loss of her house:

Me the woman he has filled with dismay . . .
Has filled me, the queen of heaven, with consternation . . .
I, the woman who circles the land—tell me where is my house.
Tell me where is the city in which I may live . . .
I, who am your daughter . . . the hierodule, who am your
       bridesmaid—tell me where is my house . . .
The bird has its nesting place, but I—my young are dispersed,
The fish lies in calm waters, but I—my resting place exists not,
The dog kneels at the threshold, but I—I have no threshold. . . .[33]

This poignant song may have been written to lament some calamity at Inanna's main temple in Erech, but beyond that, it is
perhaps the oldest known statement of the condition of the
goddess and woman as exile. Like the later Babylonian wives of
Israel sent away from their homes by the patriarchy,[34] even the
great pre-Babylonian goddess knows and sings of expulsion. In
fact, the search for a home is also one of the recurrent dream
themes in the initial analytic work of modern women, daughters
of the patriarchy.

Indeed, much of what Inanna symbolized for the Sumerians
has since been exiled. Most of the qualities possessed by the
upper-world goddess have been desacralized in the West or
taken over by masculine divinities, or they have been overly
compressed and idealized by patriarchal moral and aesthetic
codes. Thus most of the Greek goddesses were swallowed up by
their fathers, and the Hebrew goddess was also depotentiated.
What remained were particularized or minimized goddesses.
And most of the powers once held by the goddess have lost their
connection to women's life: the embodied, playful, passionately
erotic feminine; the powerful, independent, self-willed feminine;
and the ambitious, regal, many-sided feminine.

Women themselves have lived mainly in the personal realm,
on the periphery of Western culture in narrowly circumscribed
roles, often subordinating themselves to males, social position,

children. They have veiled their needs for power and passion,[35] living safely, and projecting their potency onto overburdened males whose power is culturally legitimated. Such collectively acceptable behavior for women lost its connection to the sacred as the full scale of the goddess was diminished. Concomitantly, the patriarchal superego became increasingly hypertrophic. Originally necessary to inculcate ethical sensitivity, it was strengthened by the institutional Christian Church to discipline the wild, tribal emotions of the medieval world.[36] Since the rise of Utilitarianism and Victorianism, it has so overconstricted and repressed life energies that they must now erupt, forcing, among other things, the return of the goddess into Western culture.

Thus constricted, the joy of the feminine has been denigrated as mere frivolity, her joyful lust demeaned as whorishness, or sentimentalized and maternalized, her vitality channeled into duty and obedience. This devaluation has produced the ungrounded daughters of the patriarchy whose feminine strength and passion has been split off, their dreams and ideals in the unobtainable heavens, maintained grandly with a spirit false to the instinctual patterns symbolized by the Queen of Heaven and Earth. It has also produced frustrated furies. For as Inanna lives unconsciously in women under the patriarchy's repression, she is too often demonic. Actress June Havoc's description of the women of her family provides a portrait of the goddess' ebullient energies ground down and soured:

> All the women of [our] family . . . had a common strain of ambition and strength and bitter independence; they married early, divorced quickly, and in the end succumbed to alcohol or drugs or madness. They wanted total freedom and since they didn't know how to go about achieving it, they were hideously frustrated. Men were a convenience to them: they had an inability to enjoy love.[37]

On the other hand, lived consciously, the goddess Inanna in her role as suffering, exiled feminine provides an image of the deity who can, perhaps, carry the suffering and redemption of modern women. Closer to many of us than the church's Christ, she suggests an archetypal pattern which can give meaning to women's quest,[38] one which may supplant the Christian myth for those unable to relate to a masculine God. Inanna's suffering, disrobing, humiliation, flagellation and death, the stations of her descent, her "crucifixion" on the underworld peg, and her resurrection, all prefigure Christ's passion and represent perhaps the first known archetypal image of the dying divinity whose sacrifice redeems the wasteland earth. Not for humankind's sins did Inanna sacrifice herself, but for earth's need for renewal. She is concerned more with life than with good and evil. Nonetheless her descent and return provides a model for our own psychological and spiritual journeys. Unlike Christ's story, where the destructive acts perpetrated on the savior are a product of human malice and fear, and thus capable of establishing a pattern of human revenge and scapegoating, in the Sumerian poem they are shown to have a transpersonal source. The goddess may destroy, just as the goddess may redeem. And this leads us to a consideration of Ereshkigal, Inanna's dark "sister."

IV   ERESHKIGAL

The other major goddess of this myth is Ereshkigal, queen of the Netherworld and the dead. Her name means "Lady of the Great Place Below," but before being relegated to the *kur*, the alien place outside patriarchal consciousness, she was a grain goddess and lived above.[39] Thus she symbolizes the Great Round of nature—grain above, growing, and seed below, dying to sprout again. To matriarchal consciousness she represents the continuum of life and death in which different states are simply experienced as transformations of one energy. To the patriarchy death becomes a rape of life, a violence to be feared and controlled as much as possible with distance and moral order.

In a myth describing the events which led to the birth of the moon god, these two perspectives are set side by side. For in the upper world, as grain goddess, Ereshkigal was named Ninlil and called wife of Enlil, the second-generation sky god. Ninlil was repeatedly raped by her husband in various disguises.[40] On behalf of the young goddess the gods punished Enlil for his violence by sending him to the underworld. Out of love for her consort Ninlil followed him down and became known as Ereshkigal. Enlil continued to appear as the ruling sky god in heaven, but he may have had an underworld form. Just as Zeus of the

underworld was named Hades,[41] so Enlil may well be the Gugalanna of the Descent myth, the Great Bull of Heaven, husband of
Ereshkigal, who has been killed.

From the perspective of the patriarchy, the rape of the goddess
establishes masculine rule over conscious cultural life (and
perhaps over agriculture) and relegates feminine power and fertility to the underworld. Thus when the god An seized heaven
and Enlil carried off the earth, and consciousness had space to
grow, then "Ereshkigal was seized by the Great Below as a
prize."[42] But from the perspective of magic-matriarchal consciousness, the goddess is not a prize to be carried out of life, nor
is death a rape and a destruction of life. Rather, death is a transformation to which, as the grain to the reaper, the goddess
willingly surrenders, and a process over which she rules.[43]

The poem describing Inanna's descent tells us that the first of
the rapes of Ninlil/Ereshkigal produced Nanna/Sin, the moon
god, who was born in the underworld and rises to light the
darkness and to measure time with his waxing and waning cycles. Nanna/Sin is Inanna's father (and father of the sun god as
well), and thus his mother, Ninlil/Ereshkigal, is Inanna's grandmother in the genealogy—an aspect of the boundless, primal
feminine that was raped, cut down, and still bore fruit. Ereshkigal
became a symbol of dreaded death to the patriarchy, and was
banished into the underworld. Nonetheless, the body of the
poem recalls her archaic potency, and the last line teaches the
sweetness of coming to know her as symbol of the Great Round.[44]

The fruits of the other rapes were said to have been monsters.
The Great Round produces a chaotic panoply which is monstrous
to the patriarchal, heroic world view with its emphasis on rational
order and control. Ereshkigal defies differentiated consciousness. She is paradoxical: both the vessel and the stake. She is the
root of all life, where energy is inert and consciousness coiled
asleep. She is the place where potential life lies motionless, but in
the pangs of birth; beneath all language and its distinction, she
judges and acts. She is the energy banishing itself into the underworld, too awesome to behold—like primal childhood experiences and the darkness of the moon, places of oblivion that are
the perilous ground on which daylight consciousness treads, the
primal matrix. And she holds the wisdom of that isolation and

bitterness. She is receiver of all, yet adversary and inevitable death-dealing victor. The myth shows her susceptible to initiatives from above, though she rules the Land of No Return, the realm below the horizon of consciousness.

In the Descent poem Ereshkigal is described first as enraged due to Inanna's invasion of her realm; second, as actively destructive; third, as suffering; and finally as grateful and generous. There is a quality of primal rage about her. She is full of fury, greed, fear of loss, and even of self-spite. She symbolizes raw instinctual feelings split off from consciousness—need and aggression in the underworld. And in sending her gatekeeper to deal with the intruder, she calls on a male to defend her. These images suggest that chaotic, defensive furies, such as rage, greed, and even the unleashed animus, are inevitable aspects of the archetypal underworld. They are the ways the unconscious reacts to unwelcome visitation.

The forces that Ereshkigal symbolizes are those connected not only with active destruction but also with transformation, via those slow, cell-by-cell organic processes, such as decay and gestation, which work upon the passive, stuck recipient even invasively and against his or her own will. Such impersonal forces devour and destroy, incubate and bring to birth, with an implacable pitilessness. Thus, when we are in it, Ereshkigal's domain seems unbounded, irrational, primordial, and totally uncaring, even destructive of the individual. She symbolizes the abyss that is the source and the end, the ground of all being. Ereshkigal's energies are also related to seeming stasis and the coalesced, unitive solidity of matter as a cosmic principle. They are the elementary, retaining, conserving, grounding forces closely related to the *muladhara* chakra, its instincts for survival and its fears for basic constancy and security. Such seeming stasis suggests the potential of cleansing immersion in the darkness of the unknown. But it also suggests a dissolution and slowness requiring great patience of those who enter. Ereshkigal's realm represents the one certainty of life, that we all die. Yet because of this very certainty, she is a manifestation of the most unknown and other, where active life's consciousness lies dormant.

Ereshkigal's vizier is named Namtar, "fate." Her realm has its own lawfulness before which the sky gods of Sumer bow. The "law of the Great Below" is the law of reality, of things as they are. This fearsome natural law is pre-ethical and always precedes the superego judgments of the patriarchy.

Unreverenced, Ereshkigal's forces are felt as depression and an abysmal agony of helplessness and futility, as unacceptable desire and transformative-destructive energy, unacceptable autonomy (the need for separateness and self-assertion) split off, turned in, and devouring the individual's sense of willed potency and value.[46] A woman suffering Ereshkigal has unknowingly put her negative animus superego first and been overpowered. She is split off from her primal affects, has lost consciousness of them. Yet she falls easily into the underworld as into a vortex, or she follows a beloved man with psychopathic or psychotic tendencies, who can lead her into these depths. Or she seeks the underworld compulsively, hides from life, often addicted to various modes of dulling the pains of the flow of change which are too much for her fragmented capacity. Or else she unconsciously identifies with what the culture rejects as ineffective and inferior, forcing her to introvert through a negative sense of uniqueness.[47]

In identifying with Ereshkigal, a woman can feel stuck in a timeless stasis, unable to budge, feeling the bleak despair and the emptiness of one raped by the animus.[48] Like the goddess as the great maw, receiving back all life, she may feel starved and greedy, and may suffer somatic symptoms, disturbances related to abdominal organs, to digestion, or to cellular disintegrative processes. It gives great solace to know which altar to approach when confronted with such states. But Ereshkigal does not want to be worshipped in the usual ways. Like the elementary, chthonic gods to whom sacrifices were holocausted,[49] she demands death, that is, complete destruction of the felt sense of individuality, and total transformation.

Dream images of the abysmal goddess are not infrequent during phases of analysis when the conscious ego-ideal is about to undergo mortification and be radically transformed. One woman professor's nightmare was of a black planet approaching her at the hour she was to teach, spewing vapors that made her scholarly mind go blank. She felt "completely destroyed, as if there is no me left." An elegant, competent businesswoman was confronted in a dream with the image of "a fat, ugly creature, like a termite queen, slowly writhing in waves of birth or defecation." She was appalled to see something "so hideous and bestial." A third woman who was beginning to come to terms with her considerable intellectual and emotional capacities, and had previously identified herself as a wild eccentric child, dreamt:

> I am on a subway platform, trying to scrape up a package of hamburger meat that has fallen and spilled. Nearby looms a giant, black-robed, cold, sadistic woman who watches. She is like a queen cobra. She has the amoral face of darkness. She can do anything; she's not interested in life or being nice. She's objective, efficient, of this solid earth and as ruthless as it takes.

This dream presaged a depression in which her grandiose ego-ideal was ground down to prime meat, and she was forced to accept the positive shadow's previously feared, calm strength. She slowly undertook a new career and walked out of an unsatisfactory personal relationship. Later she dreamed that the dark woman had moved into her housekeeper's room, replacing a nice, homey, ineffective woman.

We often meet this underworld aspect of the feminine in analysis when animus-identified puella women descend into what the idealistic animus has branded as evil or sick or ugly and loathsome. The regression or introversion is often so slow and deep that it may turn into a profound, deathlike depression, which can be very frightening if there is no orientation to its archetypal meanings and pattern. One previously active woman described this in her journal as

> a slow decaying of all the shoulds, a dying of the encasements of my life that has felt like rotting. I have had to accept that slowness and the destruction of what I thought was me. There is always the fear that once I sacrifice the old, social, competent me, I will be dead. Yet in this depressed place, where I have felt inertia in the embrace of uttermost matter, like cement holding me, there has been an unbinding of energy. It's been so deep I lose my sense of time—only know that my nails have grown and need cutting again. It's coming at everything slow and from below—not human and warm, but detached. Below ideas of mean or not mean.

Another said:

> I've been so low—it's been nauseous, like green meat. I've never let myself be so passive and full of the uglies, but I'm not even abashed anymore. It's a coming to know that I don't care, and so what. It

seems so cold, but it has a strength that can receive and accept anything, even pain. So now I can feel at home in the universe. It balances some place I've been scared of all my life in my mother's fierceness and my fear and hate to touch a man's penis. I had to heal me there before I could relate without being blasted or going unconscious.

When we are reduced to such depths of numb pain and depression, to timelessness, preverbal chaos and emotionality—all that we call awful or infantile and associate with the archaic dimensions of consciousness—we can know that the goddess we must serve and revere is Ereshkigal. Contact with her grounds a woman. It coagulates feminine potency to confront the patriarchy and the masculine as an equal.

Patriarchal consciousness has isolated this goddess, raped her, and relegated her to the underworld. We are enjoined against looking too closely at the awesome, destructive side of the nature goddess.[50] She has been carried out of our consciousness, and she abides in the depths of the unconscious. In her terrible form Ereshkigal never comes up. When the gods give a feast, they ask her to send someone to get her food.[51] Yet she is not antagonistic to the masculine: she is surrounded by male judges, her consorts and servants are male, and she gives birth to sons. She is easily turned from fury at Nergal, who was rude to her emissary. When he recognizes that "it was but love you wanted of me from months ago to now," she offers him marriage and rule over the Netherworld, which he accepts.[52]

Contrary to much that has been written, this myth suggests that the consciousness of the deep layers of the psyche is not an adversary of heroic, patriarchal consciousness of the sky gods. The forces and modalities of the Great Round do not wish to rule, or even to resist, hierarchical, progress-oriented, Logos modes. They do require reverence and respect. Ereshkigal rages when she is not met with respect. She is proud but she does not mount an offensive, nor does she transgress her own boundaries. She simply demands recognition as a power equal to that of the Great Above—as Nergal finally realized when he confronted her.

V   THE EYES OF DEATH

Affect and energy and lawfulness characterize Ereshkigal. She also has "eyes of death." For Inanna is killed and turned into meat by Ereshkigal in an action described in the poem with chilling awe:

The holy Ereshkigal seated herself upon her throne . . .
She fastened her eyes upon her (Inanna), the eyes of death,
Spoke the word against her, the word of wrath,
Uttered the cry against her, the cry of guilt,
Struck her, turned her into a corpse.
The corpse was hung from a nail.[53]

Here in the poem, Ereshkigal's eyes combine with word, affect, the judgment of conscience, and the act of murder. They are the eyes of death, pitiless, not personally caring. To humans who are paralyzed with fear and have lost their sense of process and paradox, her eyes can have a hateful glare that freezes life, like a mother's hate-envy that blights her child and makes an end of all beginnings. They express raw sadism and rage in its archetypal form. Or they are the eyes of depression to which all looks dead. They can also be the eyes that transfix life, the projection of our human fear or rage that seizes a moment or an image and makes it concrete and static. Such eyes bring psychosis; we see them in individuals suffering psychotic states, where the capacity to see through the tightly held fragment to the life process and spirit, in which the static frame inheres as a partial fact, is lost.

They can thus be the eyes that lose a sense of the greater whole. Or they can suggest a capacity for objectivity or unrelatedness that is life-affirming and self-affirming at a demonic level. Such a capacity is not considered feminine by our culture, but Jung, writing on the *muladhara* chakra, reminds us of the value of the negative aspect of the Self. There is an "aspect of hatred . . . [which] one would describe in Western philosophical terms as an urge or instinct toward individuation,"[54] for its function is to destroy *participation mystique* by separating and setting apart the individual who had previously merged his or her sense of identity with loved ones.

In the poem, Inanna, unveiled, sees her own mysterious depth, Ereshkigal, who glares back at her. She has an immediate, full experience of her underworld self. That naked moment is like the fifth scene in the Villa of Mysteries where the faun, looking into a mirror bowl, sees reflected back a mask of terrible Dionysus as lord of the underworld. It is the moment of self-confrontation for the goddess of active life and love.[55]

A woman dreamed: "I am handed the poison of the world. It is labelled 'uncaring.' " She had been struggling with what she thought was her lover's coldness. The dream image showed her that it was, instead, nature's coldness. And she, in identity with the victim who seeks subservient affiliations and merging through placation of her partner, would have to drink to find her communion with the goddess.

Archetypally, these implacable eyes of death see with an immediate "is-ness" that finds pretense, ideals, individuality and relatedness, irrelevant. They also hold and enable the mystery of a radically different, precultural mode of perception. Like the eyes in the skulls around the house of the Russian nature goddess and witch, Baba-Yaga,[56] they perceive with an objectivity like that of nature itself and our dreams. They bore into the soul to find the naked truth, to see reality beneath all its myriad forms and the illusions and defenses it displays.

Western science once aspired to such vision. But we humans do not have such objective eyes. We can see only limited and relative, indeterminate truths. We and our subjectivity are part of the reality we seek to uncover. Through the vision of Ereshkigal, however, objective reality is unmasked. It is nothing—"Neti, neti," as the Sanskrit says—and yet everything, the place of paradox behind the veil of the Great Goddess and the temple of wisdom. These eyes see from and embody the starkness of the abyss that takes all back, reduces the dancing, playing maya of the goddess to inert matter and stops life on earth.

These eyes obviate the patterns and ideals of habitual and collective rational consciousness—the way we see in linguistic confines, "trapped within conceptual spaces"[57]—that form the world of differentiated appearances. They pierce through to the substance of preverbal reality itself. They also see through collective standards that are false to life itself. Thus they destroy identification with animus ideals and make possible a perception of reality without the distortions and preconceptions of superego. This means seeing, not what might be good or bad, but what exists before judgment, which is always messy and emotional and full of the preverbal percepts of the near senses (touch, smell, taste). This implies not caring first and foremost about relatedness to an outer other, nor to a collective gestalt or imperative. Though seeing this way is initially frightening because it cannot be validated by the collective and can provide what Logos consciousness fears as mere chaos, it opens the way to possibilities of a totally fresh perception, a new pattern, a creative perspective, a never ending exploration.

Such seeing is radical and dangerously innovative, but not necessarily evil unless unbalanced and therefore static and partial. It feels monstrous and ugly and even petrifying to the uninitiated. For it shears us of our defenses and entails a sacrifice of easy collective understandings and the hopes and expectations of looking good and safely belonging. It is crude, chaotic, surprising, giving a view of the ground below ethics and aesthetics and the opposites themselves. It is the instinctual eye—an eye of the spirit in nature. This is the vision that Ereshkigal and Kali and the Gorgon bring to the initiate. It is the meaning of the vision of the terrible guardian head at Siva's temples.[58] This vision is awful, and yet it bestows a refined perception of reality to those who can bear it. This is the wisdom of the dark feminine that Psyche could not yet sustain, the knowledge she was to bring to Aphrodite, the Greek Inanna, to make her beautiful and eternal. Psyche saw it briefly and fell unconscious, for that age was not ready for such knowledge. Now we need to know this vision, for we are already working with its subtle energies in astro- and atomic physics.

Psychologically, this mode of seeing, this knowledge, implies that destruction and transformation into something radically new are part of the cycle of reality.[59] As one woman put it:

I see that you can't do anything without hurting someone, some sacrifice, some pain or betrayal—at least much of the time. That everything ends and begins somewhere else. Innocence is impossible.

Such knowledge is hard to endure. We try to pretty it up, cover, avoid it. But knowing this basic reality permits a woman to give up trying to be agreeable to parental and animus imperatives and ideals. It is like hitting rock bottom, from where they are irrelevant. It relativizes all principles and opens a woman to the paradoxes involved in living with the Self.

One woman forced to awareness of this vision dreamed of a beautiful lady with tiny skulls in her pupils, and through those eyes the dreamer saw into a vast night sky. Another woman had a vision of her dead grandmother with her eyes fallen into her head. She wrote, "Such eyes include everything. They see across to the ground of being and they can stand such objectivity. They mean pain is inevitable. I can't hide." As an analyst I stand by that vision when I speak my own truth, saying, "That's how I feel now; that's what I see." Such truth is my moment's valid discrimination. But like a probe, it may hurt the one seen. And it may separate me from another. But when I lose connection to the solidity of that seeming coldness, or try to stave it off as the good mother or daughter, then my ego becomes ungrounded and the coldness falls into the unconscious and comes at me or the other from the animus. When a woman in therapy projects that stony *muladhara* vision onto me, sometimes I am afraid either to be seen so coldly or to value such vision as transpersonal feminine objectivity (which I share and value as self-protection). At such times I lose conscious connection to that cold objectivity and can be petrified with fear of it. It emerges from a negative transference, and I want to plug up the other's rage.

This cool, objective eye is one basis, perhaps the left brain aspect, of feminine evaluation. It is not deceived by responsible performance or willed achievement, but finds the ineluctable facts in process, in the panoply of emotional vectors that give each moment life, and that pass as others crowd into the present. The individual has little control over these processes but may find a grounding if she can reverence change itself and find a way to move with it. Such vision is transpersonal and has the power to protect. So Athena, *gorgopis* (bright-eyed) and owl-eyed, wore the Gorgon's eyes on her shield; so Inanna later embodied the "eyes of death."

VI   THE PEG, THE STAKE, AND THE MEATHOOK

The seemingly cold yin of Ereshkigal's vision is intimately related, in the myth, to the suffering yin. Inanna hangs impaled, and Ereshkigal lies naked and groaning in misery of death or labor. She is described as:

The birth-giving mother, because of her children.
Ereshkigal lies there ill (perhaps in labor),
Over her holy body no cloth is spread,

Her holy chest like a *shagan* vessel is not (veiled)[60]
(her talons, like a copper rake (?) upon her)[61]
Her hair like leeches she wears upon her head.[62]

Suffering is also a major part of the underworld feminine. It may
be unconscious until the goddess of light awakens it to awareness, stirring the silent numbness into pain. On the magic level of
consciousness, the sufferer has no awareness of suffering.[63]

But suffering is part of the feminine. We forget that until this
century childbirth was often attended by death: thus Aztec
women who died in childbirth were equated with warriors who
died in battle; thus Anne Bradstreet wrote a poem bidding
farewell to her husband and little ones when she went into labor
with another child;[64] thus Cotton Mather and his contemporaries
saw that

the Difficulties both of Subjection and of Childbearing, which the
Female Sex is doom'd unto, ha's been turned into a Blessing, . . .
God Sanctifies the Chains, the Pains, the Deaths which they meet
withal; . . . [as] a further Occasion of Serious Devotion in them.[65]

The constant cycle of strenuous childbirths which often resulted
in death kept most of a woman's life focused on the harsh malevo-
lence of reality, on a sense of living at the brink of the abyss. So
women's creativity has gone into actual births and the arts and
sustenance of the household, all subject to wear and destruction—to devouring—and not much appreciated in the wider
cultural context. And yet these are the basic civilizing force of any
culture, immediate, personal, made in the small interstices of the
process of sustaining survival. It is no wonder, in this context,
that Jewish men thank God they were not created female. But
wounding for a woman is not necessarily pathology. It is part of
the cycle of menses and birth and daily blood life.

Ereshkigal is caught in and embodies this ordained process,
"that all life death doth end." Birth and death are intimates in the
history of women, and change and pain are inevitable. She suffers in isolation, in patient submission, enduring. She reminds us
that many of the great goddesses suffer and are wounded by
separation from child or mother or lover. They do not avoid
suffering, but face into it and express its reality. Some get stuck or
impaled. For suffering can lead to terrible passivity, a negative

inertia (like the Greek Perithous who got stuck in Hades). In Ereshkigal's realm there is a standstill where all is miasmic and inhuman and inchoate. Inanna is impaled; Ereshkigal groans. There is no hope, no effective yang answer, no way out by work or will. This is the other side of the coldness of the dark goddess. Yet here the sacrifice of activity can lead even to rebirth and illumination when it is accepted as a way to "let be." It suggests presence at its darkest level—a sense of loss, even the capacity for action—so deep nothing matters. It is the place of the powerlessness of chaotic and numb or unchanneled affect, the lonely grief and rage of powerlessness and unassuaged loss and longing, a hellish place where everything we know to do is useless, and so there is no known way out of the despair. We can only endure, barely conscious, barely surviving the pain and powerlessness, suspended out of life, stuck, until (and if) some act of grace with some new wisdom arrives. Such raw, impersonal, though potentially initiating miseries are Ereshkigal's domain.

To hang from Ereshkigal's peg can be terrible and frightening. One woman verbalized this misery: "There's pain because I was abandoned, like a spike in my heart. And all my life dead." It is to feel the abysmal bereftness of the child of the death mother, to live a life of mortification. A woman imaged in a dream her uncle's phallus as a pole on which she was suspended. She remembered his frightening physical advances and rages, but she had idealized him and was afraid to give up her own desire for men who resembled him "because that feels like home." This cruel human sadism is like Ereshkigal's pole. It stops conscious human life. Often we find ourselves getting sick or "going crazy" rather than facing the reality of such pain.

But there is another side to the image of the stake. The Great Goddess is lifeless and penetrated while she is passive, empty of life, reduced to meat. There is no motion, no obvious quickening, only the placement of the body on the peg. With a terrible fixing, Inanna is nailed down. The potential of her "myriad offices" and capacities is grounded; and this actualization seems to be part of what fertilizes a new spirit within her, just as limitation can evoke creativity.

One woman expressed her experience of the painful side of this *fixatio:*

It's as if my messy house is my cross. I'm utterly fixed—out of the fantasy of home and great life and being an important person. Just hanging there, and the old labels don't apply. I've lost all control of the way things used to be, and the pulling myself up by the bootstraps, and the shoulds. I stick to tiny details that nail me down. They are supports to get me through a pain that's not even dramatic and desperate, but just numb. There is no meaning, no comfort. I can only wait and wait. And it's not even waiting for rescue in the old way.

This forty-eight-year-old woman had spent much of her life hoping to be recognized, hoping finally to be mothered, hoping to be acclaimed by a knight on a white charger who would redeem her passivity. Through analysis the quality of the inertia changed. She felt she could sacrifice her habitual dramas, her frantic, unconscious activity, and withdraw into the small details of her everyday life. She identified the humiliation she felt as akin to Christ's crucifixion, for she knew no way to have the cup taken from her, and she did not yet know the story of Inanna or feel connected to the feminine. After many months of focus on the incarnated facts of existence, she began to see that what she had sought was present within those facts when she was able to see them from a new perspective. Through sensory awareness work, she began to honor her body with clothes that had color and texture. She found her feelings opening up in the transference relationship with her therapist. She began to value her incarnated and feeling life, and she could finally look back on her depression as a gift bringing her a new sense of her existence.

Another aspect of the incarnation potential in the stake was articulated by a woman who spoke about a newly awakened sense of the reality of her body:

A woman is nailed to the cross when she begins to menstruate. That's why I hated it, pretended it was nothing. Then, with the energy of a bull, a woman has to take in that cross, allow it to pierce her and let herself be swung between its two horns. It's the order of nature for a woman, and a different kind of cross from the Christian, for we have to swing between the prongs through time. I always considered it dirty and the moodiness and pain of my period a real sacrifice, but I can see now—through my daughter's experience—that the energy there is the equal of phallic energy, only there are two prongs, making one bowl.

In spite of her conscious disgust for menstruation, this woman had an instinctive sense of the "bull of the mother," and her statement recalls the great horned altar at Crete and the horned moon god as lord of woman.[66]

There is a possible connection between this sense of the horned god and the Gugalanna of the myth, who can be seen as the transpersonal "bull energy of the menstrual cycle." He is "killed" or actively deprived of his menstrual effect when a woman becomes pregnant. There may be a suggestion, from this perspective, that the Descent myth has reverberations concerning a central mystery of feminine experience, pregnancy. Certainly submission to the mystery of bodily experience is one way in which a woman, even the goddess, is "nailed down" into incarnated existence—nailed into reality to find her own firm stance. In this sense, the pole suggests an aspect of the impersonal feminine yang energy. It makes firm, nails down into material reality, embodies, and grounds spirit in matter and the moment. It is thus supportive, a peg to hang onto through life's flux.

The stake is also like a phallus or dildo of the dark goddess, or the sexual member of Gugalanna, her husband, who was killed. It provides an opening penetration that is the instrument of the goddess' initiation, like the impersonal phallus of any man at the temples of Inanna/Ishtar. That rite, as Esther Harding saw, freed the energies of sexual intercourse for service to the goddess.[67] Because the receptive yin is by nature empty, there is a danger that women feeling their own emptiness, especially in a patriarchal culture, will seek fulfillment through actual male partners and sons, or through serving the collective ideals of the animus in prostitution to the fathers. They will envy the penis and seek it to satisfy their longing for power; or they will try to lose their sense of impotence in worship of the man who gives sexual joy and the possibility of blissful merging. Awareness of the inner space can make a woman feel empty—like an oral cavity, lifeless, hollow, as if without food or substance due to lack of mother or lover. She then craves to be filled and is susceptible to abject dependence on an outer or animus impregnation. She can lose her own soul in the bliss of melting into her lover.

A woman's hunger to merge with the masculine as animus or outer man, her idealization of the masculine as the true spirit to which she will submit, and her need to be filled with patriarchal authority or parented by the masculine, is changed through her inner intercourse with the stake of the dark goddess. Too often the woman cannot distinguish between her unmothered need for the mother and her need for a male partnership. Perhaps because so many women were nourished by the patriarchal animus of the caretaker, or because they found their brothers and fathers warmer or more valuable, they continue to seek strength and mothering from men and their own animus, even devaluing feminine nurturance when it is available for themselves. Ereshkigal's stake fills the all-receptive emptiness of the feminine with masculine yang strength. It fills the eternally empty womb/mouth and gives a woman her own wholeness, so that the woman is not merely dependent on a man or child but can be a full and separate individual unto herself. She can stand by her own "no" and "yes," her own solid stake. Ereshkigal's pole impregnates a woman with this new and holy attitude to life.

Our culture has clearly discouraged women from claiming impersonal feminine potency. The concept is considered monstrous. Thus women are too often encouraged to be docile and "relate with Eros" to sadistic paternal animus figures, rather than claim their own equally sadistic-assertive power. Such a *coniunctio* with the phallus of the goddess is not a substitute for the later marriage of feminine and masculine, but it clarifies the lesser *coniunctio,* and means that the greater one can be genuine and passionate. For when a woman can feel her own individual self-connected stance she can be open to receive another into her own integral, strong vessel.

All the women I have quoted here have begun to serve the dark feminine. They have experienced a new energy to stand firm on ground they feel belongs to their individually experienced reality, and to stand against the collective, patriarchal animus, even if they are seen as obnoxious or unpolitic, even if they have to destroy the old sentimental forms of loving and the sense of well-being they once got from being merely agreeable and loyal and good and "healthy." For until the demonic powers of the dark goddess are claimed, there is no strength in the woman to grow from a daughter to an adult who can stand against the force of the patriarchy in its inhuman form.

VII   THE BIPOLAR GODDESS: TWO SISTERS, TWO ENERGY PATTERNS

I first came to the myth of Inanna's descent through another woman's initial dream: "I go under the water to the bottom of the sea to find my sister. She is hanging there on a meathook." This woman had been identified with the values of the patriarchy. She was in graduate school, trying to be heroic and smart and charming, but she was full of anger and fear, and could only relate to men if they were homosexual. Her dream suggested her need to search for qualities of the multifaceted, passionate, and strong feminine suspended deep in the unconscious, and to return them to conscious life, for her sister is analogous here to Inanna and the dreamer's capacity for fruitful, trusting relatedness. She had lived with a sense of being alien and exiled as if in hell, and felt closer to Ereshkigal's dark realm than to the energies symbolized by the image of Inanna. At first I understood the meathook as vicious callousness, which we connected to her family experience and to her animus. I did not find the Inanna amplification until the unpeeling of her schizoid defenses had been underway for two years, and she was well on her way into the underworld herself. I was grateful, then, for the myth's teaching that the terrible slowness of the process, gate by gate, was the right pace.

Ereshkigal is called Inanna's sister in the poem. She is her shadow, or complement; together the two goddesses make the bipolar wholeness pattern of the archetypal feminine, the mother-daughter biunity of the Great Goddess. The pattern is analogous to the star Inanna, above and below. The goddess of the Great Above symbolizes all the ways life energies engage actively with one another and flow together, including connections that are loving and disjunctions that are passionate. Below, and too often repressed, is the energy that turns back on itself, goes down into self-preserving introversions. It is the energy that makes a woman able to be separate unto herself, to survive alone.

Psychologically, we see these two energy patterns in the empathic and self-isolating modalities that are basic to feminine psychology. They appear in relation to all inner and outer partners—children, creative projects, lovers, even to a woman's own autonomous emotions and perceptions and thoughts. The active desire to want another, to wrap the partner in loving and warring embrace—that is Inanna; the circling back and down, disinterested in the other, alone, even cold—that is Ereshkigal.[68]

It is not pathological to be inconstant, this myth tells us; rather, it is a service to the bipolar goddess of life and transformation. Many women feel guilty about separating themselves from others or being inconstant, and they fall into depression. Or they cling to relationships, even when being related to others undermines their own integrity (until the Self enforces its demands through unconscious coldness, or feistiness), because they do not recognize the bipolar wholeness pattern.

The bifurcation often appears in dream images of patriarchially oriented women as a splitting of the female body at the waist, the upper part suggesting the more nurturant and culturally and personally "good" and "related" sides of a woman; the lower part, the "ugly," "smelly," and impersonal "negative" aggressive and impassioned sides. Our cultural divisions have not the same content as do those of the Sumerians, for Inanna celebrated her vulva with open delight and relished her power. And even within our culture there are general and individual differences. What is repressed by intellectual, achieving daughters of the patriarchy is not always what is devalued and ignored by women immersed in the roles of mother and wife.

In relating to the images of the feminine presented in the Descent myth, some women find themselves gripped by the erotic and active-assertive side of Inanna; they are able to feel their own previously feared energies mirrored in this upperworld goddess. It is as if they have to redeem the potential of joyful sexuality and/or active assertion from the underworld of their psyche. Other women, already comfortably conscious of their erotic and/or assertive capacities, may need to meet the potentials of patient receptivity and gestation imaged in the figure of Ereshkigal. They may have to "descend" temporarily from their accepted patterns of behavior into a period of introversion (or actual pregnancy or depression), in order to continue the process of realizing their potential wholeness.

But no matter how the pattern is imaged or incarnated, it is there, and it is bipolar; alternation, the oscillating way, is a function of the feminine Self. The experience of descent is central to the inconstant, rhythmic quality of the feminine mode as it proceeds through time, manifesting first one phase, then another.

Both goddess images represent phases of one whole that needs to be seen and honored.

So this myth teaches us the life-enhancing *circulatio* pattern. Inanna marches into the underworld with determination, going actively and consciously towards her own sacrifice. Likewise, modern woman has to acquiesce and cooperate in her introversion and necessary regressions into the underworld magic and archaic levels of consciousness. She must go down to meet her own instinctual beginnings, to find the face of the Great Goddess, and of herself before she was born to consciousness, into the matrix of transpersonal energies before they have been sorted and rendered acceptable. She sacrifices what is above to and for what is below.

But there are two goddesses, and between Inanna and Ereshkigal, as in all significant relationships, a cross-fertilization is implied. Inanna brings differentiated awareness and activity to stir up Ereshkigal's realm; she effects a conscious suffering, perhaps a birth. In return she receives her own death and rebirth, the capacity to witness, and a new strength in introverted presence. Above ground Inanna is like a cornucopia, pouring forth, passionately initiating. Below she is passive, herself an initiate. She is dissolved and becomes the receiver of life's processes; her decay is an underworld gestation, not of child but of Being itself in its seemingly most negative mode. Simultaneously, Ereshkigal becomes active and aware. The cross-fertilization between the two goddesses has a profound effect on each of them and on their creative capacities; it ultimately changes the relationship between upper and lower worlds.

VIII THE DESCENT

The motif of descent is commonplace in Jungian work. It applies equally though differently to both women and men, although I am here dealing only with women's experience of the process.[69] We make descents or introversions in the service of life, to scoop up more of what has been held unconscious by the Self in the underworld, until we are strong enough for the journey and willing to sacrifice libido for its release. The hardest descents are those to the primitive, uroboric depths where we suffer what feels like total dismemberment. But there are many others imaged as descents into tunnels, the belly or womb, into mountains and through mirrors. Some of the easier ones may be necessary to loosen rigidities and raise energy, before we can risk the shattering descents to the depths of our primal wounds to work on the psychic-somatic level of the basic hurt.

These deepest descents lead to radical reorganization and transformation of the conscious personality. But, like the shaman's journey or Inanna's, they are fraught with real peril. In therapy the therapist hopes to "manage" and companion the descents with help from the unconscious, but some fall beyond the therapist's capacity or open into the unseen crevasses of psychotic episodes. All descents provide entry into different levels of consciousness and can enhance life creatively. All of them imply suffering. All of them can serve as initiations. Mediation and dreaming and active imagination are modes of descent; so, too, are depressions, anxiety attacks, and experiences with hallucinogenic drugs.

The causal meaning of Inanna's descent has puzzled scholars. In the earliest version of the myth it has nothing to do with raising Dumuzi/Tammuz, for she has not yet even sent him down. The later Ishtar versions suggest the goddess wants to raise the dead, and Ereshkigal's reaction to the intrusion of the Queen of Heaven implies the dark goddess' fear to lose something she has been holding onto, something that has been dead to the above world. The myth may even suggest her fear to confront herself with another level of consciousness and to feel her own misery, to come to an awareness of suffering.[70]

Scholars have been inclined to dismiss as a mere excuse Inanna's stated reason for her descent:

My elder sister, Ereshkigal,
Because her husband, the lord Gugalanna had been killed,
To witness the funeral rites . . . so be it.[71]

But I think those words hold the truth: Inanna descends to witness the funeral rites of the lord Gugalanna. The name Gugalanna means "great bull of heaven." The bull is a symbol of masculine primordial energy, the fertilizing power of nature.

"The lord Gugalanna had been killed." Gugalanna is, I think, the underworld aspect of Enlil. The wording of the poem suggests that Inanna must witness the repressed shadow of the sky god, must see that Enlil was a rapist and was banished to the underworld for his violence. The sky god fathers are not purely admirable. The patriarchal gods also have an underside, a large shadow split off into the unconscious. The poem's image suggests that this shadow is bull-like passion, raw desire and power, sadistic bull-dozing violence, demonic bullying. That stubborn, bullish, defensive shadow of the gods is a fact of the patriarchy, and its ideals overwhelm the feminine and struggle to control and hold their own in life, charging ahead, uncaring where they destroy playful sensitivity and empathetic relatedness. Inanna's descent implies her confrontation with this archetypal patriarchal shadow. She must see the limits of the fathers and be witness to what was repressed; she must refind Ereshkigal.

For modern women, the death of the bull of heaven implies that what once sustained and fertilized the animus-ego can no longer function. The ancestral father principle has been depotentiated, and with it animus ideals and imperatives which functioned to provide an identity for the father's daughter. The disidentification can occur in several ways. When a woman can look behind the facade of the idealized father as model, she can begin to see the human fragility that it concealed, and she can then become free of the compelling magnetism of the ideal. "What I thought was such strength and vitality and intelligence in my father turns out like the Wizard of Oz. He's just a little man behind the curtain who could barely manage his business, trying to puff himself up," said one woman as she confronted the facts of her personal father's life. Another dreamed of her minister father as an Inquisitor, and was able to look at the archetypal shadow behind the Christian virtues her father had instilled in her. She said with astonishment and intensity as she confronted the dream image, "They burned women." For the first time she could look at the sadism involved in the patriarchal ideals she had worshipped, and see them as enemy of the feminine and herself. When a daughter of the fathers sees that the virtues and concepts that had hitherto sustained her are irrelevant to her own personality, she can also begin to let them go, using the clear eye of Ereshkigal's objectivity.

The desire to witness the death of the bull of heaven brings Inanna to her descent. The next part of the myth implies her death-marriage. Her death and impalement on the phallic post of the dark goddess represents her union with the yang side of the mother. In the myth Inanna goes down as if dressed for a wedding, even wearing the ointment "Let him come, let him come" on her eyes and the breastplate "Come, man, come" on her body. She seems to want at first to use her seductive powers to try to raise the dead, to reanimate the bull of heaven. But she goes to witness the funeral rites (saying, "so be it"), as if also foreseeing and acquiescing to her own death. It is her funeral, also, and she prepares for it. Thus she can open herself to receive the potent forces dormant in the underworld. As initiate, she courageously surrenders to her own sacrifice, in order to gain new power and knowledge.[72] Like the seed which must die in order to be reborn, the goddess of the granary submits. Like the good metal and good stone and good boxwood of the poem, which are broken by craftsmen in the creative process,[73] Inanna allows herself to be broken for a new creation.

Such a sacrifice is the basis of primordial fertility rites. Inanna offers herself in sacrifice, witnessing to the death of fertility and bringing herself as seed. She offers her own libido to replenish the lost source. Hers is the voluntary immolation upon which continual creation depends. As Eliade points out:

The myth of the birth of edible plants . . . always involves the spontaneous sacrifice of a divine being. This may be a mother, a young girl, a child or a man. . . . [In this extremely widespread mythological motif] the fundamental idea is that life can only be born of another life which is sacrificed; the death by violence is creative in the sense that the sacrificed life becomes manifest . . . at another level of existence. The sacrifice brings about a gigantic change.[74]

The rites of the Earth Mother involve a hieros gamos and/or violent death. In the collective rituals the one sacrificed is the scapegoat of the community. The victim is offered to the earth goddess in order that she bestow "good crops, seasons, and health."[75] It is "the sowing which fecundates the Earth-Mother."[76] According to Erich Neumann:

the mother's sacrifice of the male, her son, was preceded in earlier times by a sacrifice of the daughter. . . .

The victim is a woman and on another day a young girl, playing the part of earth goddess [as the corn]; she is beheaded, and her blood is sprinkled on fruit, seeds, and so on, to guarantee their increase. . . .

> The essential elements in this fertility ritual are the beheading of the woman as goddess, the fructifying sacrifice of her blood, the flaying of her body, and the investment of the . . . priest in her skin.[77]

Such rituals were widespread. There is evidence that they took place in ancient Mexico, among the Pawnees,[78] and probably among the forerunners of the Sumerians. Perhaps the immolation of pigs in Athens, and their dismemberment when they had become fertilizing rotten flesh, is a later adaptation of this same necessity to sacrifice something of the earth to the earth so that new life may rise.

We know that when Inanna was in the underworld, nothing grew or copulated. The earth was barren. The goddess had withdrawn in sacrifice to herself as the first scapegoat. From the perspective of this sacrifice we can see that Inanna maintains the balance of life. From "highest heaven" she goes to "earth's deepest ground." To the extent that she was high, she must go low; from extraverted, active, to inert passive meat; from differentiated and ideal to undifferentiated and primordial. Only thus can the balance demanded by the Great Round be maintained. It is an exchange of libido for the purpose of renewal.

We can see from this myth that the original scapegoat had nothing to do with a sin offering. Ethics were not involved, only the necessity under the natural law of the conservation of energy to maintain a balance of energy in the overall system of life. Nothing changes or grows without the food of some other sacrifice. This is the basis of women's experience of childbearing and of all blood mysteries that create and maintain life. This law is known to matriarchal consciousness and to modern physics. It is the basis of psychology and transformation of any kind, and Jung's libido theory is based upon this profound and cosmic fact.

Psychologically, the processual aspect of the exchange is experienced as painful and slow. We feel identified with whatever aspect we are closest to and can rarely find the partial relief provided in moments of enlightenment when we can see the pattern from a transcendent perspective. Jung writes of the descent to the plant level as "the downward way, the yin way . . . (to) earth, the darkness of humanity."[79] It is to this descent that the goddess Inanna and we modern women must submit, going into the deep, inchoate places where the extremes of beauty and ugliness swim or dissolve together in a paradoxical, seemingly meaningless state. Even the queen of beauty becomes raw, rotten meat. Life loses its savor. But the process of change, even the rotting, is sacred, for it represents submission to Ereshkigal and the destructive-transformative mysteries she symbolizes.

The process by which the stellar goddess submits herself to concreteness and incarnation involves her unveiling. This motif suggests the removal of old illusions and false identities that may have served in the upper world, but which count for nothing in the Netherworld. There one stands naked before the all-seeing eyes of the dark goddess. The unveiling means being stripped bare, unveiling the goddess to herself—the original striptease. It suggests a need to be utterly exposed, undefended, open to having one's soul searched by the eye of death, the dark eye of the Self. Such unveiling is immensely hard for a daughter of the fathers, for it means giving up both defensiveness and the illusions of identity provided by the regalia of the upper world, those roles and marks of power and status earned from the patriarchy which serve as surrogate or persona-identity to a woman who is handmaid to the fathers and the animus.

The descent and return of the goddess Inanna, like the Eleusinian mysteries, conveys the message of unquenchable indwelling life. Scholars think that the Sumerians and Akkadians did not believe in reincarnation, although the Akkadian Ereshkigal kept the water of life and used it to restore Inanna's corpse. The motif has perhaps more to do with rebirth and re-illumination of consciousness. Inanna sheds her old identities, is reduced to primal matter, and then is reborn. Similarly, individuals undergoing initiation in a sacred process shed their old identities and enter new ones. The unveiling is part of the initiation process.

This unveiling motif may also suggest the preparatory stages for temple prostitution. Like modern nuns, who are divested of their secular identity, the priestesses of Inanna's temples may have undergone a similar process—even to dying in the initiation on the cross of the impersonal phallus of any man, which opened them to experience their sexuality as an aspect of their service to the goddess.

From yet another perspective, the disrobing of Inanna suggests her and her initiate's awareness of different levels of consciousness. The seven garments of queenship lie on her body at the levels of the kundalini chakras. In different versions of the myth, she wears a crown, rod or ear pendants, a necklace, breast stones, a gold ring or hip girdle, bracelets, and a garment of ladyship (called breechcloth in the Akkadian version). As she divests and reinvests herself of these objects, attention may have been called to the corresponding chakra.[80] She is brought down to naked *muladhara*—the rigid, inert material of incarnation, the bare ground of facts and bodily reality—from the crown with its bliss-ful uniting of opposites (Inanna as the goddess presiding over such relations) and cosmic consciousness into the pelvis, down to the root chakra where potential life sleeps and is restored in another paradoxical uniting of opposites.

The seven gates of Ereshkigal's house have parallels in Egyptian material, but are perhaps more accurately related to the seven positions of the planet Inanna/Ishtar during her descent and return. The Sumerians kept accurate astronomical observations of planets, including the returns of Venus,[81] each with its different metallic and psychological correlations.[82] The gates are also stages of an initiatory and sacrificial way like stations of the cross. As a motif they appear in modern dream material in many guises. One woman dreamed of an innocent Marilyn Monroe figure falling through seven balconies to a bloody death. The dream presaged a severe depression and the dreamer's introduction to eruptive primal affects that opened the depths of her psyche.

Before her descent Inanna prepared the strategy for her rescue, and instructed Ninshubur to carry it out if she did not reappear from her journey after three days. She had foreknowledge that she would need help if she got stuck in the underworld. This motif is familiar from many mythologies and from clinical practice.

Ninshubur is the spokeswoman of the Self, the one who has heard Inanna, keeps track of the days, and cries out of her deep feeling that the goddess must be roused. Ninshubur is, for me, a model of woman's deepest, reflective-of-the-Self, priestess function, one which operates as simple executrix of the Self's commands, often when the soul is most threatened. In the poems mentioning her, Ninshubur has no life of her own, no specificity beyond her capacity to serve. She simply carries out precisely and competently what the goddess asks of her. In her profound, egoless obedience, she is almost invisible; indeed she dresses like a beggar at Inanna's bidding. Yet on the "faithful servant" Ninshubur's integrity and reverence and capacity for action depend the turning in the myth that restores the reborn Inanna to the world of the Great Above. As the goddess says in the poem, "Because of her, my life was saved."[83]

Inanna tells Ninshubur to go first to the sky god, Enlil, the high father of all, then to Nanna-Sin, her own father, the moon god, then to Enki. Why does she not send Ninshubur to her mother or to Ninhursag, the earth mother? The poets of her culture saw Inanna, already and unfortunately, valuing masculine power more than that of the mothers. Perhaps it is because she is the gods' hierodule, or because she feels their greater cultural potency. In any case, in her search for the necessary attitude to help her in extremis, she is wrong in her first choices. They are seemingly powerful but actually incapable or ungiving sources.

We see this search for help from the wrong sources often enough in therapy when patients insist on appealing to those who will reject them on principle (saying "such needs are infantile"), or to those who have a different world view or awareness or typology. Because the powerful parental archetype was initially projected onto those who could not adequately validate the individual, the seeker continues to expect help from such ungiving sources. Only after trying repeatedly, and staying stuck in the hell of feeling deprived and resentful, or even of turning against the need impulse itself (by identifying with the aggressive collective god, the superego), can such individuals learn to turn away. Indeed, much of therapy involves learning to abandon the old patterns and to turn toward truly nourishing and self-validating sources. Only in the process of learning to fill the archetypal parental structure with new content can a person realize that it is not his or her need or appetite for life that is at fault, but the fact that it was aimed toward the wrong source.

The sky god and moon god refuse or do not dare to rescue Inanna from the underworld. They embody impersonal patriarchal respect for law and order, far removed from the modalities of their "daughter" Inanna and the dark feminine. They see Inanna, through the projection of their own bull-like shadow, as merely ambitious, one who "craves" too much. And they cite the rule that one who goes to the Great Dwelling stays there.[84] They seem almost spiteful, glad that she got her comeuppance. Thus the superego and those living by its tidy laws retaliate against or abandon those individuals and appetites daring to move beyond collective, conventional confines. There is no help for the wayward from the powers in control.

IX   THE CREATIVE MASCULINE

There is one "father" in the Descent myth who is helpful: Enki. His name means "lord of the earth" (like Poseidon). He is the wily god of water and wisdom, ruling the flow of seas and rivers, and living deep in the abyss. In several myths he is especially close to Inanna. In this myth he initiates the process of her release.

Enki is the generative, creative, playful, empathetic male. Like Mercurius he includes the opposites and is not bound to the principle of law. Although Enki is said to have created the *me*, those ordering principles of the upper world and civilization, his order is creative, not static and preservative. He is the culture bringer, not the preserver of the status quo. His wisdom is that of improvisation and empathy. Having a bisexual breadth (in one myth he was said to undergo an eightfold pregnancy), he can penetrate into any necessity, even into the underworld.

Enki often mediates between the world of the fathers and the feminine. Always he flows creatively with life, and therefore has the potential to totally restructure the system from his own impetus. In the Descent myth he cracks the inertia of the legalistic-defensive paradigm by a totally new approach. Rather than abiding by the precedents and laws, he initiates a new process, by resorting to what was hitherto ignored: he moves with feeling.

From some dirt under his fingernail Enki creates two little servant-mourner figures, a *kalatur* and a *kurgarra*. These are described as "sexless devotees"[85] or "creature[s] neither male nor female."[86] They are perhaps hermaphroditic or androgynous, polymorphous creatures, who participate in the Great Round by their own lack of sexual differentiation. The opposites, male and female, are not yet set apart in them. Thus they do not embody consciousness as discrimination based upon cutting apart, separation, and antagonism, but consciousness as empathy and mirroring. So they can creep up to Ereshkigal, unchallenged through all the gates; "Like flies, they slipped through the cracks of the gates."[87] They are humble, nonheroic creatures, without definition or even the need to be separately defined, and without any sense of what we would call ego-needs. These little asexual creatures represent the attitude necessary to draw a blessing from the dark goddess.

What they are told to do by Enki is just what therapists do for patients in those abyss places that are preverbal and primal, where psyche and body meet the borderline, and where all is timeless and spaceless and the patterns of the magic level of consciousness hold.[88] These creatures move in close to the goddess, ignoring the ways of upper-world law and distance. Then they witness and they mirror with empathy. They see and feel, and they groan with Ereshkigal. Honoring the goddess, they express the suffering of existence that she now feels; for consciousness has come into her realm and with it consciousness of pain. They affirm her in her suffering. They have been taught by Enki to trust the life force even when it sounds its misery.

Complaining is one voice of the dark goddess. It is a valid and deep way of expressing life in the feminine soul. It does not, first and foremost, seek alleviation, but simply states the existence of things as they are felt by a sensitive and vulnerable being. It is one of the bases of the feeling function, not to be seen and judged from the stoic-heroic superego perspective as foolish qvetching and passive whining, but just as autonomous fact: "that's the way it is." Enki's wisdom teaches us that suffering with is part of reverencing.

Enki's mourners moan with Ereshkigal. When she says, "Woe! Oh my inside!" they echo her with, "Woe! You who sigh our queen. Oh, your inside!"[89] Their echoing makes a litany and transforms the pain into poetry and prayer. It makes out of life's dark misery a song of the goddess. It establishes art as a reverent and creative and sympathetic response to the passions and pains of life. And it shows the potency of such a litany. For with their mirroring song they ransom a goddess of life. From Ereshkigal pours forth not more destruction but generosity. The goddess of nature is grateful for the humble mirroring and for hearing the song of herself. Precisely empathetic expression moves her. She answers the little creatures:

> Who ever you are,
> [Because] you have said: From my inside to your inside,

From my outside to your outside,
If you are gods, I shall pronounce a [kindly] word for you,
If you are men, I shall decree a [kindly] fate for you.[90]

In the Ishtar versions of the Descent poems, Enki's way of approaching the feminine permits Ereshkigal to produce her essence, the water of life, which she holds in the underworld. It turns the cause of the inertia toward its own life-giving side. It stirs the tomb to bearing, shows us that the unconscious suffers and brings forth life.[91] Like the Gorgon whose blood kills or heals, Ereshkigal can destroy or create and heal, depending on what attitude we take to the dark goddess.

In the older versions of the myth Enki provides his servants with the food and water of life from his own store. And Ereshkigal, grateful for their reverent mirroring, turns towards them and appreciates their help and grants rewards. She offers them "a kind fate," and "the water-gift, the river in its fullness," and "the grain-gift, the field in harvest." They ask for the corpse that hangs from the nail. Ereshkigal, all-knowing, names it, "the corpse of your mistress," and she gives it to them. She is beneficent, transformed, generous. A miracle has occurred through Inanna's sacrifice and Enki's finding of the right attitude. The fertility of the bull of heaven that had died is reborn in the dark womb.

To the goddess it is no shame for a woman to be submissive. But as Marie-Louise von Franz has pointed out, such willing service is not always the way to gain what is necessary from the goddess of nature. Sometimes she must be approached with active, heroic courage rather than heroic submission. Gretel had to push the dark goddess into the oven of transformation. Sometimes she must be endured or avoided or cleverly fled from. The appropriate way to approach the dark goddess seems to depend on the conscious personality of the visitor and on what qualities are to be gained from the dark side of the instinct and image pattern. For the proud, passionate and active goddess Inanna, submissive sacrifice, humility, and passive mirroring are the compensatory ways to set her free.

X   INANNA'S RETURN

Inanna is restored to active life and rises from the underworld reborn. But she returns demonic, surrounded by the pitiless small demons of Ereshkigal, whose duty it is to claim the dead. In the myth they are to claim the underworld's substitute, and Inanna with "the eye of death" is to choose her own scapegoat. She has met Ereshkigal and knows the abysmal reality that all changes and life demand sacrifice. This is exactly the knowledge that the eternally maiden daughters of the patriarchy have fled from, wanting to do things right in order to avoid the pain of bearing their own renewal, their own separate being and uniqueness. Inanna comes up loathesome and claims her right to survive. She is not a beautiful maid, daughter of the fathers, but ugly, selfish, ruthless, willing to be very negative, willing not to care.

The problem for Inanna on her return is the substitute for herself. Whom can she choose as her scapegoat? The law of the conservation and sacrifice of energy permitted her release. In the myth this law is revealed to be the foundation of the year-god rites. As we have seen, only by sacrifice can the rupture of the wholeness pattern be repaired. On one level we can see that only her best beloved consort is equal to Inanna. Indeed, in a love song she fashioned for Dumuzi she tells him:

> You, beloved, man of my heart,
> You, I have brought about an evil fate for you. . . .
> Your right hand you have placed on my vulva,
> Your left stroked my head,
> You have touched your mouth to mine,
> You have pressed my lips to your head.
> That is why you have been decreed an evil fate,
> Thus is treated the "dragon" of women. . . .[92]

Dumuzi's love of the goddess had brought him prosperity and great joy, but he had dared intimacy, and that entails a price. In the later mysteries it is forbidden to look upon the goddess' face and live. No mortal can endure the awesome face of reality and survive unscathed. Dumuzi has done that and more. Thus he has already been made sacred, or "sacrificed." The goddess takes him as an initiate, in her underworld aspect. This is the esoteric and psychological mystery of his sacrifice. Inanna challenges her equal to make the same descent she has endured, perhaps to claim the same strength and wisdom.

When we depend on the other for our validation, we remain compliant or erupt only unconsciously. But being willing to send down Dumuzi means daring to stand for our own reality—daring to aim where we know there is a complex—even if it sends the other into defensiveness so his or her ego is sacrificed in the underworld. This is the extraverted, challenge-to-the-beloved side of the confrontation with Dumuzi. On the introverted side, the ideal most cherished must be sacrificed, given up to the goddess. The beautiful agreeableness of the love goddess and the human father's daughter, the identification with spirit and with having things easy and innocent—those animus ideals must be redirected toward the dark goddess herself and changed profoundly in her service, in order that the woman as herself, in service to her Self, may survive. The beloved Dumuzi here represents the favorite animus attitude of the old king whom the feminine soul must render to the Self or kill as the primary source of her own validation and identity.

On her return Inanna finds Dumuzi unconcerned for her plight. He is "dressed in noble garments . . . sitting on a lofty throne."[93] He does not grovel at the sight of the goddess surrounded by demons. He does not descend from his throne. As consort and year god, he has been spared the pains of the barren land. He seems unconscious of the goddess except in her fertility and Aphroditic aspects, and he basks in his role as favorite, godlike and regal in his ignorance. On him Inanna vents her hatred and vengeance, the demonism of the returned goddess. On him she "fastened the eye of death, spoke the word against him, the word of wrath."[94] In the world of light she repeats the actions of her dark sister, fully embodying in herself the underworld, death-dealing aspect of the goddess.

Before Inanna comes to the city of Erech and finds Dumuzi, three other figures—Ninshubur and her own two sons—appear to her, all of them dressed in sackcloth, throwing themselves at the feet of "mother" Inanna. They are afraid and servile, and she spares them from the demons. This part of the myth points up the psychological problems of women who identify with the culture's perverted ideal of mushy, self-abnegating relatedness as a means of gaining validation. They let their own needs be turned aside when they are seen as motherly or commiserating. They lose true relatedness by allowing themselves to be merged with others. Such merging is simply a way of avoiding confrontation. It keeps a woman's strength, which she needs to foster her individual integrity, in the underworld.

"Take him away," Inanna decrees. And the demons, instruments of fate "who accept no gifts," bind and beat Dumuzi. His torture is not unlike Job's or Christ's agony. And like his mythological descendants, he appeals to god to spare him. Through suffering Dumuzi awakens fully to the reverence of fear and to his mortality. Wrenched from his regal, godlike state, he is made suddenly aware of time's limit and human insecurity and death. In confronting the dark aspect of the goddess Inanna, he feels fear and pain, and these feelings teach him awe of the goddess and the value of his mortal life. He tries to save himself. He offers his tears. He appeals to Utu, the solar god, who arranged his marriage to Inanna. He asks to be transformed into a snake. And Utu hears him. Utu makes Dumuzi sacred. He sacrifices Dumuzi's human incarnation and grants him the undying form of the snake, immortal consort of the goddess, symbol of the energy of life.

In other myths—"The Most Bitter Cry,"[95] "The Dream of Dumuzi," and "The Return"[96]—the story ends in different ways. Two new elements are added: Inanna's reaction to the death of her consort, and a new character, Dumuzi's sister Geshtinanna.

In these other myths the Great Goddess sings in grief over the loss of her beloved:

Inanna laments for her young bridegroom,
"Gone is my husband, sweet husband, . . .
My husband has gone among the . . . plants, . . .
My husband who has gone to seek food, has been turned over to the
    plants . . .
. . .who has gone to seek water, had been turned over to the water.
My bridegroom, like a hand crushed . . . , has departed from the
    city. . . ."[97]

She weeps that he has been "taken captive," "killed," and "no longer bathes," "no longer treats the mother of Inanna as his mother," "no longer competes with the lads of his city," "no longer performs his sweet task among the maidens of his city." Inanna is bereft. She mourns her beloved. Even she cannot escape the profound sadness that change incurs in the feeling heart. As an instrument of fate, she causes the sadness; but she also suffers it and relieves it. In the underworld she was unconscious of her own transformation while Ereshkigal groaned. In the Great Above, Inanna suffers the separation from her beloved.

Other songs throughout the dynasties of Sumer describe Inanna's joyful reunitings with Dumuzi in his renewed incarna-
tions as king of her land and city. "On the day of 'sleeping, / On
the New Year, the day of rites," she takes others to her bed in the
sacred marriage rite, celebrating the cycle of undying life.[98] The
Great Goddess rejoices and mourns as her own process, of life-
death change through time, brings her new mortals and takes
them away in an eternal round of consorts (until Gilgamesh
defies his role, spurns her offer of the sacred marriage, puts the
institution of kingship on a new basis, and upholds the deroga-
tion of the goddess).

Inanna, like Ereshkigal, is an archetypal energy pattern. Each
generation of humans is altered and affected by contact with the
enduring bipolar goddess and needs to find or create life-
sustaining balances within their grand pattern. For humans must
ever be shifting, struggling and flowing, to stay in equilibrium by
including enough of Ninshubur's realism and service to survive
in the mundane world. It is a never-ending play, a balancing act,
without a fixed or even ideal end.

The problem is even more complicated when seen from the
human perspective. For all her archetypal intensity, Inanna lacks
our capacity for personal human connection. She is served by any
mortal in the role of Dumuzi. She is the goddess, unrelated except
to her own inherent necessities and to the other impersonal
intensities. We humans have a harder problem, for we are also,
being small and time-space bound, embedded in a network of
personal intimacies. We serve and are patterned and fueled by
the archetypal energies, the goddesses, but we also care about
ourselves embodied on earth and about the other fragile creatures
whose destinies we share. Not only do we struggle to stay in
conscious relation to the archetypal realm and to avoid identification with any particular archetype in order to keep the balance
fluid and life enhancing; we must also stand for Inanna as goddess of passions and affects, of love and war, as the goddess who
supports our personal, time-bound life on earth. We must also
serve her by sustaining the earthly and human realm and its
embodied necessities. For we find the goddess in and through
our personal connections, incarnated in the place where we suffer our passions: in daily life. And this, as the myth of "Dumuzi's
Dream" suggests (see below), also serves Inanna, the great,

impersonal goddess. For through our passions and sacrifices, the goddess is given back her beloved, and life can flow forth from her holy womb. The very nature of earth's life, and of the goddess herself, prevents the possibility of her having an undying, single partner. The goddess' fructifying consort is mortal, a god-man, a man made god in his service to her. He embodies the life-death bipolarity of the eternal process of change. That frightens and disgusts the side of us that, like Gilgamesh, wants eternity and stasis. But as the goddess is also matter, there is no stasis and no eternity of form possible for material life. We must gain our eternity in another way, not by clinging to the embodied identities we call heroic ideals. We must go beyond Gilgamesh's and the patriarchal ego's denigration of the goddess as fickle and learn to serve her rather as inconstant. This is the primary psychological task to which our age is called.

XI GESHTINANNA

In the myth of "Dumuzi's Dream" we are pointed in this direction by a new character introduced into the myths, the shepherd king's sister, Geshtinanna, who brings us out of the dramatic intensity of the sweeping mythic forces. She bridges the vivid, overwhelming energy patterns laid forth in the Inanna material and the patterns of the smaller, earthly, human, personal world. She points us to a possibility of keeping our reverence for the goddess of life and death, beyond the patriarchy, but at the price of willing acceptance.

Geshtinanna, Dumuzi's sister and daughter of Enki and his wife, the reed goddess, is a wise woman, "a tablet-knowing scribe . . . who knows the meaning of words, . . . who knows the meaning of dreams."[99] In the poem, the shepherd Dumuzi has a dream in which he imagines the destruction of his work and himself. He sees a single reed bowed in mourning and two reeds cut down. He calls upon his sister to interpret his vision. She sees it as foretelling their mother's mourning and their own destruction and she urges her brother to flee. She sees "the demons coming against" him, and vows to protect him with her silence even if she is tortured on his behalf. Later when he flees to her house and is seized for the last time, she laments wildly and searches for her brother.

Like Ninshubur, but in service to the human dimension, Geshtinanna does what she can to redeem the one lost to the underworld. She follows the destiny she saw in Dumuzi's dream. But she does it as a mortal woman, and she does it through the goddess, not through the high gods. With Inanna, whose friend she is in other myths and whose love for Dumuzi she well knows,[100] she finds Dumuzi's grave and grieves. Then with full consciousness, and following the pattern established by the goddess, she offers to take her brother's place in the underworld. She acquiesces to her own cutting down.

Both she and Inanna descend after they suffer a separation from and loss of a vital partner. (Thus graves have always been considered entrances to the underworld, to the depths of the unconscious.) But unlike Inanna, Geshtinanna offers herself not out of the goddess' love of adventure and strength. Instead, her motivation is human passion, both of love and grief. And Inanna is so moved by her offer of sacrifice that she transmutes Dumuzi's sentence and mitigates the destiny laid out for Geshtinanna in the dream. She decrees that brother and sister shall alternate, each spending six months in the underworld and six months on earth. The goddess allows them to embody the process of her own cycle—the descent and return, return and descent in endless rearrangement of life's pattern.

There is a poem, too, in which the shepherd Dumuzi introduces Geshtinanna to sexuality, showing her incest among the animals of her sheepfold. She is the earthly, "root stock" sister of the gemini pair. She represents endogamous libido in kinship that is an intimate, personal connection to the masculine; she and her brother are born together out of the same womb and die together, the two cut down in the same image. Thus Geshtinanna personifies the woman who can be a sister-comrade to mortal man. She is caring in a way that goes beyond the goddess' impersonal capacity, seeing life's fragile patterns with human wisdom, and is willing to share another's burden out of grief and love; she serves the reborn goddess, but can have her own standpoint as well.

Geshtinanna comes into the story after Inanna's descent and return. She does not feel the defensive need of a daughter of the fathers to receive payment of a returned gratification every time she makes some self-sacrifice for the masculine. Her capacity for intimate relatedness is more specific and embodied in earthly feeling—beyond the goddess' impersonal, queenly rhythms and primal affects. She can read the messages of the unconscious, yet she can stand firm even against demons. She is an image for one who can mediate between the human and transpersonal realms and share the burden of weaving them together.

Geshtinanna seems to symbolize the product of Inanna's descent and return; she is a budded offshoot of the goddess' encounter with her own dark sister, a new "root stock of the vine" of life. Yet, compared to the Great Goddess, she seems humble and humanly conscious. As daughter of Enki, she is supportive of the feeling dimension. She shelters her brother in his fear and dependency, and she responds creatively to his destiny, for she is close kin to his fate and feelings. Unlike the god-man consort, she is "a wise woman," made conscious both by her brother's fear and by the dream. But she is strong enough to mitigate and to take upon herself human suffering, through conscious, loving sacrifice. She offers herself to the goddess, her friend, out of passionate love for her human brother. Thus she does not flee from her fate, nor does she denigrate the goddess of fate as do Gilgamesh and the patriarchy. She volunteers. In her courageous, conscious acquiescing, she ends the pattern of scapegoating by choosing to confront the underworld herself. Willingly, she offers to serve Ereshkigal as well as Inanna.

Her image is Christlike, yet more personal than Christ's, and deeply feminine. He gave his life for all men in a grand gesture. She offers herself, courageously accepting her own destiny, for one man she cares for, her brother, whom she calls "beloved man."[101] Hers is a small, personal answer, an individual and individualized response. By this creative act she serves Inanna's process of life and her own incarnated constellation of the goddess of love and war—her own personal feelings. On this earth specific, here-and-now evaluation is the limit of our experienced feeling function. We may extrapolate from it, but that is the scale on which we experience it.

Geshtinanna is not a grand model, a single answer to the process of descent and return. She is herself, and her response is specific to her own feelings and her own fulfillment. She simply shows us the problems and her own resolution. But, for me, she conveys the possibility of an incarnated capacity to serve both the goddess and human life. She is a result and an embodiment of the whole initiation process involving the creation of Inanna's renewed darkness and passion and remorse and Dumuzi's divine kingship and human dependency and fear. She feels personally, and she can be lovingly related to the masculine as a partner. She is also willing to serve both the light and dark aspects of her own depths and those of the goddess. As she is portrayed in the poems, she lacks the vibrancy of Inanna. She also does not yet know Ereshkigal's domain, for she has not yet made her own descent. There is no struggle in her character between her instinct to relate to her beloved and her instinct to stand alone and for her own depths. But she is willing to dare the descent. And that is what many modern women are called upon to do by their dreams and feelings.

We can wonder what will change in Geshtinanna, how she will be different on her first return and on all the ones thereafter, for each descent is a new process, and she may return with different balance each time. We can wonder how any human woman or anima is to be transformed through the rhythm of service to Inanna and the world of the Great Above—with its active passions, extraverted and collective relationships, and creative expression—and to Ereshkigal and the world of incubating dark and seeming stasis, where the collective unconscious works upon us and we come to our aloneness rooted in the goddess and *muladhara*. It is for us to endure the phases of descent-ascent-descent, as a service to both aspects of the feminine instinct and spirit patterns. It is hard to say and feel "Holy Ereshkigal, sweet is your praise!" Yet that is as essential as it is to welcome back the full range of the upperworld feminine, symbolized by Inanna, to the above, conscious world. Acknowledging Ereshkigal can lead us to find meaning in pain and loss and even in death, just as we need to reaffirm the meaning in Inanna's passionate joy and combat and ambition. All of these are valid and holy experiences for women.

Embodying the process of descent and ascent, alternating with her brother-animus, enduring and embracing the play of opposites, Geshtinanna stands outside the patriarchal mode. Her stance is ever creative, ever relative and flexible. It cannot be reached deliberately as an ideal but only by suffering the individualized feelings and passions that in her represent her service to the goddess, and by enduring the descents and returns demanded by the goddess. In the form of wine Gestinanna symbolizes a new feminine spirit and an old, yet ever-new, consciousness of process. Every new crop of the vine must descend for fermentation into the underworld and come up transformed as the fruit of underworld transformation. As with the ever-new wine, taste and quality will vary; each year's crop will be different from another's. The only standard is a process of earth's organic rhythms, which is why the taste and quality must vary. And that variability is the point—part of feeling-discrimination and its joy and sorrow.

As a forerunner of Dionysus, Geshtinanna points us towards a new kind of individuating ego that celebrates and acquiesces in the transformation processes of life and death, that embodies an ever-changing balance between transpersonal and personal,[102] and that dares to encounter the shadows in the underworld in order to return to life feelingly and humanly embodying, not repressing, their energies.

There are problems with the facts of Geshtinanna's fate as a paradigm for modern women. Her fate—as decreed by the goddess—can give us faith in the process of change, which is a help in letting go of old consciousness and being willing to live into new psychological spaces. Like many of us, she chooses to serve her own individual destiny (as it was conceived in ancient Sumer). But we would probably not long be able to accept a fate that prevented our living out a more conscious relation to the partner (or animus). Sumer solved such problems of relationship by positing an alternation of conscious and unconscious positions. Geshtinanna and Dumuzi do not again meet; they pass twice a year in the endless cycle, and we get no hint of psychological development, of the accretion of wisdom as the years turn.

The implication for modern women is that only after the full, even demonic, range of affects and objectivity of the dark feminine is felt and claimed will a true, soul-met, passionate and individual comradeship be possible between woman and man as equals. Inanna is joined to and separated from her dark ancestress-sister, the repressed feminine. And that joining and separation, with Ninshubur's and Enki's and Dumuzi's help, brings forth Geshtinanna—a model of one who can take her stand, hold her own value, and be lovingly related to the masculine as well as directly to her own depths; a model of one who is willing to suffer humanly, personally, the full spectrum that is the goddess.

Modern women have a long history that is becoming more and more conscious. We can feel the effects of our long struggles in the patriarchy and in the underworld. And we must, as Jung put it, "dream the myth on." There are no paradigms that exactly fit our situation. The ancient tale of Inanna tells us only what forces we must serve. How each of us is to find her own individual balance as we descend-ascend and ascend-descend—that is still to be lived and written. The Inanna mythologems of descent and return reintroduce two great goddesses, two primal feminine energy patterns and their partners, and the possibility of an individual human response to bring them into incarnated, personal life. The story presents a model for health and for healing the split between above and below, between the collective ideal and the powerful bipolar, transformative, processual reality underlying the feminine wholeness pattern. The images of the myth can orient us on the path as we suffer the return to the goddess and renewal, following first in the footsteps of Inanna, then of Geshtinanna.

vi The Common Language of Women's Dreams: Colloquy of Mind and Body

CAROL SCHREIER RUPPRECHT

A whole new poetry beginning here.[1]
ADRIENNE RICH

Why study dreams? Because it is the nature of human beings to dream. Each of us has several dreams each night, spends a total of four full years of life in the REM (Rapid Eye Movement) state of dreaming sleep, and experiences an estimated 150,000 dreams in a lifetime.[2] Dreams mediate among all the various dimensions of human experience: mind and body, feminine and masculine, conscious and unconscious, image and behavior, as well as past and future, the individual and the collective, the personal and the transpersonal. They offer a holistic view of the human person, one that can guide women's search for self in these last decades of the twentieth century.

Contemporary culture offers two very promising sources—the neurophysiology of sleep and dreaming and analytical (Jungian) psychology—for study of the dream as a psychophysical unit and as an expression of the fundamental unity of the many other spheres of human experience listed above. Because both of these disciplines focus on preconscious and unconscious phenomena, they can give us a view of human nature that is neither gender-biased nor culture-bound.

The current literature in both fields, however, suggests that this potential may never be realized without an ongoing feminist review which complements, supplements, and interprets the emerging data and theory to reflect the actual experiences of real women living now. With the impetus of such a review, women may begin the work of naming their own experience of the unconscious world, experience which has been made known primarily through the perspective of theorists, researchers, analysts, therapists, and teachers who have been predominantly (and in the experience of some women, exclusively) male.

The purposes of this essay are several. Section I is a review of the dream theories most valuable for feminism which have been formulated in recent decades in the neurophysiology of sleep and dreaming and in analytical or Jungian psychology. Section II shows how these theories are linked through their re-recognition of mind-body symbiosis and how that link may stimulate feminist thought. Section III offers a feminist critique of dream data collection and theories that have been predicated on unexamined assumptions about gender. Section IV proposes an archetypal approach which will help women not specifically trained in either discipline to understand their own dreams as well as these new processes of investigation.

Putting this material on dreams in an archetypal perspective has the aim not to produce solutions or resolutions, but to generate new hypotheses, stimulate new kinds of experiments, increase awareness of gender effects among experimenters and subjects, and foster further interdisciplinary exchange between neurophysiology and analytical psychology. Within the field of neurophysiology, I will examine the "activation-synthesis" hypothesis of dream formation. In analytical psychology, I will look at the hypothesis of a "collective unconscious" comprised of "archetypes." The first theory is the recent proposal of two psychiatrists, J. Allan Hobson and Robert W. McCarley, conducting research at the Massachusetts Mental Health Center. The second theory originated with Swiss psychologist C.G. Jung (1875–1961) and is being reformulated and carried forward in the new interdisciplinary field of archetypal theory by the psychologist James Hillman and others.

Obviously only a very limited sample from the literature in these fields can be introduced here. In the area of neurophysiology I will focus on two articles from the *American Journal of Psychiatry* (AJP) that present the activation-synthesis argument. These articles were chosen because they challenge Freudian dream theory and received greater response from readers than any article previously published in the history of the journal. They are also condensed enough in form to be accessible to general readers and to stimulate the kind of dialogue between science and psychology that their authors advocate.

It would have been impossible to select out of the more than twenty volumes of Jung's published work that material which focuses on dreams, because the dream theory is at once both base and context for all of Jung's other major concepts. My principal sources here are volumes VIII and IX of the *Collected Works (CW)*, in which Jung describes his hypotheses and discusses mind-body relations in terms of the archetypal nature of spirit and instinct.

In juxtaposing material from neuroscience and analytical psychology, a system of mutual checks and standards of verification becomes possible. Such a system has the value of a dynamic balance between subjectivity and objectivity. It counters the tendency of science to make truth claims based on its purported objectivity by forcing it to examine the gender-based, and possibly gender-biased, perspectives of its practices and practitioners. And it offsets the inevitable and acknowledged subjectivity of psychological theory that grows out of the personal psychology of the theorist by insisting on an examination of concrete biological evidence.

I

> The remarkable correlation between the REM sleep state and dreams remains one of the best documented and richest examples of mind-body correspondence and thus a very promising avenue for understanding how the mind and body relate to each other.[3]
>
> ROBERT W. MCCARLEY AND EDWARD HOFFMAN

As this decade proceeds, the pace of sleep and dream research threatens to render each new report obsolete before it comes into public view, but current work of most interest to feminists is that of J. Allan Hobson and Robert W. McCarley. These two psychiatrists developed the "activation-synthesis" hypothesis of the dream process and presented their theory in the *American Journal of Psychiatry* in December 1977.

The article, which provoked an unusually strong reader response, was titled "The Brain as a Dream State Generator: An Activation-Synthesis Hypothesis of the Dream Process." In that article and in one published the previous month in *AJP*, "The

Neurobiological Origins of Psychoanalytic Dream Theory," the authors posited a complex and inextricable bond between neurophysiological processes in the brain, specifically those originating in the pontine brain stem, and many of what they labelled "formal features of the experience of dreaming," such as number of dreams, duration, intensity, periodicity, imagery, cause of arousal from sleep, dream amnesia and recall.[4]

Hobson and McCarley, building on the earlier research of Aserinsky (1953), Kleitman (1953, 1955), and Dement (1957), who identified several phases in sleep correlated with eye movement—the now familiar REM and NREM (Non-Rapid Eye Movement) phases—introduced their theory this way:

> The activation-synthesis hypothesis that we will begin to develop in this paper asserts that many formal aspects of the dream experience may be the obligatory and relatively undistorted psychological concomitant of the regularly recurring and physiologically determined brain state called "dreaming sleep." It ascribes particular formal features of the dream experience to the particular organizational features of the brain during that state of sleep. More specifically, the theory details the mechanisms by which the brain becomes periodically activated during sleep and specifies the means by which both sensory input and motor output are simultaneously blocked, so as to account for the maintenance of sleep in the face of strong central activation of the brain. The occurrence and character of dreaming are seen as both determined and shaped by these physiological processes.[5]

Three aspects of Hobson and McCarley's theory greatly affected the reception and impact of their first published article in the *AJP* and persuaded me of the value of their work for feminist thought. One is their almost polemical promotion of a dialogue between neurophysiology and psychology. Two is their positive emphasis on mind-body isomorphism in Freud's thought and their recognition of this as the heuristic link between the two disciplines. Three is their attempt not only, as one might expect from laboratory researchers, to describe their procedures and results, but also to assess and challenge Freud's theory of dreams: "Sharing Freud's conviction that mind-body isomorphism is a valid approach, we will now review modern neurophysiological evidence that we believe permits and necessitates important revisions in psychoanalytic dream theory."[6] Further, they call for an alternative psychological dream theory more congruent with contemporary neurophysiological understanding.

Hobson and McCarley argue against Freud's notions of repression and distortion as primary forces in dream formation, his notions of disguise, concealment, displacement, and condensation, and his distinction between the manifest dream and latent dream thoughts. They claim the primacy of neurophysiological determinants in both the origin and formation of dreams. This claim is later modified to a call for "equal time" for neurophysiology in the dream formation process, but it is still advanced in the context of an attack on Freud.

Why do Hobson and McCarley present their material in the form of a critique of Freud likely to provoke sharp reaction from psychoanalysts? First, they believe that all of Freud's concepts are predicated on a view of the brain as a passive entity reacting to external influences rather than a neuronally active system that is self-enclosed, self-generating, and motivationally neutral. Second, their research seems to have led them to the conviction that cooperation between neurophysiology and psychology is essential for the forward movement of both disciplines. Psychoanalysis, because it looks for the origin of dreams in psychic conflict, rather than in natural processes, does not seem to be a psychology capable of such cooperation.

A holistic view of human experience, the authors imply, becomes possible only when accurate, mutually validating evidence from mind and body is available. (Their concurrent argument, that Freud, having based his neurobiology on erroneous nineteenth century assumptions, inevitably developed an erroneous psychology of dreams, is not persuasive.)

Hobson and McCarley make no mention, in their first article, of any other psychological theories of dreaming that have challenged Freud on bases similar to theirs or any additional theories of dreaming that reinforce their laboratory observations. Any reader familiar with the work of Swiss psychologist C.G. Jung, however, would be immediately struck by correspondences between the activation-synthesis hypothesis of dream formation and the dream theory central to Jungian, or, as Jung himself called it, analytical, psychology.

Among respondents to the 1977 articles, one reader was quick to supply precedent and context from Jung. James Hall is a

Jungian analyst, medically trained psychiatrist, and author of a book which was also published in 1977, *Clincial Uses of Dreams: Jungian Interpretations and Enactments*. With Jung in mind, Hall wrote in his letter that in contrast to Freud "there are other voices in the broad psychoanalytic tradition which view dreams as conflict-free in origin."[7] Hobson and McCarley had stressed this natural etiology in claiming that the dream process has its origin

> in sensoriomotor systems, with little or no primary ideational, volitional, or emotional content. . . . The sensoriomotor stimuli are viewed as possibly providing a frame into which ideational, volitional, and emotional content may be projected to form the integrated dream image, but this frame is itself conflict free. Thus both the major energetic drive for the dream process and the specific primary stimulus of the dream content are genotypically determined and therefore conflict free in the specifically psychodynamic sense of the term.[8]

When Hobson and McCarley responded to the first flood of letters to the editor of *AJP*, they cited Jung as supportive precedent for the ontological naturalness of the origin and formation of dreams: "To me dreams are a part of nature, which harbors no intention to deceive, but expresses something as best it can, just as a plant grows or an animal seeks its food as best it can."[9]

Why is the dream theory central to analytical psychology favored by these psychiatrically trained neurophysiologists who hold such strong reservations about Freud? A large part of the answer lies in Jung's general view of the psyche (the totality of psychic processes, conscious and unconscious) and hence of dreams as naturally occurring, undistorted, accessible phenomena of mentation. Jung's description is very like the neurologists' description of dreams as neuronally active, self-generating, motivationally neutral phenomena. For Jung the dream experienced while one sleeps (Freud's "latent dream thoughts") and the dream reported when one is awake (Freud's "manifest content") are proximate enough to be considered a single phenomenon: the dream. Like the neurophysiologists, Jung asserts that the reported dream is not a disguise or substitution or distortion of the experienced dream. The dream is a product of the natural cooperation of all elements of the psyche, not a result of conflicts between parts of the system, such as the instincts seeking expression and the superego exercising repression.

This natural cooperation, in which conscious and unconscious achieve a dynamic, mutually compensatory self-regulation, demonstrates the psyche's innate impulse toward holism, or the fullest development of the person, through the process Jung called "individuation." This claim that the self-generating, self-regulating psyche moves naturally toward holism was not advanced by Hobson and McCarley themselves, but by James Hall in his letter to the *AJP*. He states that in Jungian theory dreams are not only conflict-free in origin but are also "oriented toward psychological growth, problem solving, and the lifelong process Jung called individuation."[10] Hall's view is shared by many earlier psychologists, even those who worked under the sway of Freud, such as P. Bjerre. Bjerre asserted in 1936 that "the dream should be viewed in terms of its constructive forces toward personality integration rather than as an attempt at libidinal satisfaction on an infantile level,"[11] a view growing out of his comparison of these constructive forces in the psyche with other healing mechanisms in human biology.

Like research on the dreaming brain, then, Jungian theory invites us to consider dreams as products of the well-functioning psyche-soma rather than the damaged or blocked psyche or the diseased brain. It also invites us to view dreaming as a creative process. Jung's concept of the prospective function of dreams—their ability to point toward future events and depict as yet unrecognized potentials—and of the processes he named "active imagination" and "amplification" underscores the creative dimension of dreaming.[12]

Neurophysiologists share Jung's interest in this creative dimension. Hobson envisioned the brain as a camera projector in his article "Film and the Physiology of Dreaming" for the new journal *Dreamworks*, a journal described by its editors as:

> an interdisciplinary quarterly devoted to the art of dreaming. We believe that the dream process lies at the root of human creativity and that the dream bears an essential relationship to all waking art forms. The purpose of this journal is to bring together the latest thinking on the dream process from many fields—aesthetics, anthropology, criticism, neurophysiology, philosophy, psychology, religion—and to gather dream reports and adaptations from artists working in various media.[13]

In the article Hobson demonstrates that whether the mind and body are isomorphic, symbiotic, analogous, or simply parallel, they may be considered fruitfully as systems which, when juxtaposed, illuminate each other in ways no single treatment of the separate system can. He goes on to demonstrate a way in which creative attention to imaginal processes can bridge the gap between science and psychology.

The interdisciplinary mode of discourse sought in *Dreamworks*, as well as in this collection of essays, is essential to archetypal theory. Archetypes manifest themselves without regard for disciplinary boundaries and logical categories, often appearing simultaneously in several areas of an individual's life—in dreams, art, work, relationships, thought, and body. The energy archetypes release is focused in a specific way, usually through certain images, yet its effects are broad and pervasive in all dimensions of conscious and unconscious life.

Through the dialogue between neuroscience and analytical psychology, we learn that the process by which archetypes reach consciousness has an analogue in the brain activation process during dreaming sleep, accounting for what the waking ego regards as bizarre elements of the dream. Several activities within the brain, kept distinct when the person is awake, occur simultaneously during sleep. The resulting dream record of these overlapping activities appears to the waking ego as strange, irrational, and illogical. Using an archetypal perspective, however, the ego can come to recognize that the dream reflects, in its own logic and language, a more complex and complete reality than that readily available to ego-directed consciousness.

The most promising approach to archetypal events, then, as to dreams themselves, is one of circumambulation from a variety of perspectives. "There is an associative field, and the combined total of the associations, while always shifting and regrouping, establishes certain parameters within which an archetype reveals itself."[14] These associations may be drawn from or need to be amplified by a variety of disciplines, because in their isolation from each other the disciplines may reiterate inaccurate, or at least inadequate, information based on values that are no longer acceptable to society. New facts and different values may result from such multidisciplinary convergence, leading to truly interdisciplinary work with a capacity to encompass and be extended by new ways of thinking.

While new neurophysiological data is the basis of Hobson and McCarley's disavowal of Freud, the hypothesis of a collective unconscious is the most dramatic example of Jung's departure from Freudian dream theory. The collective unconscious, comprised of archetypes, is the core concept of analytical psychology and its dream theory. While the personal unconscious corresponds in many ways to Freud's id, Jung postulated a collective level of unconscious processes, described with varying degrees of clarity and shifts of emphasis throughout his work. This part of the psyche carries the universally human psychological material, material deriving from what Jolande Jacobi calls "the inherited possibility of psychical functioning in general, namely from the inherited brain structure." She cites this description in her survey, *The Psychology of C.G. Jung:* "The term 'brain structure' . . . points to the connection between the psyche and biology. For the psyche, as it presents itself—as it is experienced by us—is inseparable from our physical being."[15]

This hypothesis of a collective unconscious Jung derived directly from his experiences with dreams, his own and those others shared with him; he collected over sixty thousand dreams before making his idea public. These dreams often included images, places, characters, events, or tones which the dreamer could not connect to anything from his or her own past experience, either through travel, participation, reading, or communication with other people, ruling out the possibility of cryptomnesia or hidden memory. Again and again Jung was able to trace the dreams' content and form to ancient images, places, characters, events, and tones.

The neurophysiological study of dreams, it seems, will be capable of corroborating the existence of a collective unconscious. As research becomes increasingly refined, for example, as the REM period of sleep becomes differentiated into several levels of subtly varying physiological activity, dream form and content may be found to vary within these levels in a form detectable through laboratory experiments and technology. These levels may range from the immediate, personal "day residue" to material more impersonal, archaic, and unknown.[16]

One other major Jungian concept, upon which many of Jung's hypotheses ultimately rest, is also of interest in feminist dream research. This principle, often ignored in writing on dreams, is "synchronicity," the meaningful coincidence of outer event and inner image. For example, a person caught in a slow process of change and becoming impatient dreams of a turtle. She also encounters a large turtle crossing the roadway on her way to work, and returns home to find in the mail a letter, on stationery with a turtle design, from a close friend with whom the dreamer has had no recent contact. The friend "coincidentally" reminisces about a period in his life when he was stuck in an impasse and nothing but patient, steady plodding had enabled him eventually to leave it behind.

Synchronicity, for Jung, supplemented cause and effect as an explanation of certain events, and it supplemented the temporal and spatial order of the world as we consciously construct it. Synchronicity also appears to have a neurophysiological counterpart in the "desynchronized" D-state of REM sleep, which McCarley describes as "a distinctive temporal and spatial organization of brain activation" markedly different from the organization of the slow-wave NREM synchronized sleep state or the waking state. ("Synchronicity" is a misleading term, perhaps, and should not be confused with "synchronized" or "synchronous." The former refers to "the simultaneous occurrence of two meaningfully but not causally connected events," events which appear initially to be discrete and random.[17] The latter terms refer to a regular and quantifiable temporal order involving simultaneous and possibly causally connected events, as in the firing of neurons.) The characteristics of REM sleep may be found to correspond to those of synchronicity, establishing another mind-body link.

In synchronicity, two or more events (the turtle in the road and the turtle stationery) occur which are not logically or causally connected. From the standpoint of the ego as the center of consciousness, these appear to be discrete events which are only coincidentally connected by occurring at the same or a proximate time. From the standpoint of the unconscious, however, the conjunction of these events is experienced as meaningful and carries archetypal force. Similarly, in the desynchronized phase of dreaming sleep, the centers of the brain primarily concerned with distinguishing and differentiating among events on temporal, spatial, and logical grounds, are substantially deactivated. As a result patterns of brain activation occur in which usually separate events, images, and objects merge, overlap, and intersect in ways that seem—in the retrospective view of the awakened dreamer—bizarre. These ways make sense, however, on a different level and in a compelling way, to the sleeping dreamer.

Jung's challenge to the authority of Freud provides another common bond between analytical psychology/archetypal theory and the activation-synthesis hypothesis of dream formation. Until a recent wave of criticism from various sources, Freud's voice in dream theory had been authoritative in the psychiatric community of the United States and, for the most part, undisputed. Hobson and McCarley, with no avowed feminist outlook or intent but with a holistic view of dreams and dreaming, issued a specific challenge to the authority of Freud and the dominance of psychoanalytic psychology. (Even in the earliest stages of sleep and dream laboratory research in the 1950s, Freud's theories had begun to be called into question, for example by William Dement.)[18] This challenge of the neurophysiologists, though arrived at by very different means, substantiates feminist criticism of Freud.

As a pioneer among advocates of a positive, heuristic, and holistic view of the dream process, Jung often spoke of the realm of human experience as holistic, of "the archetype as linked with image in . . . a psychoid continuum rooted in the material world."[19] Feminists wary of Freud, however, have been equally wary, for somewhat different reasons, of Jung. As feminist critics of Jung, myself included, began to demonstrate in the midseventies, it is easy to disparage analytical psychology by revealing its particular brand of gender bias. Jung was given to contradictory and often extreme statements, among them the following: "In men, Eros, the function of relationship, is usually less developed than Logos. In women, on the other hand, Eros is an expression of their true nature, while their Logos is often a regrettable accident."[20] Despite such extreme statements in Jung's writing, however, archetypal dream theory does offer a way of seeing that goes far beyond historically enculturated sexism, even though Jung and his early successors failed to make much use of this potential. Under the influence of a new climate of feminist consciousness and a growing body of archetypal theory fostered by James Hillman, mainstream and orthodox

Jungians like Edward Whitmont, June Singer, and James Hall have begun to loosen previously dogmatic and prescriptive categories associated with gender.[21]

Thus the fundamental dream theories of analytical psychology and archetypal theory are being and will continue to be reinforced, corroborated, extended, and opened up for further inquiry by the discoveries and hypotheses of the neurophysiology of dreaming. With their emphasis on the ontological naturalness of dreams, creativity, interdisciplinarity, synchronicity, the collective unconscious, and the challenge to Freud, these two fields can be of great value to feminist inquiry.

II

We view ourselves as adding a new structure of meaning to dreaming consciousness [awareness] which becomes a rich field for exploration of new mind-body relationships and so expands our knowledge of what it is to be human.[22]

J. ALLAN HOBSON AND ROBERT W. McCARLEY

The relationship between neurophysiology and psychology envisioned by Hobson and McCarley presumes a symbiotic or, for the time being at least, an isomorphic relation between mind and body. Hobson, in an interview for *Science 80*, identified the chief appeal and challenge of their work this way: "The most important thing is that sleep research reminds us once again that mind and body are one."[23] Scientific knowledge led even an early psychoanalyst like Karen Horney to sense a pattern of isomorphic relation between mind and body. Her orthodox Freudian view was modified by her knowledge of embryology and she came to believe that "striving toward self-realization is inherent in the biological system of the organism."[24]

It is ironic that the two neurophysiologists point to Jung as supportive precedent for their work, since the human body often disappears in analytical psychology, especially where Jung and Jungians are reacting to Freud's emphasis on the body and its sexual features. Moreover, this de-emphasis on the body has led to certain feminist criticism of Jung, for it allowed him to hypothesize unremittingly about feminine and masculine principles, about the anima and the animus, without ever referring to female and male persons who inhabit verifiably different physical forms. Jung was prolific in discussing feminine and masculine principles (especially the former in men). He was less comfortable with and less attentive to male and female biological attributes, and the possible effect of biological differences on the psychology of men and women.

The medically trained Jung, however, did struggle early in his career with the instinct-archetype relationship and tried to explain biologically the origin, transmission, and recurrence of archetypal patterns. In an essay, "On the Nature of the Psyche," written in 1947 and revised in 1954, Jung wrote: "Psychic processes, therefore, behave like a scale along which consciousness slides. At one moment it finds itself in the vicinity of instinct, and falls under its influence; at another, it slides along to the other end where spirit predominates and even assimilates the instinctual processes most opposed to it."[25] Furthermore, instincts and archetypes are so similar in their autonomy of function that it is logical to hypothesize a link between them:

> The instincts are not vague and indefinite by nature, but are specifically formed motive forces which, long before there is any consciousness, and in spite of any degree of consciousness later on, pursue their inherent goals. Consequently they form very close analogies to the archetypes, so close, in fact, that there is good reason for supposing that the archetypes are the unconscious images of the instincts themselves, in other words, that they are *patterns of instinctual behavior.*[26]

Jung never abandoned his interest in the somatic basis of psychic phenomena. In his last work *Man and His Symbols,* published posthumously in 1964, he writes: "Here I must clarify the relation between instincts and archetypes: what we properly call instincts are physiological urges and are preceived by the senses . . . at the same time they also manifest themselves as fantasies and often reveal their presence only by symbolic images (archetypes)."[27]

Jung, however, seemed incapable of, or uninterested in, applying such observations about the physical to his own life as a male or incorporating them into his theory about male and female psychic experience. He encouraged serious attention to the phenomena of the unconscious, but it remained for scientific advances in dream research to attempt to validate psychological experience on the physical level and to establish parallels, analogues, congruencies, and isomorphisms between physical and psychological processes.

Feminists have much to gain from a holistic method of inquiry as practiced by Jung and Hobson and McCarley. But the value of this new approach in expanding our knowledge of what it is to be human depends on the way we resolve a paradox; the major dream theorists of our century have at best ignored (as Hobson and McCarley do) and at worst misconstrued (as Jung does) the experiences of women. Some have used dream theory to reinforce gender stereotypes rather than to understand women, their bodies, their roles in society, and their relationships with each other and with men. What has been defined as "human" has really only been "male," and even perhaps an incomplete definition of maleness.

For example, the debate among respondents (all were male) to the *AJP* articles on the activation-synthesis hypothesis proceeded on certain assumptions about mind-body dynamism. Some of these assumptions strike the female reader as puzzling and completely inapplicable to her experience. When psychoanalysts wrote in to differ with Hobson and McCarley, their arguments were circular in a way that effectively, if not intentionally, excluded women. Among the respondents to the 1977 articles, Philip D. Walls argued that it does not matter whether Freud's neurobiology was accurate or not, contrary to Hobson and McCarley's claim that the neurobiology was inaccurate and therefore Freud's dream psychology was flawed. Freud, Walls said, did not derive his theory from science but from case histories and clinical experience which, his followers have found, are sufficient validation of the rightness of his theory.[28] The reasoning here is sound, but the premise contains a basic fallacy. If the measure of effectiveness of psychoanalytical theory lies in its being confirmed by clinical practice and if the assessment of that effectiveness lies in the hands of the clinical practitioner, a self-fulfilling prophecy can readily occur. What comes to be seen in the practice is what theory predicts will appear. When things appear which are not accounted for by the theory or which contradict it, they are either not noticed at all, or they are construed as the patient's psychopathology. Thus there is no outside standard by which to verify one's findings because the confirming "evidence" comes from clinical data that is reputedly the original source of the theory.

Since the beginning of psychoanalysis, a disproportionate

number of analysts have been male and a disproportionate number of patients have been female. The legitimate complaints of the female patient about constricted social roles, self-images, and sexual behavior have frequently been labeled as personal psychopathology. Indeed, psychoanalysis has shown an impressive and alarming capacity to disarm its critics, especially female critics, by analyzing them away, that is, by responding to them as if they were patients. Thus feminist criticism is seen as evidence of psychopathology and dismissed, and both the substance and style of feminist criticism are categorized and explained away in terms like "penis envy" and "deficient superego." Criticism based in scientific experimentation on the physical body conducted by male psychiatrists, such as that done by Hobson and McCarley, will be harder for psychoanalysts to refute by labeling its proponents as psychopathological.

It still remains for feminists to ensure that the new dialogue between science and psychology is one in which women's voices are heard. One of the goals of this essay is to spur participation in the dialogue by making women aware that it is going on and especially by calling their attention to the discussion of mind-body relationship.

A holistic perspective on the mind-body issue is essential for feminism for several reasons. The tendency in Western European culture and in the United States, notably in religion, philosophy, and depth psychology, has been to identify the female with body, with base matter, and, by extension, with evil.[29] The conceptual reunification of mind and body will ensure that neither is ever considered the exclusive, or even preeminent, province, literally or symbolically, of one sex.

In addition, so many events in women's lives—the onset, recurrence, and cessation of menses, pregnancy, lactation, childbirth, abortion—have major effects in both the psychological and biological spheres simultaneously that only a holistic view can take account of women's experience. In the fields of analycial psychology and the neurophysiology of sleep and dreaming, the shift away from medical and psychological pathology is a happy one for feminism since it orients us toward acquiring knowledge rather than curing disease and it excludes from research prior definitions of health and illness, normality and deviance.

The addition of dreams to the mind-body paradigm gives us a

unique temporal inclusiveness. As Rosalind Cartwright has noted, dreams give us a twenty-four hour perspective on "what are the continuities that are stable across the three states of waking, sleeping, and dreaming, and what things appear to be reversed or complementary from one state to the next."[30] Also, if we begin with the dreams of children, we will have an opportunity to do longitudinal studies examining gender difference before extensive cultural conditioning has occurred and before, during, and after the physical changes of puberty lead girls and boys to different self-perceptions and differences in treatment by society.

III

> Male/female differences are apparent in dreams and REM sleep from childhood to old age.[31]
>
> ROSALIND CARTWRIGHT

> If anyone dreams that he is wrapped in swaddling clothes like a little child and takes milk from a woman, whether or not he is familiar with her, it means he will have a long illness, unless his wife is pregnant. But if a woman has such a dream, it foretells that she will have a little daughter. If a young woman dreams that she has milk in her breasts, it signifies that she will conceive, carry, and bring to birth a child. But for a poor man without a livelihood, it foretells an abundance of money and possessions, so that he will be able to feed even others.[32]
>
> ARTEMIDORUS DALDIANUS

The excerpts above come from texts on dream theory that appeared in print almost two thousand years apart. The first is from Rosalind Cartwright's *A Primer on Sleep and Dreaming* (1978), the second from the *Oneirocritica*, or *The Interpretation of Dreams*, by Artemidorus, a Greek writing in the second century A.D. Throughout these two thousand years, dream theory has displayed a fundamental assumption, now explicit, now implicit, that gender is a frequent, predictable source of difference. This difference can appear whether one is looking at the dreaming process, the experienced dream, the reported dream, or the interpretation of dreams. Men and women, one would inevitably deduce from recorded dreams and dream theories, often dream different kinds of dreams; when they dream dreams similar in content and form, the dreams often have different meanings; when they have similar dreams, they often report the dreams differently.

Dreams appear to be a rich field for exploring gender differences, then, but much research up until now has been gender-biased when it has been gender-conscious. When noting or commenting on gender differences in dreams, many theorists offer tantalizing glimpses of their personal and cultural biases, and contemporary theorists are no exception. Furthermore, the sex of experimenters and subjects, dreamers and interpreters, has been shown to influence collection and interpretation of material, and even reports on scientific research results have been shown to be affected by the sex of the reporter. One dream researcher notes: "There was a strikingly high degree of disturbance of ego scores in the dreams of those subjects whose sleep sessions had been presided over by an experimenter of the opposite sex."[33]

Gender bias is even evident in studies where gender is ignored and where claims of an objective method are most insistent. An example is the "content analysis" method of dream research, the creation of Calvin Springer Hall, whose theory and data form the basis for much dream research undertaken in the last thirty years. More than any dream research on any scale to date, Hall's research has been gender-conscious. His books are filled with gender specific descriptions of dream content, most notably in the chapter on "The Conflict of Sex Roles" in *The Meaning of Dreams* (1953) and articles like the one titled "Strangers in dreams: An empirical confirmation of the Oedipus Complex" (1963).[34]

Hall's litany of striking contrasts between men's and women's dreams is intriguing, but it makes us skeptical of his methods of collecting and categorizing dream reports. Content analysis with Hall almost invariably confirms central psychoanalytical tenets such as the Oedipus complex and women's inferior superego and ethical capacity, culturally sanctioned roles, and stereotypical behavior and attitudes.

First let me cite some of the interesting gender differences Hall appears to have uncovered. Phallic symbols in dreams occur in images and in contexts of impairment and aggressiveness in males, and of impairment and rejection in females. In aggression dreams, women dream more often of being victims, men more often of being aggressors. When men dream of themselves as victims, they are victims of misfortune, not aggression. Men's dreams show more physical aggression, women's more verbal aggression. Male dreamers engage in more aggression with strangers than with people known to them, while female dreamers have an equal number of aggressions with familiar and unfamiliar persons.

Most strangers in dreams of both sexes are male, as are most threatening characters and most perpetrators of violence. Bodily disabilities and injuries or defects to something belonging to the dreamer were three times more numerous in males' dreams than in females' dreams.

> There is an interesting and virtually universal difference in the frequency with which males and females dream about other males and females. Male dreamers dream more often about other males than they do about females. The ratio is about two males to one female. Females dream about males and females in equal proportions. This difference has been observed in children as well as in adults, and in various ethnic and nationality groups.[36]

Men's dream encounters with other men are more often aggressive and negative than their dream encounters with women which are often friendly or sexually intimate. Women's dream encounters with men and with women are aggressive or friendly in equal proportions. In addition, Hall writes, "Men, as might be expected, have more physical activities in their dreams than women do."[36] Women are more preoccupied with color and value judgments in their dreams; men are more preoccupied with size. Women dream more about swimming than men do.

These differences reported by Hall have been used to support many kinds of explanations and the reliability of his data has been unquestioned, despite his clearly stated bias toward orthodox psychoanalytic theory and the stereotypical gender assumptions that underlie his work. The latter are reported along with the dream data as given:

> Women dream of being in familiar indoor settings—usually their own houses—more often than men do. Men dream of being out-of-doors more frequently than women do. These differences reflect the differences in the working life preferences and activities of the two sexes.[37]

Hall reports other "typical" dreams: "getting married and having

children (especially by women)"; as well as typical wish fulfillment dreams: "adolescent boys of performing outstanding feats
in the playground or battlefield"; "young men of becoming
famous, young women of wearing beautiful clothes and jewels,
older women of living in spacious mansions."[38]
Hall moves readily from the reporting to the interpretation of
his data, which always confirms the theory he supports. The
"fact" that men and women dream differently about aggression
and victimization provides confirmation, for Hall, of Freud's
theory of different superego functioning in men and women:
men take more responsibility for their misfortunes, which they
see as arising from something within themselves, while women
seek external causes and assign blame outside themselves.

It is interesting that females dream more often of being victims of
aggression, and males more often of being victims of misfortune.
This difference may be explained by the Freudian theory that the
conscience of the woman differs from the conscience of the man.
Her conscience is said to be more externalized. This means she is
less likely to accept responsibility for her misdeeds. The male conscience is more internalized, which means he is more likely to
acknowledge his own guilt and to blame himself for his misdeeds.[39]

That this was written almost twenty years ago seems little excuse
for Hall's failure to consider many now obvious contingencies of
men's and women's lives. Nor can we dismiss the body of his
work, as it still forms the basic pool of data for dream researchers,
and is even used by Hobson and McCarley. Perhaps the reason
women dream of themselves as victims is rooted in physical and
cultural realities such as their comparatively smaller size and
lower muscle to body weight ratio that make them more vulnerable than men to crimes of violence, including rape. Moreover,
Carol Gilligan's new study on ethics suggests that the process of
moral reasoning may differ significantly between women and
men. There are "two ways of speaking about moral problems,
two modes of describing the relationship between other and
self," she writes, and these may prove to be gender specific.[40]
Hall concludes that female dreamers' attitudes toward others
indicate ambivalence because they dream equally about familiar
and unfamiliar, same-sex and opposite-sex persons. It does not
occur to him that it would be equally plausible to conclude that
women are more balanced in their interactions with others and

men imbalanced. Many other challenges to Hall leap readily to mind, and yet his data continues to find uncritical acceptance among otherwise insightful, scrupulous dream workers. Even Susana Ortiz, whose thesis "Dreams in Pregnancy" serves later in this essay as an example of promising feminist research, cites Hall as one of her sources.

It is not only in the area of reporting dream content, however, that dream research shows such gender bias. An androcentric view is held by many experimenters and influences all aspects of the experiments. Most researchers and reporters I have encountered in my years of research on dreams have been men. When they have been women, they have been women trained in a male-dominant system of general medicine, especially psychiatry. Furthermore, the typical subject in the experiments I have studied has been a white, right-handed male and his data have been regarded as the norm against which data from all other subjects is measured.

Research reporters, as well as experimenters, can be guilty of gender bias when they omit or de-emphasize data about women. Initial reports of the Hobson-McCarley hypotheses failed to focus, as the researchers themselves had, on pontine brain stem activity as the basis for observing dream mentation as it corresponds to physiological activity. In the following statement, the researchers appear to be at least tentatively phallocentric: "Perhaps the outstanding example of the inter-relationship between the physical phenomena of REM and the psychological aspects of dreams may be the male erection, McCarley says."[41]

Both researchers and reporters need to report the sex of both experimenter and subject as part of their data and to acknowledge that, if and when it becomes necessary to interpret on the basis of gender, any view of one sex's experience by the other is a partial view and warrants inclusion of the other sex's view on the same data. For example, a feminist perspective which starts by calling attention to gender bias in research could enhance, clarify, and challenge the rich material in the most recent report (July 1981) of activation-synthesis research. In the article "REM Sleep Dreams and the Activation-Synthesis Hypothesis," the effect of the sleep lab environment on the dreamers and the dreams is not discussed, although this environment has been shown to modify dreams significantly. Furthermore, there is no mention of the sex of the subjects (who are elsewhere identified as male) or of the experimenters, although the sex of the participants has been shown also to influence all aspects of dream collection, including recall, content, and length.

> The longest dream reports were contributed by the two subjects who had their sleep sessions in conjunction with an experimenter of the opposite sex. . . .
> These findings are in agreement with Whitman's accounts of the unusual amount of sexuality content in the manifest dreams reported by female subjects in sleep-laboratory experiments to a male experimenter.[42]

While penile erection may be the most externally visible phenomenon of physiological response during sleep, certainly women's many physiological processes, such as vaginal engorgement, menstruation, pregnancy, lactation, and menopause, are equally measurable phenomena for sleep and dreaming research, especially given the elaborate and sensitive technology now available in sleep laboratories. The cyclic, often predictable, and easily monitored nature of many of these processes would make them useful in research. Comparatively little research along these lines and even less research that includes an awareness of gender has been conducted. Yet even when such research has been carried out on a small scale with carefully limited scope and intention, it has yielded fascinating results and has deepened our understanding of the dynamic archetypal relationship between image and behavior. In her nursing thesis study of dreams in pregnancy, Susana Ortiz found a clear correlation between the dreams and the behavior of pregnant women: "The greater the anxiety in dreams, the better the subject coped in childbirth."[43] The women in Ortiz's study dreamed more often than is reputedly usual for women about bodily injury and impairment, violence and threat (to self, not the fetus), and hostility directed outward. Such dreams, in the culture of the United States, are considered to be more characteristic of men than of women.

Ortiz followed the women in her study through the last trimester of pregnancy and through the birth and a brief postpartum period. She concluded that "handling anxieties related to childbirth events in dreams serves to help a woman prepare herself psychologically for the real crisis. Anxiety scores were found to be significantly and positively correlated to coping behavior scores."[44] In reading Ortiz' reports, one is most struck by the way even such a time-limited study of a small sample of subjects engenders in the researcher a respect for dream-behavior symbiosis and mind-body complementarity.

While Ortiz relies on dream theorists other than Jung (he is mentioned once, cited from a secondary source), she ends with a conservative yet suggestive statement that reflects an archetypal mode of thought:

> Although effective adaptive behavior is largely guided by cognitive functions (Lazarus, 1966), these must be preceded by a thorough understanding of the complete "picture" and all its related variables. If we accept that all human situations have conscious and unconscious elements, then certainly we cannot assume the "picture" complete until both elements have been considered. It is reasonable to think that perhaps dreams serve the function of scanning the unconscious elements for us.[45]

Thus dreams can be seen as contributing to the integration of conscious and unconscious, to the development of a holistic perspective on health. In addition, the absence of dreams, through curtailment of an individual's typical sleep patterns for example, has been shown to have negative as well as positive effects on mind and body. Some studies suggest that it is not just loss of sleep or deprivation of dreaming time but interruption of or failure to complete the whole psychophysiological process of dreaming sleep that leads to a hallucinogenic state akin to psychosis (seen, for example, in marathon disc jockeys and flagpole sitters). Similarly, "the vast hormonal changes taking place during a normal pregnancy are accompanied by very real changes in sleep patterns," changes which may play a part in post-partum depression.[46] As we learn more about psychophysical interaction, we will be able to treat mind and body together rather than attribute certain symptoms exclusively to emotional problems to be treated with counseling or to physical causes to be treated solely with medication.

The conclusions of Ortiz and others concerning the content of women's dreams do not coincide exactly with those of Calvin Hall, who reports women's preoccupation with their appearance and with the possibility of a defective infant.

Dream content changes during the later stages of pregnancy. Themes of being physically and sexually unattractive, and apprehension that husbands might find other women more attractive, are quite common in the dreams of pregnant women. There are also many anxiety dreams of giving birth to a malformed baby.[47]

Ortiz, along with others, reports that there is frequently a total evasion of the childbirth event in dreams, and that in dreams of anxiety it is more often the woman herself, rather than the fetus or newborn, who is threatened. Convincing evidence of the pregnant female's preoccupation in dreams with the fetus is not available.

From this single sample of research on dreams of women in a significant psychophysiological situation, we can turn briefly to the dreams of children. Gender-based dream differences have been found to be widespread among even very young children and have shown certain distinctive changes over the life of the child up to and through puberty. Dream researchers David Foulkes, L. Breger, and Rosalind Cartwright, like many others, report such differences as early as five or six years. Boys dream more unpleasant dreams, which are full of adult male strangers. Girls' dreams are more pleasant and more often include parental figures, both father and mother. At ages seven and eight, the unpleasantness for boys decreases and for girls increases, with the dreams of both showing an increase in adult male strangers.

The high incidence of threatening adult males in the dreams of children and adults of both sexes may reflect the conscious and unconscious activity of men, their roles in society, and the perceptions of them by others, particularly women and children. The cultural image, in the collective consciousness, of the male as protector may have its obverse, in the collective unconscious, of the male as threatening aggressor. The pervasiveness of the dream image of threatening adult male seems to suggest generalized anxiety about male power and its uses among humans in our culture. It is possible that the threat-laden image of the adult male could be mitigated by men's increased participation in child care and greater attention to their capacities for gentleness and nurturance. That image also may reveal males' fears of their own capacity or potential for forceful use of physical power.

When we reflect on reported differences in dreams between the sexes and compare them to similarities and differences in the behavior of women and men in society, we can begin to see the advantages of a feminist theory that includes dreaming. Any noticeable correlation, or lack of correlation, for example, between Foulkes's discovery of gender differences in dreams of children[48] and Nancy Chodorow's theory of gender differences in child development, advanced in *The Reproduction of Mothering*, would allow us to identify with greater certainty patterns of significant gender difference. This would, in turn, necessitate serious reconsideration of both research methodologies and cultural conditions.

Are little boys just more frank in reporting their darker dreams, or are they living up to perceived cultural expectations of aggressiveness? Are little girls more inclined to report positive experiences in dreams to please the questioner? If conscious and unconscious experience are complementary and compensatory, is conscious life on the whole less pleasant (or less stimulating, less challenging) for little girls than for little boys? Or do dreams in children function homeopathically, reiterating and reinforcing waking life? Do boys' and girls' dreams have to do with different realities in their social lives or with different ways of processing the same realities?

We can begin to investigate such questions only when we establish nonsexist environments for the study of dreams—the dreams of women and men, girls and boys—and we can only profit from past investigations when we approach them with a raised feminist consciousness that is buttressed by rapidly growing pools of data and new modes of inquiry.

IV

> We need a dream-world in order to discover features of the real world we think we inhabit (and which may actually be just another dream-world).[49]
>
> PAUL K. FEYERABEND

In the beginning of this essay I promised to propose an archetypal approach for women not specifically trained in neurophysiology or psychology that would give them access to their own dreams and to those processes of investigation. To fulfill that promise I want to introduce some personal, anecdotal accounts of dreaming.

A feminist archetypal approach to dreams begins with an attitude that sees women's experience as valuable but not yet fully known to us, the self as dynamic and evolving, and the unconscious as a powerful force for both self-knowledge and the energy to seek that knowledge. With this attitude we neither ignore gender differences in dreams nor set out to prove their presence or something about them. Indeed, at first it may be best just to be aware of gender effects and their influence on one's own imaginal life without referring to the lives of others, especially men.

For access to your own dreams, begin by valuing them, paying attention to them, taking them both as seriously and as playfully as you take everything else in your life. Keep a dream journal. Follow Hillman's recommendation to "befriend" your dreams.[50] Live with them, carry them around with you; paint or draw or dance or sing them; get acquainted with your dream population, menagerie, language, and geography. Be aware of the way physiological changes affect your dreams.

Dreams become more meaningful when they are seen as part of a series. The series of dreams in one night, in one month, or one year will often show a lateral homology, that is, a continuity across apparently disparate forms and contents, which reflects archetypal patterns in your sleeping and waking life. Use the Jungian processes of active imagination and amplification to involve your waking self in your dream life and to facilitate the flow of energy between conscious and unconscious. Active imagination is a directed process of transforming energy patterns of the collective unconscious into images available to consciousness. This creative, often playful, process includes spinning out in fantasy those images already available through dreams, i.e. developing, extending, and following through images which in the dream are partial or suggestive or powerful or ambiguous. Amplification is another creative process, one which broadens and enriches dream content by finding analogies in art, folklore, fairy tales, myth, legend, and other sources of archetypal material. In contrast to Freud's "free" association, amplification is a limited, controlled, and directed association process which circumambulates the dream, focuses exclusively on it, and includes only material specifically connected to the dream content.

I first became aware that my dream life was influenced by my gender in some fundamental ways long before the advent of feminism, after several years of analysis with a male Jungian analyst. That clinical experience has been valuable beyond my expectations: the relationship was based on mutual trust—psychological wounds were healed, and my life was enriched. But there were several months in which I seemed to be spinning my wheels, and I even had dreams which supplied that image. Sessions were pleasant, interesting, but they were not really going anywhere. At that point my analyst suggested I work for a while with a female analyst to see if that would break the stalemate. (In some Jungian training centers, same-sex and cross-sex analyses are recommended.)

I was skeptical of the influence of the therapist's gender, but just before my first scheduled session with a female analyst and throughout the first several weeks of our meetings, my unconscious released a flood of material which had never come up before in my dreams. It was material primarily about my female self, my grandmother, mother, daughter, sisters, aunts, and schoolgirl friends. Not only the content but also the form and tone of my dreams changed.

I gradually became aware, through recounting such experiences at meetings, conferences, and lectures around the country, that many women had similar stories to tell. One reported the following interesting event:

> My dream is turning into a nightmare. As dream ego I have in three successive incidents performed a strong, positive, effective action. Now, feeling snakes crawling all over my head, I begin to beat and claw at them, screaming "Kill the snakes! Kill the snakes!" My thrashing and screaming wake my husband who then, with difficulty, rouses me from sleep. Half-awake, I reach for my bedside dream journal and record my dream. In the morning my husband advises me to see our doctor soon, for my headaches are surely getting worse if they are so painful that they make me beat and clutch at my head and scream out in my sleep, "My head aches! My head aches!" Startled, I consult my dream journal and find that I had, indeed, written my dream cry as "Kill the snakes!", which is the way I remembered the dream.

This anecdote, far richer in detail and meaning than summarized here, raises several questions for which we do not now have even tentative answers. Some of those questions are associated with gender: Had the dreamer actually "translated" her vigorous, aggressive attack on the snakes, as she came into partial consciousness, into an acceptable physical pathology, a headache? Had the husband, wishing to deny the ugliness and horror of the actual nightmare, "translated" her words into a form and meaning acceptable to him, congruent with his image of his wife (reported by her) as timid and neurasthenic? Why had the dreamer wanted to kill the snakes? The Medusa is a strong mythological image of the powerful woman: Why did the dreamer fear the snakes? Why did this dream come at this particular time in the dreamer's life? Was the woman's fear a component of the dream itself or of the waking state?

Another anecdote, which may serve as a caveat rather than a stimulus to questions, was supplied by Annis Pratt in the original draft of her essay for this volume. It follows as she wrote it:

> I owe the birth of my two daughters, an immensely empowering experience in and of itself, to the distorted interpretations of a (Jungian) therapist. One particular dream, of a hungry, pathetic infant that I needed to nourish, but which kept dwindling away into a speck of mud or a safety pin or button, recurred often enough to seem crucial to my crisis at that time, so the therapist decided that the sad little child symbolized my unborn children and indicated a need for me to develop my *anima*, or feminine, maternal side. I realize now that the poor little thing was my own manifestly unmothered self, calling up a capacity for maternity that should have been applied, posthaste, to my own personal needs. The therapist, on the other hand, built a case for having babies and for resisting the promptings of my career or *animus* side. Bearing two daughters brought out powers which I was eventually to apply to myself, and so empowering were my pregnancies that I took my doctoral examinations and wrote my dissertation and first book under the influence of my surging hormones. I do not think that the therapist would have anticipated the special blend of maternal and intellectual power that rendered me goddess-like in my biological and academic effectiveness; by that time, needless to say, I had given him up.

Another anecdote was supplied by a member of the audience at an archetypal theory panel during the 1980 National Women's Studies Association Conference. The woman was struggling with the question of sexual identity and was focusing on her pull toward lesbian relationships. She brought to her male therapist a dream in which she had a satisfying relationship with a man much younger than herself. The therapist identified this dream as symbolizing her progress toward heterosexuality, a goal he saw as desirable. The dreamer felt uncomfortable with this interpretation and as her life evolved, it came about that she was to be her fullest self in relationship with another woman. In retrospect, she felt the dream had been symbolic of her having gained enough strength (represented by the young man) to act on her intuition and desire by choosing a lesbian relationship despite the difficulties it would bring into her life in society. At the time of the dream she had had the intuition that it signaled strength and freedom to choose, rather than literal confirmation of heterosexual behavior, but this interpretation had been unacceptable to her therapist.

What is important in these two tales is not a choice between a feminist "right" interpretation and another "wrong" one, but rather the freedom to pose and explore all possible interpretations, including those which are unfamiliar, unsanctioned by society, inconsistent with accepted theory, or challenging to the personal or professional views of a particular psychological theorist or practitioner.

These personal accounts lead me to make a second set of recommendations to readers seeking access to their own dreams. Form or join dream-sharing groups made up exclusively of women. If you choose to work with a therapist or analyst, male or female, choose carefully a person who will honor and accept your reality even when that reality appears to conflict with cultural expectations or with "evidence" from psychological research and clinical practice. Remember Jung's injunction—the opposite of Freud's—that the dreamer's resistance to the interpretation of a dream means not that the hidden complex has been stirred but that the analyst hasn't "got the dream right." Until an interpretation wins the dreamer's full assent, it isn't "right."

Read widely but selectively and critically among books on dreams. So many studies, experiments, and theories take the ego standpoint only. The ego categorizes, seeks consistency and coherence, and often imposes these where they are not immediately evident. The ego is associated with the forebrain and cognitive functions that characterize waking activity, while the lower centers of the brain are involved in sleep and dreaming. To approach dreams from the point of view of the ego only is to transfer to one sphere of the self an activity of a very different sphere that has its own inner organization and language. If we consider only the cognitive level in dream study, we reduce processes like dreaming and pregnancy to one-to-one correspondences between physiological phenomena and psychological phenomena.

In dream study, research, and theorizing it will be essential to remain open to new manifestations of the archetypes which may not conform to previous manifestations or which have not been completely grasped by the ego. Because our conscious views are partial, time-bound, and from the ego standpoint only, they need to be balanced by the perspective of the unconscious which is expressed primarily for most people in dreams and fantasies and also can be found in art, literature, and all works of the human imagination.

The neurophysiological study of sleep and dreaming, a science of the mind, is completed by archetypal theory which offers an imaginal view of the body. Charles Rycroft observes that "dreaming is a sleeping form of imagination" and that images are not created out of nothing. Many dream images, he notes, are fragmentations and recombinations of images derived from external objects, including the body.[51] Philosopher and archetypal theorist Edward Casey has taken similar ideas even further in his studies of imagination.[52] Jung, who called the dream the "self-portrait of the psyche," felt that the dream could also have a mirroring relationship to the body. Dreams can help us in the diagnosis and prognosis of physical illness; dreams may allow us to detect disease and make progress in healing even before the illness is detected by medical technology or registered by waking consciousness.

Ortiz' research shows us that dreams have an adaptive function; they help women through psychophysical processes such as pregnancy. By looking at women's dreams, *with them,* we may be able to predict which women will need special support during events such as childbirth. If deprivation of sleep-dreaming time during the post-partum period can be shown to be an element in depression and even psychosis, we may be able to help women avoid such outcomes. For a young married woman I knew, with a small child and a new-born, a deepening post-partum depression led to suicide before anyone sensed the extent of her incapacity to recover mentally and physically from the birth.

Dreams could also be useful in counseling women about choices involving their bodies. My experience with college students who have had abortions has shown that this experience may have powerful psychological effects on a young woman which often show up in dreams and nightmares. This is not to say that counseling that includes the dream perspective would lead to a decision not to abort, but it could help a woman prepare emotionally for the event and work through the psychophysical after-effects. It would be helpful for women to know that, whatever constraints on or sanctions of abortion exist in society, abortion seems to be connected with profound archetypal processes in the unconscious that need to be considered and incorporated into the experience.

REM research has led to another discovery with yet to be explored gender implications. REM sleep serves the function of establishing neural circuitry in the brain; thus the infant passes at least 50 percent of sleep time in REM dreaming phases. REM sleep also has been linked with cognitive and imaginative capacities. Since REM sleep maintains neural activity, and vice versa, and since deprivation of such sleep and its concomitant dreaming processes results in disorientation, dysfunction, and even psychosislike behavior, then the observation that REM sleep differs noticeably between males and females requires further investigation.

All humans experience a decrease in the amount of REM sleep from infancy to old age, but the process of decrease varies markedly in women and men. After an initial sharp drop from infancy to puberty, women experience a gradual decrease until the age of twenty, and then the amount remains stable throughout the life span. Men, on the other hand, experience a gradual decrease from puberty to middle age (thirty-forty) and then another significant decrease in old age. Certain stages of REM sleep actually disappear in the elderly man.[53] The physical and psychological health of the elderly are certainly affected by this variance in sleep and dreaming patterns. Any study of the elderly, especially on gender-specific issues, will be incomplete unless it encompasses dream findings and thus defines its subjects as living through conscious and unconscious, mind and body, image and behavior. Such an approach can be especially valuable with elderly persons confronting death. Jung's work suggests that the aging body may deteriorate, but the unconscious goes on energetically, producing dreams, sometimes reflecting the physical changes, sometimes going on as if it will continue to exist even when bodily functions cease. Examining dreams of women and men on the Jungian model allows us to see the interconnection of image modes (dream, unconscious) and behavior modes (waking, conscious) and, in addition, to see how these modes have been interrelated throughout time. Thus the dreams of the elderly may put them in touch with a collective experience of timeless human events like death that could mitigate personal fears.

It is also possible and useful to construe the archetypal view as enabling sharper separation between, rather than the unity of, image and behavior. If the dreaming brain is seen as an enclosed, self-regulating system with most external stimuli input and motor output blocked, dreaming as an activity of that brain can be recorded, observed, and analyzed separated from behavior, apart from motor activity and social interaction and even the self-conscious and possibly inhibiting awareness of the sleeping, dreaming subject. The dream state, by offering at least a temporary disconnection from social behavior, provides a unique arena for examining the mental processes by which men and women dream.

Not all psychologists or scientists are as ready as Hobson and McCarley to respond to the imaginal dimension, however, and where they are not, the archetypal perspective must be supplied as a corrective by the individual woman herself. One area of research bearing on gender that would benefit from the application of an archetypal perspective is personality theory.

Within the last decade, descriptions of mental health established in the United States psychiatric profession and catalogued in the *Diagnostic and Statistical Manual of Mental Disorders*, or *DSM*, were found by psychological investigators like Sandra Bem to be heavily gender-loaded. For a long period of time, maleness had been widely held to be the norm of mental health. Those characteristics identified within the medical profession as healthy correlated with characteristics attributed primarily, and sometimes exclusively, to men: independence, decisiveness, aggressiveness, leadership capacity, and instrumentality (in contrast to expressiveness). Bem designed and applied a series of tests which demonstrate such common, gender-linked attributions.[54]

Though the tests of mental health that revealed this gender bias are now seldom used, the evidence is strong that we all live, or have a sense of living, in a male-dominant culture. Though dominated by individuals who meet its standard of mental health, the culture is not always characterized, in the opinion of many women (and many men), by sanity, balance, and wholeness. There arose from this difference in perception the feminist expression: "A healthy woman is a crazy person." To be herself, her own version of sane, balanced, and whole, a woman must be out of sync with her culture. This is the view of the conscious world.

In the unconscious world, however, things look different. Applying the previously mentioned measures of health and normalcy to dreamers, we find that "a healthy man (in the conscious world) is a crazy person (in the unconscious world)." A man whose behavior meets the prevailing standards of sanity has dreams, in form and content, which often correspond closely to dreams of the mentally retarded, the mentally disturbed, and the brain-damaged. On the other hand, women's dreams often show forms and content labeled positive on normative scales of mental health. The norm of mental health has been, then, not normal, but only one set of associations based on masculine gender and conscious life. To get a wholly healthy person, therefore, in our current culture, one would have to construct a person from man's consciousness and woman's unconsciousness.

Are the conscious and unconscious complementary, as archetypalists maintain? Do dreams portray what is missing from the conscious attitude? The whole portrait of any individual, then, would have to include mind and body, sleeping and waking states, conscious and unconscious, and findings so far lead us to suspect that the healthy individual would combine, in a variety of ways, elements we now label as "feminine" and "masculine."

The colloquy of mind and body conducted in the dreams of women, and men, needs to be listened to carefully and openly. It offers an alternative to negative etiologies for natural processes, constricting theoretical categories, authoritative stances, and premature foreclosure on questions of gender. When we participate in this colloquy, we need not exclude elements that do not fit the "laws" of nature and culture or denigrate each individual woman's experience as idiosyncratic. Examining the congruences between the neurophysiology of sleep and dreaming and archetypal theory will allow women access to processes that are beyond the control of others (and even beyond their own conscious control) and beyond cultural conditioning. Thus each woman may hope to discover her truest self. The process of dreaming is continually renewing—every night brings new dreams—and continuously self-correcting and self-regulating. Dreams can be an empowering resource for women in a culture that fosters unhealthy adaptive behavior because body and mind will signal the harm in such adaptation. All a woman must do is learn to watch for the signals, listen to the colloquy and become an active participant in it.

vii | Feminist Archetypal Theory: A Proposal

ESTELLA LAUTER AND
CAROL SCHREIER RUPPRECHT

I. UNCONSCIOUSNESS-RAISING

The range and diversity of contributions to this collection and their common commitment to both feminism and archetypal thinking indicate that feminist archetypal theory is a viable mode of inquiry and not a contradiction in terms. As feminists we want to do more consciousness-raising about women's issues in general, including the relationship between patriarchal theory and women's experience. As archetypal theorists we want to do some *un*consciousness-raising (a term suggested by Annis Pratt), specifically about women's images in dreams, art, literature, myth, religion, and therapy. Our proposal for a feminist archetypal theory is based on the essays included in this volume and years of correspondence, conferences, and conversations with feminist archetypal thinkers around and outside of the United States. This final essay, however, is the product of an exchange between the co-editors and would not necessarily be endorsed by the other contributors to this volume. It is a proposal rather than a conclusion because we see our enterprise as prospective.

Why do we need a feminist archetypal theory? Despite the explosion of information about women in recent decades, we still know relatively little about our mental processes in relation to our behavior. We have an increasing supply of data on the work we do, the money we earn, and the political offices we hold, but very little knowledge about patterns that may exist in our perceptions, imaginings, and cognitions. All of the evidence is not in on the issue of sex differences. Just as research on the absence of significant differences seems to become conclusive, new questions (for example, about lateralization of the brain in males and females) renew our belief in sex differences. Meanwhile, we postpone the search for a clearer understanding of female experience in order to avoid establishing any categories that might serve once again to confine women.

Feminist studies have identified contemporary culture as thoroughly masculine in spheres such as norms, values, laws, and even language. This masculine dominance raises the concern that any woman seeking knowledge of herself, to say nothing of seeking Self and wholeness, will be forced from the outset of her search to encounter that dominance head on. Women have what anthropologists call a "muted" culture and our experiences, as we move to own and articulate them, appear as the unknown, the "wild," to the dominant culture.[1] Its members, perhaps threatened, may marshall their considerable force against such movements. And an additional effect of such continuous subordination within the culture is the truncating of women's hope that female experience even exists.

While sociological, economic, and political spheres of feminist activity are inevitably bound up in and thus limited by the dominant culture's vested interests and efforts at control, we believe that the imaginal sphere of life may proceed without so much interference from outside. Unfortunately, the division of feminist inquiry into separate spheres can lead to competition for resources, support, and attention; workers in one area may tend to ignore or denigrate those in others. In the archetypal view the areas are interdependent and fully complementary. For women in the arena of imagination to ignore sociology, economics, and politics is to content themselves with abstractions lacking a "local habitation and a name." For women in the sociological, economic, and political arenas of action to ignore the psychological dimension of themselves and their disciplines is to cut themselves off from a unique source of awareness of the "why" and "how" of their own personal behavior and of the seemingly ineradicable social forms and attitudes which they seek to change. Only when the feminine is regularly taken to and brought back from an archetypal level can individuals gain (or regain) the strength that comes from contact with the collective unconscious. The movement toward the collective unconscious by individuals is part of the general participation in the collective consciousness which we call society or culture.

Those of us working for battered women's shelters, against sexual harassment, for reproductive rights, and against sexual inequities of all kinds are having to deal, consciously or not, with archetypal images and patterns and energy. These issues, which focus on the reproductive and cognitive capacities of the female body, show us the interdependence of conscious and unconscious dimensions of our lives.

The interdependence of these spheres of activity mirrors the interdependence of the many disciplines through which women are seeking knowledge of themselves. Interdisciplinarity is essential to feminist inquiry. We cannot recover fully our lost history; too many documents have been destroyed or were never able to be made by women at all. *All* aspects of women's experience have been ignored or distorted or denied. The force necessary for feminist ideas to take hold in any culture permeated with the masculine must be great enough to overcome all the forces resisting these ideas, including women's own enculturated inhibitions about their own worth and work. Such force will accumulate only when evidence from many fields converges. Since we do not now have and cannot immediately acquire evidence tested in time, the bulk of our evidence must come from what is currently available; this will be so until feminist scholars have had time to record a history of women, establish documents, conduct studies, and test hypotheses.

We want to bring together the labors of the clinic, the laboratory, and the library, the work of analysts, analysands, and academics. This means putting academic women more in touch with the processes of the unconscious, as Sylvia Brinton Perera does so eloquently in this volume, and putting clinicians in touch with scholarly writing and thinking about their work and their analysands. Such a collective study also means getting more female analysts to write about their experiences, as they re-value the cognitive, ego-directed thinking functions, so that others can share in the insights they have gained. If they do not write on their own, they may want to collaborate with their academically trained sisters. To be abstract is not necessarily to deny the experiential; professional scholarship need not exclude the personal.

We hope we have shown that feminists must include both the personal and the professional, the experiential and the intellectual, the much touted but increasingly doubted "objectivity" required by our male mentors and the clear, felt "subjectivity" of our own experience. In this way we will affirm both individuality and collectivity. Feminist archetypalists can also show that moving to the collective unconscious enables a subsequent movement to collective consciousness. As Inanna's story demonstrates, one does not descend to the underworld to stay there but eventually to return; in fact, as Perera notes, our aim should be to set in motion a regular process of descent and ascent, a dynamic exchange among all aspects of ourselves.

We were surprised to find, as we reread the manuscript prior to composing this final chapter, how much our contributors actually shared with each other and with us. The differences seem to be primarily ones of style and focus. Our basic similarity lies in our call for a reformulation of existing theory, but we also seem to share the belief, expressed by Jean Shinoda Bolen, that "women are acted on from without by stereotypes and from within by archetypes." What follows, then, is our explication of the theoretical issues raised in our introduction which derive from our redefinition of the concept of archetype. In this chapter we will clarify our relationship to previous theorists, explore our role in the mind/body, nature/culture controversy, and take a look at the future of feminist archetypal theory.

II   "ANIMITY," OR LEARNING TO LIVE WITH
THE FATHERS AS EQUALS

It should be clear from the essays we have included that we are unwilling to discard or ignore all the work done in the Jungian tradition (or any other tradition) because it is "corrupted" or "contaminated" by patriarchal theories. Jung's ideas, nevertheless, pose some difficulties for women. One of them is his tendency to reify concepts, so that archetypes seem to be fixed entities with a life of their own rather than cultural hypotheses about psychological processes. This tendency, coupled with his habit of thinking in terms of rigid oppositions (masculine/feminine, Logos/Eros, anima/animus), has been particularly detrimental to women, who have often been placed in categories by the male-dominated culture without being consulted about their actual experience. This situation was exacerbated by Jung's belief that the feminine as it appeared in works by men was the same as the feminine in actual women. Thus, he did not see the need to examine products of the female imagination or consider the masculine bias of the many mythic and religious documents which he used to substantiate his theory of archetypes. As Sue Cox notes, Jung gained partial acceptance from feminists because he argued that both sexes exhibited masculine and feminine characteristics and because he valued the feminine highly.[2] But his concept of the feminine, as Annis Pratt observes in her essay, has often been just another device to "swallow up the experience of women." The difficulties with his androgynous ideal have been discussed in an early issue of *Women's Studies*.[3]

On the positive side, however, Jung's concept of individuation as a lifelong task for the person, and his notion that individuation is an elaborate and subtle process of developing the recessive potentials in the person, is a positive aspect of his system for both sexes, but particularly for those women who have more flexible life patterns.[4] This drive toward wholeness still allows for significant periods of regression, not "in the service of the ego" so much as in the interest of allowing all the elements of the psyche full play. Since healthy child-rearing may depend on a good deal of regression, this aspect of Jungian theory could have a significant impact on women (and men) involved in child care. Perhaps the most positive element of all in Jung's theory is his attitude toward the unconscious. It is seen not as a repository of repressed contents but as a multi-faceted field of energies, some known and suppressed and others unknown to the conscious layers of the psyche.[5]

Jung has been much criticized for not emphasizing the role of sexuality in determining the contents of the unconscious, but, in fact, as Carol Schreier Rupprecht has argued, Jung assumed the inseparability of body and psyche. The great benefit of his theory is that he does not presuppose that the unconscious is determined by any of the semiotic systems of culture. The unconscious is a generative system with its own energies that operate with some degree of independence from conscious mechanisms of the psyche. Using Jung's theory, thus, it is not difficult to justify the search for a "female imaginary."[6]

No discipline is better suited than archetypal theory to the study of patterns in our imaginative processes and their products. Not only does archetypal psychology assume that such patterns matter as much as other facts about women, but its practitioners have developed a sensitivity to different kinds of subjective reality that can help us understand women's reported experiences. For example, it is relatively commonplace now for archetypal psychologists to assume that our innate capacity to form images operates along a spectrum.[7] At one end of that spectrum is the mode of imagining most in keeping with everyday existence in which social, economic, and political behavior occurs. This is the mode of normal waking consciousness expressed in the images of things and events we know, have known, and can readily call to memory. Moreover, these images are often thoroughly acceptable to the imaginer's culture, their content being known collectively through widespread patterns already manifest in the culture and conscious to everyone. These images contribute to our sense of shared experience and cultural harmony, but there is always the danger, as Demaris Wehr reminds us, that the culture will confer ontological and normative status on such images, turning them into stereotypes.

Another mode of imagining involves a different relationship to culture. It is visionary, and it occurs in fantasy (what Jungians call "active imagination") and at times in literature and art. The visionary image, which partakes of both consciousness and unconsciousness, may be unfamiliar to those in the cultural mainstream, but it often wins acceptance. Sometimes it represents the unique experience of a single individual, but often, Jungians have discovered, it anticipates or signals the appearance of an image from the collective unconscious. The resurgence of nearly forgotten images of goddesses in twentieth-century poetry and visual art by women is an example, for it seems to have occurred in response to existential crises rather than as a conscious product of scholarship.

At the other end of the spectrum of imagining is the encounter with the utterly unknown which occurs unexpectedly in dreams. It is this kind of experience that led Jung to formulate the concept of the "objective psyche" with its central tenet of a collective unconscious. The images that arise in such encounters provide us with the clearest evidence we have of the limited nature of individual consciousness and, perhaps, human culture. As women, we know even less about our dreams than our fantasies, and we will not have a clear understanding of ourselves until the full spectrum of our experience is known. The model of human imagining drawn by archetypal psychology will prevent us from stopping prematurely at conscious knowledge in our search for patterns in women's experience.

In using Jungian or archetypal psychology, of course, feminists must separate wheat from chaff by continually referring to the experiences of real women, and not just white middle-class women of European stock but women of different races, ethnic and cultural backgrounds, and historical periods. Even within the Jungian tradition the process of sorting has begun. In a recent essay Edward C. Whitmont, Chairman of the Board of the C.G. Jung Training Center in New York, acknowledges the limitations of Jung's early attitude toward Logos and Eros. Whitmont points out that Jung himself saw his opinion as preliminary and tentative. His successors, unfortunately, turned this tentative hypothesis into a formula they then rigidly applied to men and women.

Whitmont consigns both the Eros/Logos and anima/animus distinctions to early Jungian thought. Acknowledging the influence of archetypal psychologist James Hillman and the current behavior of women and men, he maintains that these distinctions are too simplistic, even for the time in which they were made, and quite inappropriate now in light of our new understanding of gender:

> Instinct, soul and spirit, anima and animus, are archetypal principles that pertain to both sexes equally. . . . Women can be and always could be deeply involved with and psychologically determined in their conscious outlook by Logos and out of touch with their affects; men can be immensely sensitive to instinct, feeling, and affect and quite at loss in respect to Logos or for that matter to any other of the masculine archetypes. . . . Either sex may partake in any of the masculine or feminine determinants in various constellations or degrees, comparable to a zodiac wheel in which any of its sections can be accentuated to different degrees in different people.[8]

Later in his essay, Whitmont introduces Robert Ornstein's list of "intuitive" characteristics associated with yang and yin and cautions that our "accustomed definition of Yang and Yin as creative and receptive respectively" may be too narrow: "Perhaps a more adequate rendering might be the idea of exteriorization, diversification, penetration and external action for Yang, and inherence, unification, incorporation, activity and existence for Yin."[9] He then speculates on the possibility that the left and right hemispheres of the brain are sex-linked. The best news, from a feminist point of view, is that he turns away from lists altogether finally to give a woman's description of the yin dimension of her experience which he proposes to call the "Medusa aspect" or "transformative dimension," in reference to the work of Karen Elias-Button.[10] A dialogue between feminism and the Jungian tradition appears to be emerging.

We hope that this newly emerging dialogue will take the form of a friendly exchange among equals. We believe that our work in this anthology is post-Jungian in that it seeks to go beyond Jung to explain and affirm the facts of women's experience through history. But we want to carry on this activity with "animity," a term Carol Schreier Rupprecht has coined to describe the process of "befriending the soul." Rupprecht intended the term to replace the divisive, dichotomous terms "anima" and "animus" and to counter the tendency to see those who challenge prevailing theory, women in particular, as filled with "animosity" (see Estella Lauter's essay in this volume). If we are indeed on friendly terms with our own souls, at home in our own bodies, in contact with the realities of our experience, and if we can create our own theories out of that experience, our dialogue with the fathers can proceed as a conversation among equals. This attitude extends not only to Jung, but to Frye, Lévi-Strauss, and others mentioned in our essays, as well as to Freud, whom we will treat later in this chapter.

III   THE "ARCHETYPAL EYE" LOOKS AT MIND AND BODY
AND SEES THEORY AS FANTASY

In the early seventies when the Boston Women's Health Collective titled their self-help book about women's health *Our Bodies, Ourselves,* they were not accepting the dictum that anatomy is destiny but rather affirming and reclaiming their bodies on their own terms.[11] For the patriarchy had, in the words of one of Perera's analysands, "cut us off at our ankles from the earth." Women were becoming aware that their bodies had been described in research informed only by male fantasy for so long that even their own sense of their bodies had been affected. Feminist archetypal theory adds to this new awareness of the structure and function of our physical bodies the awareness of our images and fantasies of those bodies, and the sense that it would be useful to know how our bodies have been construed by patriarchal culture in the past into forms unrecognizable to us.

Analytical psychology has generally denied women access to the realm of spirit (Logos) and assigned them to the realm of body (Eros) and then, along with much of the Western European tradition, denigrated the realm to which they have been assigned. Because Logos was seen as the source of culture, women also became relegated to nature. This pattern is familiar to anthropologists who study currently functioning societies, and the pattern has been a point of feminist debate within anthropology, a debate launched in part by Sherry Ortner's work in the early seventies: "Is Female to Male as Nature Is to Culture?" Her answer is an emphatic no.[12]

Even Jung rebelled at times against the denigration of the female body through its association with matter and evil and its concomitant separation from spirit. He greeted with glee the decision of the Catholic Church to raise the stature of the Assumption of Mary because for him it heralded a recognition that "even her human body, the thing most prone to gross corruption" was elevated, effecting the possible reunion of matter and spirit. What Jung called the "abysmal side of bodily man," earth and the feminine body, was also validated.[13] It is interesting, however, to compare this raising to the heavens of an essentially passive woman (and virgin mother) arranged by a male god (and a pope) with Inanna's voluntary, unaided descent to the underworld.

Why has the association of female with matter, and hence with evil, persisted throughout the centuries? Because underlying the history of science and medicine is a fantasy about women shared by male observers that has run its course for hundreds of years without being seriously tested against the facts.

James Hillman goes back to Genesis, that is to myth, for the roots of the fantasy. "The psychological history of the male-female relationship in our civilization may be seen as a series of footnotes to the tale of Adam and Eve"; using an "archetypal eye" (one acquired through "profound appreciation of history and biography, of the arts, of ideas and culture," not focused on persons and cases),[14] Hillman strips away the facade of scientific objectivity. He demonstrates that male fantasies of superiority and male fears of the female have colored theorizing and experimentation in Aristotle, Galen and the Stoics, Leonardo da Vinci, William Harvey, Paul, Jerome, and Thomas Aquinas. Supposedly objective facts were reiterated in theory and "rediscovered," "verified," and "proven" in experiments. One of the more bizarre but influential "facts" that was established was the presence in semen of minute forms of men, complete with heads and limbs. The homunculus implied that only male seed exists—if there were female seed, it was not necessary for reproduction (the woman serving only as passive vessel)—and that semen was superior to menstrual blood because of its spiritual quality. Hillman concludes from his survey of texts since ancient times that "theory-forming is thus as free and fantastic as the imagination; it is limited perhaps even less by observational data than by the archetypal *a priori* dominants of the imagination, the preformation of ideas acting as preconceptions that determine how and what one observes."[15] Hillman later revised the deterministic concept of archetype implicit in this statement from 1972, but even in its unrevised form, it proved useful in unmasking the fantasy of female inferiority underlying reproductive history.

Moving from the realm of the body to that of the mind, we find a similar absence of scientific objectivity in the study of intelligence through the centuries, which has posed an even more serious problem for women. Stephen Gould echoes Hillman's observations and conclusions in *The Mis-Measure of Man*, a study of the "science" of phrenology and other means of measuring and quantifying intelligence up to and including Binet's IQ tests. Gould notes in his preface his deliberate use of the nongeneric term "man" to dramatize the fact that all of the studies and experiments had been done on males and all of the conclusions were presumed to apply to all humans. Thus scientists moved from denigration to omission of women. Gould's analysis destroys the myth of scientific objectivity under which so much of the work he examines proceeded and demonstrates the force of cultural myths and male fantasies in the choice of topics for research, in the collection and description of data, and in the interpretation of that data and the application of theories derived from it.[16]

Hillman's and Gould's books should be required reading for all persons currently engaged in research on hemispheric specialization in the brain. Researchers already seem to be falling into the same kinds of errors we now find so ludicrous in past "scientific" discoveries and hypotheses, including fantasy descriptions of maleness and femaleness, this time localized in the brain. In so doing, they are continuing the long tradition of left-right analysis of the body, which nearly always includes a valuing of one side over the other. Hillman refers to this traditional theme in his book because it played a role in theories about reproduction. One particular theory explained what place the fetus would occupy in the uterus: " 'On the right boys, on the left girls.' This statement, attributed to Parmenides, was passed on to us by Galen. It compares to a similar one from Anaxagoras, passed on by Aristotle."[17] In such pairing, left was almost always female and inferior; right was almost always male and superior. The persistence of theories based on this principle into our time alerts us to its archetypal basis and the need to re-evaluate "data" being accumulated and interpreted for its enculturated gender bias.

Although the history of scientific thought has generally worked against women, as women undertake scientific study that highlights their own experience, they must be wary of becoming trapped in their own fantasies, of replacing a male bias in research with a female bias and male denigration of women with female denigration of men. As Hillman argues, "Fantasy especially intervenes where exact knowledge is lacking; and when fantasy does intervene, it becomes especially difficult to obtain exact knowledge."[18]

The energetic repudiation of gender difference by early feminists grew understandably out of their awareness that to be different from men in our culture was to be inferior. If our research and study and re-visioning of previous research ultimately suggest that there are significant gender differences, we do not want our fantasies to stand in the way of this truth. If there are differences, we will be able to understand the meaning of such differences. We will value women's experience as much as men's and insist that explanations about what it means to be human in society include our experience. We will recognize a spectrum of gender differences rather than accept another rigid dichotomization. To be rooted in the body and to be aware of the body's needs and effects is not necessarily to be determined by them. We embrace the possibility of a female epistemology that is rooted in the experience of living in a female body but do not accept it as binding. We want to remain open to change. We must be free to construe the evidence, when it is compelling, as a description of what is or has been, not of what will or must be.

IV   THE FUTURE OF FEMINIST ARCHETYPAL THEORY

Feminist archetypal theory involves several key elements: a commitment to raising the unconscious, a deontologized concept of the archetype, a post-Jungian approach to the female psyche, a spirit of "animity" toward ourselves which allows us to engage our forebears in productive dialogue, and an affirmation of the psychophysical unity of the human person. We look forward to the participation of many others in emending and extending our proposed theoretical framework. Each of the essays included in this collection suggests a direction to be taken in testing our ideas and generating new dimensions of a feminist archetypal theory.

Demaris Wehr suggests the project of seeing through "nomic" formulations, such as existing descriptions of the anima or the feminine with our eyes open to the patriarchal imprint they bear. Examples of this kind of project include Adrienne Rich's *Of Woman Born*, which deontologizes the archetype of the mother,[19] and Christine Downing's *The Goddess*, which works through the author's relationship with several archetypal figures.[20]

An even more ambitious project would be to examine the societies that produced certain formulations to see how they reflect and express societal needs.[21] We might search for the historical moment when Eros became associated with women's essential nature, instead of serving as the godlike embodiment of a male perspective in Greek myth, in order to see if this association arose to encourage women to tend the home fires and thereby to insure the survival of the species.

Estella Lauter's work suggests that it will be fruitful to examine the images created by women in the nonverbal arts (newly available in a growing number of historical surveys of visual art, music, and dance) in order to understand their relationship to the gender-linked archetypes that have long been familiar. Such efforts will yield redescriptions or additional descriptions of archetypal patterns that accord with reported female experience. With these new descriptions in mind, a woman who dreams of herself as Medusa will not automatically see herself as a "terrible mother"; instead she may see her dream as expressing a need to find the source of her own creative energy so that she is less vulnerable in her mothering. This kind of activity will be useful as long as the new descriptions we arrive at do not become reified. Study of nonverbal works of art by women will also serve to test the credibility of theoretical formulations concerning the experiences of women. When we use present descriptions of archetypal patterns as road maps to be redrawn according to the evidence of female experience, we are bound to locate patterns that have not yet been fully or accurately described. Again, as long as we do not assume that these patterns are binding or that we have discovered the essence of woman, we have much to gain from calling attention to the undescribed nodes of female experience. Lauter's book on myth-making in women's poetry and visual art explores these possibilities. A similarly inductive approach to studying archetypal patterns is embodied in Annis Pratt's recently published book, *Archetypal Patterns in Women's Fiction.*[22]

Pratt's essay here articulates the interdisciplinary nature of our enterprise; that is, she shows us how archetypal interpretation of women's literature is both psychological and anthropological. The principle behind her work (and ours) is that hypotheses confirmed by many disciplines and tested in many media approach truth as closely as we are capable of doing. The program of research implied by her essay is formidable. We would need to survey all of the works of women in order to find their patterns. Then we would have to engage in both biographical and cultural studies to find the roots of those patterns and establish a dialectical relationship with our feminine archetypal code. Such an ambitious task will require the collaboration of many scholars. Pratt herself is currently engaged in a study of women's poetry, following the course she advocates here.

Sylvia Brinton Perera's essay encourages further research into myths about women that were recorded in periods before our present symbol system was formed. But it is also a model of a new kind of research based on the conjunction of dream, experience, and scholarship. At one point Perera says that her quest began as an inquiry into an analysand's dream of being impaled on a meathook; at another she says her own needs as a therapist led her to explore her own roots more fully. Multiple beginnings are characteristic of archetypal work.

Perera could not have progressed very far in her quest, however, if she had not had access to Kramer's writings on the myths of Inanna. We must not underestimate the importance of the labor of traditional scholarship in our enterprise. We need to gain the linguistic and archaeological skills that will assist us in unearthing our past, in recovering lost texts and translating, editing, and annotating those texts and others that have been distorted by transmittal via patriarchal culture. Merlin Stone and Diane Wolkstein exemplify two different approaches to this process.[23]

Much of the work still to be done lies in reinterpreting sources, such as Kramer's, in which rich material is made available but is not yet thoroughly interpreted in the light of women's actual experience. Perera provides a model for a kind of interpretation that does not ontologize the myth under consideration. She never doubts the truth in Inanna's story, but she does not assume that is *the* truth for all women. She uses myth as a touchstone for an interior journey that still needs to be described in our own terms. And she searches for the language of that new description in women's dreams.

Carol Schreier Rupprecht suggests that we value our dreams by recording and befriending them. Since they contain material beyond the control of self and others that is inaccessible through any other means, we retain the power to interpret them ourselves, to translate them into our own language. She urges us to use our dreams to complement the perspective of the ego; in this way, we will understand the phenomena of the physical world both literally and symbolically. We may even be able to see mirrored in dreams the health or illness of the body; the information from dreams can supplement our conscious observations of the physical.

Before accepting any interpretations of women's dreams, we need to know how they are influenced by the settings in which they are studied and by the researchers involved. We need to examine the assumptions under which experiments are set up and conducted and how those assumptions affect the conclusions that are drawn.

Rupprecht also hopes for further archetypal study of findings about sex differences in the amount of REM sleep experienced from infancy to old age and in hemispheric specialization in the brain. She argues for a reformulation of personality theory that includes unconscious as well as conscious elements in the person and reflects the experiences of healthy women. When information from sleeping and waking states, from the body as well as the mind is included, a holistic portrait of the healthy person will become possible. This, too, is an ambitious program for research in a field that has been far less responsive to feminist concerns (perhaps because its female population is so small) than have the disciplines of literature, religion, art history, and anthropology.

In addition to recommending that our readers follow in the fields of their choice the leads given by the essayists in this volume, we want to call attention to several pressing tasks still to be undertaken if feminist archetypal theory is to grow and not become mired in internecine disputes.

First, we need to consider the impact our formulations will have on earlier attempts to infuse a female perspective into Jungian psychology. Many women with keen minds have been followers of Jung, and several of them have written eloquently about the feminine; a few have also written about the concerns of women. Mary Esther Harding's concept of the virgin is widely used by feminist interpreters of literature and religion.[24] Adrienne Rich criticizes Harding, however, for failing "to give full weight to the pressure on all women . . . to remain in a 'giving' assenting, maternalistic relationship to men."[25] Estella Lauter also criticizes her for judging the virgin unattractive unless she serves Eros. But in the interest of developing the richest possible theory, we need to re-examine the material Harding has amassed in the light of post-Jungian thought.

Similarly, Nor Hall could be criticized for restating Toni Wolff's theory that the feminine is structured by four archetypes: the mother, the amazon, the hetaira, and the medium.[26] To be sure, Wolff's theory is an improvement on Neumann's reduction of the feminine to two axes, the maternal and the transformative, both related to children and men.[27] And it is true that Hall admits that the images she found actually spill out of the categories she uses. But we need to re-examine her wonderful material in a less categorical frame.

Christine Downing's autobiographical and scholarly book *The Goddess* presents another sort of challenge, for she is an analyst and a scholar of formidable sophistication in both the feminist and the archetypal traditions. Nonetheless, in her personal mid-life odyssey to discover the meaning of the goddesses who appeared in her life or in her dreams, she often essentializes the goddesses; she finds herself in them and them in her, not so much as embodied possibilities, as Perera recommends, but as essential truths. She goes a step further than Hall, maintaining that the female personality is made up of many goddesses rather than a few types of women. But we must examine carefully the idea that the goddesses represent something which is eternal in the female person, and in particular Downing's latent assumption that the Greek pantheon represented the whole person. Nevertheless, Downing's book has much to teach us about female experience.

In addition to combing the works of female scholars and therapists writing in the Jungian tradition, we need to come to terms with the Freudian tradition, to establish a rapprochment, if possible. The problems with Freudian, as with Jungian, theory are well known. The notions that we are bedeviled by penis envy or lack a superego seem ludicrous to most women even after those formulations have been filtered through the metaphorical interpretations offered by the French psychoanalyst Jacques Lacan and his followers.

Freud seems to posit male sexual issues as the definitional base of human identity, ignoring the realities of female sexuality as we now know them after decades of research by women. Furthermore, the equating of the unconscious with materials repressed in childhood presents problems, as does his view of the nonevolutionary nature of human development. Freud's view seems to freeze the adult in childhood issues, as if childhood were the only time our lives can go awry and the return to childhood scenes the only way that healing can occur.

Nevertheless, Nancy Chodorow has demonstrated the feminist potential of Freudian theory when it is filtered through adequate sociological data.[28] In this collection Perera suggests that penis envy is a function of a woman's more or less temporary feeling of emptiness in a patriarchal culture rather than an inescapable aspect of womanhood. In the myth of Inanna, Ereshkigal's stake gives her the strength to stand alone. Perera interprets the peg in the myth as an aspect of the "impersonal feminine yang energy." It belongs to the dark goddess and serves as a way to ground the spirit in matter and the moment. "It is thus supportive, a peg to hang onto through life's flux," rather than a symbol of masculine sexuality or culture.

Other theorists in the post-Jungian tradition deserve mention as well. In a paper presented at the 1982 meeting of the American Academy of Religion, Naomi Goldenberg urged feminists to look into the theories of D.W. Winnicott, particularly his definition of the psyche.[29] The Argentinian Gloria Bonder has already begun to use Winnicott's object relations theory. Carol Schreier Rupprecht described Bonder's work in a report on the International Interdisciplinary Congress on Women.

In fact, [Bonder] talked about having adopted, and adapted for women's studies, a concept—transitionality—borrowed from the work of an English pediatrician-turned-psychoanalyst, D.W. Winnicott. Transitionality, Bonder asserted, is a permanent process in life (not merely, as Winnicott observed, a developmental stage in the infant), and it is a process more characteristic of women than of men. She defined transitionality as that type of subject-object relationship which is neither total fusion (confusion of boundaries) nor total separation, but a relationship that is paradoxical, intermediate, and dynamic. In ideological (i.e. male) discourse, the object either is or is not; in transitional discourse the certainty of this distinction is challenged. Thus one need not, indeed can not, differentiate subjectivity and objectivity so sharply. All objects are subjectively experienced as part of the subject, yet not *as* the subject; that is, object and subject are not coterminous but *are* and *are not*, simultaneously. Since the potential to create may be rooted in the experience of relationships, a wider sense of their possible scope and variability can release creative energy and facilitate scholarship, especially scholarship of the kind, in content and method, which can lead to new understanding of women, and of so-called "female subjectivity."[30]

Bonder thus engages in two activities that feminist archetypal theory supports: taking from male theorists what is valuable and modifying it or adding whatever is necessary to make such theory applicable to women's experience, and rejecting the mental process of analytic separation, categorizaton, and claims of objectivity in order to include the effects of unconscious processes on cognitive ones.

Another direction that we consider essential to the growth of a viable theory is cross-cultural and international in scope. We need to go in all directions of the compass to study "muted" cultures. One impressive theme of the International Interdisciplinary Congress in Israel was the commonality of problems and hopes among women in radically different national, cultural, racial, and economic settings. In order to find out more about the phenomenon of female experience, we need to look more carefully at our common experiences through the eyes of anthropologists and other scholars of non-Western culture, religion, and art. Because patterns that appear the same to the uninitiated observer may have very different cultural resonances, we need to collaborate with the women from such cultures in our interpretation of each other's images and artifacts.

We come to the end of this chapter and this project with mixed feelings. While our original conviction about the value of and necessity for feminist archetypal theory has deepened, we have also become acutely aware of all we hoped to accomplish and didn't, of all that remains to be done.

In its present form, our work is still too multi-disciplinary. We hope that it will become fully interdisciplinary as the disciplines of psychology, literary criticism, art criticism, religion, and others ask the same questions and examine the same patterns of women's experience from many perspectives. We hope that our articulation of feminist archetypal theory is ground-breaking, not in the sense of laying a foundation for a building but in the sense of preparing new soil for the flourishing of new hybrid plants. We hope our work resembles the "Transcendental Etude" envisioned by Adrienne Rich in these lines:

Such a composition has nothing to do with eternity,
the striving for greatness, brilliance—
only with the musing of a mind
one with her body, experienced fingers quietly
pushing dark against bright, silk against roughness,
pulling the tenets of a life together
with no mere will to mastery,
only care for the many-lived, unending
forms in which she finds herself.[31]

Notes

Introduction

1. C.G. Jung et al., *Man and His Symbols* (Garden City, N.Y.: Doubleday, 1964), 25.
2. Ibid.
3. C.G. Jung, *Memories, Dreams and Reflections,* ed. A. Jaffé, trans. R.F.C. Hull (New York: Random, 1961, 1963), 161–62.
4. C.G. Jung, *Collected Works* VIII, par. 321. (*The Collected Works of C.G. Jung,* trans. R.F.C. Hull, are published by Princeton University Press in the Bollingen Series XX and are hereinafter cited as *CW* with volume and paragraph numbers following.)
5. Ibid.
6. Jung, *Man and His Symbols,* 50.
7. Ibid.
8. Naomi Goldenberg, "Archetypal Theory After Jung," *Spring: An Annual of Archetypal Psychology and Jungian Thought* (1975), 199–220.
9. James Hillman, *Re-Visioning Psychology* (New York: Harper & Row, 1975).
10. Goldenberg, "A Feminist Critique of Jung," *Signs: Journal of Women in Culture and Society* 2, No. 2 (1976), 443–49.
11. Jung, *CW* X, par. 117.
12. Goldenberg, "Feminist Critique," 449.
13. Jung, *CW* IX, part 2, par. 27.
14. Jung, *CW* IX, part 2, par. 29.
15. Goldenberg, "Feminist Critique," 447.
16. Jung, *CW* IX, part 2, par. 29.
17. See Jolande Jacobi, *Complex, Archetype, Symbol in the Psychology of C.G. Jung,* trans. Ralph Manheim (Princeton, N.J.: Princeton Univ. Press, 1959); *The Psychology of C.G. Jung,* trans. Ralph Manheim (New Haven, Conn.: Yale Univ. Press, 1943); and Violet S. de Laszlo, ed. *Psyche and Symbol: A Selection from the Writings of C.G. Jung* (Garden City, N.Y.: Doubleday, 1958).
18. Goldenberg, "Feminist Critique," 448.
19. Ibid.
20. Goldenberg, "Feminist Critique," 449.
21. James Hillman, "An Inquiry into Image," *Spring: An Annual of Archetypal Psychology and Jungian Thought* (1977), 83.
22. Hillman, "Inquiry," 84.

23. Erich Neumann, *Art and the Creative Unconscious*, trans. Ralph Manheim (Princeton, N.J.: Princeton Univ. Press, 1974), 82.

24. Rachel Blau DuPlessis, "The Critique of Consciousness and Myth in Levertov, Rich and Rukeyser," in Sandra Gilbert and Susan Gubar, *Shakespeare's Sisters* (Bloomington: Indiana Univ. Press, 1979); see esp. 299–300.

25. James Hall, *Clinical Uses of Dreams: Jungian Interpretations and Enactments* (New York: Grune and Stratton, 1977), 116.

26. Carol Schreier Rupprecht, "The Martial Maid and the Challenge of Androgyny," *Spring: An Annual of Archetypal Psychology and Jungian Thought* (1974), 278.

27. Hall, *Clinical Uses*, 130.

28. Hall, *Clinical Uses*, 116.

29. Ibid.

30. Eric Gould, *Mythic Intentions in Modern Literature* (Princeton, N.J.: Princeton Univ. Press, 1982), 63.

31. Erich Neumann, *The Great Mother*, trans. Ralph Manheim (Princeton, N.J.: Princeton Univ. Press, 1955), 81.

32. Nancy Chodorow, *The Reproduction of Mothering* (Berkeley: Univ. of California Press, 1978), 110.

ii

1. See Goldenberg, "Feminist Critique." Also see Goldenberg, "Archetypal Theory after Jung"; Carol Christ, "Some Comments on Jung, Jungians and the Study of Women," *Anima* 3, No. 2 (Spring Equinox 1977), 68–69; Goldenberg, "Feminism and Jungian Theory," *Anima* 3, No. 2 (Spring Equinox 1977), 14–18. Responses to Christ and Goldenberg can be found in *Anima* 4, No. 1 (Fall Equinox 1977).

2. Peter L. Berger and Thomas Luckmann, *The Social Construction of Reality; A Treatise in the Sociology of Knowledge* (Garden City, N.Y.: Doubleday, 1967); Berger, *The Sacred Canopy: Elements of a Sociological Theory of Religion* (Garden City, N.Y.: Doubleday, 1976).

3. Berger, *Sacred Canopy*, 3.

4. Berger, *Sacred Canopy*, 4.

5. Berger, *Sacred Canopy*, 5.

6. Berger, *Sacred Canopy*, 8–9.

7. Berger, *Sacred Canopy*, 17.

8. Ibid.

9. Berger, *Sacred Canopy*, 19.

10. Berger, *Sacred Canopy*, 32–33.

11. Thanks are due to one of my students at Harvard Divinity School, Lorna Hochstein, for sharing this insight with me.

12. Edward C. Whitmont, *The Symbolic Quest: Basic Concepts of Analytical Psychology* (Princeton, N.J.: Princeton Univ. Press, 1969), 179.
13. It does offer social criticism in some other areas, however, such as war, which is seen as the corporate "shadow projection" of one nation unto another.
14. Jung, *The Collected Works* VII, pars. 389–90. *(The Collected Works of C.G. Jung*, trans. R.F.C. Hull, are published by Princeton University Press in the Bollingen Series XX and are hereinafter cited as *CW* with volume and paragraph numbers following.
15. Jung, *CW* IX, Part I, par. 91.
16. Jung, *Memories*, 392–93.
17. Jacobi, *Complex, Archetype, Symbol*, 37.
18. Jacobi, *Psychology of C.G. Jung*, 41.
19. Rudolf Otto, *The Idea of the Holy* (New York: Oxford Univ. Press, 1958), 1.
20. Otto, *Idea*, 10.
21. Otto, *Idea*, 12–13.
22. Ibid.
23. Otto, *Idea*, 14–15.
24. Otto, *Idea*, 21.
25. Otto, *Idea*, 23.
26. Otto, *Idea*, 31.
27. In an article entitled "Religion and Modern Thinking" which appeared in the German periodical *Merkur* (February 1952), Buber criticizes the religious nature of Jung's thinking. Buber says Jung oversteps "with sovereign license the boundaries of psychology in its most essential point" (Martin Buber, *Eclipse of God*, New York: Harper & Bros, 1952, p. 104). Buber defines Jung's psychology as a modern form of Gnosticism, primarily because Jung conceives of God as a *conjunctio oppositorum* in which good and evil are bound together. Buber's reply is close to my own criticism of Jung's divinization of the human psyche:

> The psychological doctrine which deals with mysteries without knowing the attitude of faith towards mystery is the modern manifestation of Gnosis. Gnosis is not to be understood as only a historical category, but as a universal one. It—and not atheism, which annihilates God because it must reject the hitherto existing images of God—is the real antagonist of the reality of faith. Its modern manifestation concerns me specifically not only because of its massive pretensions, but also in particular because of its resumption of the Carpocratian motif. This motif, which it teaches as psychotherapy, is that of mystically deifying the instincts instead of hallowing them in faith." (175–76)

28. Jung, *CW* VII, pars. 400, 403.
29. Jung, *Memories*, 395.

30. Much as Jung disavowed himself as a theologian, he did consider theological matters to a great extent in his work. The entire concept of the collective unconscious rests on Jung's understanding of the way the Divine is manifested in human life. Jung's major theological point is that the Christian concept of God as all-good and all-powerful is erroneous. Jung's theology and psychology mutually derive from and reinforce one another. Jung was preoccupied with theological problems from an early age, especially the problem of evil and its coexistence with an omnipotent, good God. From an early religious experience (the cathedral vision, at age eleven) Jung took comfort in what he felt God had revealed to him: that God, too, has an evil side and that God had willed Adam and Eve to sin. God's evil accounted for the evil in humanity, since people are created in the image of God. Since God contains both good and evil, Jung reasoned, He needs human evolution in order to evolve Himself more fully. The placing of good and evil on the same level—ontologically, psychologically and theologically—is the fundamental Jungian tenet that allowed Jung to elevate to the level of the Divine so many opposing and neurotic interhuman and intrapsychic phenomena.

31. C.G. Jung, *CW* VII, par. 331. Many feminists have seized on such extreme statements as the following:

> A woman possessed by the animus is always in danger of losing her femininity, her adapted feminine persona, just as a man in like circumstances runs the risk of effeminacy. These psychic changes of sex are due entirely to the fact that a function which belongs inside has been turned outside. . . . With regard to the plurality of the animus as distinguished from what we might call the 'uni-personality' of the anima, this remarkable fact seems to me to be a correlate of the conscious attitude. The conscious attitude of woman is in general far more exclusively personal than that of man. Her world is made up of fathers and mothers, brothers and sisters, husbands and children. The rest of the world consists likewise of families, who nod to each other but are, in the main, interested essentially in themselves. The man's world is the nation, the state, business concerns, etc. His family is simply a means to an end, one of the foundations of the state, and his wife is not necessarily *the* woman for him (at any rate not as the woman means it when she says 'my man'). The general means more to him than the personal; his world consists of a multitude of co-ordinated factors, whereas her world, outside her husband, terminates in a sort of cosmic mist." (Jung, *CW* VII, par. 338).

32. Emma Jung, *Animus and Anima: Two Essays* (Zurich: Spring, 1974), 20.

33. Of course, from a Jungian standpoint the collective unconscious, by definition, cannot be a reflection of the surrounding society. Jung is quite clear on this point:

> Looked at from the outside, the psyche appears to be essentially a

reflection of external happenings—to be not only occasioned by them, but to have its origin in them. And it also seems to us, at first, that the unconscious can be explained only from the outside and from the side of consciousness. It is well known that Freud has attempted to do this—an undertaking which could succeed only if the unconscious were actually something that came into being with the existence and consciousness of the individual. But the truth is that the unconscious is always there beforehand as a system of inherited psychic functioning handed down from primeval times. Consciousness is a late-born descendant of the unconscious psyche. (Jung, CW VIII, par. 676)

On the question of which level is causative—the psychic (or spiritual, as Jung also calls it) or the material level—Jung is clearly, although not philosophically, idealist. He sees the psyche as causative and would have to say that culture derogates women *because* of an archetype (the animus or negative anima) and not the other way around. More recent scholarship on the psychological characteristics of minority and oppressed groups, however, suggests that the concept of internalized oppression, rather than innate inferiority or a propensity toward self-devaluation, accounts for their self-derogation. Furthermore, our everyday observations tell us that no one, male nor female, comes equipped with enough self-confidence to value themselves properly without encouragement from outside.

34. See, for example, Sarah Pomeroy, *Goddesses, Whores, Wives, and Slaves* (N.Y.: Schocken, 1975) and Sheila M. Rothman, *Woman's Proper Place* (New York: Basic Books, 1978).
35. Emma Jung, *Animus and Anima*, 19.
36. Mary Daly, *Beyond God the Father: Toward a Philosophy of Women's Liberation* (Boston: Beacon, 1973), 8.
37. Emma Jung, *Animus and Anima*, 76.
38. She flirts with such an identification, but she actually avoids making it. For examples of Emma Jung's relative caution on this issue, see *Animus and Anima*, 55, 59. Ulanov does not do this, either, in her recent book *Receiving Woman: Studies in the Psychology and Theology of the Feminine* (Philadelphia: Westminster, 1981).
39. Christ, "Some Comments," 68.
40. Ibid.
41. Jung and Jungians are not totally unaware of these three social facts. For them, however, social reality is always derived from the psychic (i.e. archetypal) level and is always of secondary importance.
42. Goldenberg, "Feminist Critique."
43. Some of the authors who do make the distinction are Christ, "Some Comments," Whitmont, *Symbolic Quest*, and Ann Ulanov, *The Feminine in Jungian Psychology and in Christian Theology* (Evanston, Ill.: Northwestern Univ. Press, 1971).

44. Jung, *CW* VII, pars. 296–301.
45. Jung, *CW* VII, par. 296.
46. Jung, *CW* VII, par. 298.
47. Jung, *CW* VII, par. 340.
48. Jung, *CW* VII, par. 300.
49. Marie Louise von Franz, *The Feminine in Fairytales* (Zurich: Spring, 1972), 1–2.
50. Jean Baker Miller, *Toward a New Psychology of Women* (Boston: Beacon, 1976), 11.
51. They do not rate relatedness high on a scale of values. See Carol Gilligan, "In a Different Voice," *Harvard Educational Review* 47, No. 4, 481–516.
52. Carol Christ has already spoken of the way the anima functions in the psyches of men, in an appropriate application of the anima theory.
53. Ulanov, *The Feminine*, 195.
54. Of course, this very fact illustrates a thorny aspect of Jung's psychological and theological thinking. While he claims to be an empiricist, and neither a metaphysician nor a theologian, in his own use of the categories Jung fails to distinguish consistently between ontological and psychological dimensions—even though he makes this distinction theoretically, as illustrated by his statement, "The religious point of view understands the imprint as the working of an imprinter; the scientific point of view understands it as the symbol of an unknown and incomprehensible content" (quoted in Ulanov, *The Feminine*, 125). Yet, even Ulanov admits that: "For Jung, 'God' designates a psychic, not an ontological reality, even though he does not always make this clear. The empiricist is limited to what is observable; beyond that resides mystery, which he does not presume to classify. For the empiricist, metaphysical truth and religious experience are essentially psychic phenomena, that is, they manifest themselves as such and must therefore be investigated, criticized, and evaluated from a psychological point of view. . . . A serious criticism of Jung's insistence on separating the empirical from ontological statements is that his own theories and results do not support the separation. . . . Ontological assertions are unavoidable because one's mode of approach in all its details is itself a piece of the reality one perceives as well as one of the means of giving it its shaping and identifying qualities" (126-27).
55. Berger, *Sacred Canopy*, 19.
56. Daly, *Beyond God*, 23.
57. Daly, *Beyond God*, 156.
58. See for example Christine Downing's essay, "Coming to Terms with Hera," *Quadrant, Journal of the C.G. Jung Foundation for Analytical Psychology*, 12, No. 2 (Winter 1979), 26–47.

iii

1. Jung's long essay, "Approaching the Unconscious," completed only ten days before his death, stands as his last attempt to make his theory accessible to the common reader.
2. Toni Wolff, *Structural Forms of the Feminine Psyche* (Zurich: C.G. Jung Institute, 1956), 11.
3. Kay Larson, " 'For the first time women are leading not following'," *ARTnews* 79, No. 8 (Oct. 1980), 64–72.
4. This assertion rests in part on interviews done by University of Wisconsin students and deposited in the Special Collection on Wisconsin Women Artists, Golda Meir Library, University of Wisconsin-Milwaukee.
5. Elsa Honig Fine, *Women and Art* (Montclair, N.J.: Allanheld & Schram/Prior, 1978); Germaine Greer, *The Obstacle Race* (New York: Farrar, Straus & Giroux, 1979); Ann Sutherland Harris and Linda Nochlin, *Women Artists 1550–1950* (New York: Knopf, 1976); Eleanor Munro, *Originals: American Women Artists* (New York: Simon & Schuster, 1979); Hugo Munsterberg, *A History of Women Artists* (New York: Potter, 1975); Cindy Nemser, *Art Talk* (New York: Scribner's, 1975); Rozsika Parker and Griselda Pollock, *Old Mistresses: Women, Art and Ideology* (New York: Routledge & Kegan Paul, 1981); Karen Petersen and J.J. Wilson, *Women Artists: Recognition and Reappraisal* (New York: Harper & Row, 1976); Charlotte Streifer Rubinstein, *American Women Artists: From Early Indian Times to the Present* (Boston: G.K. Hall, 1982); Eleanor Tufts, *Our Hidden Heritage* (New York: Paddington, 1974). Four sets of slides prepared by Karen Petersen and J.J. Wilson were published by Harper & Row in 1975: *Women Artists: A Historical Survey; Women Artists: Images—Themes and Dreams; Women Artists: Third World; Women Artists: Twentieth Century.* Four more sets prepared by Karen Petersen and Mary Stofflet were released in 1980: *American Women Artists: The Nineteenth Century; American Women Artists: The Twentieth Century; Women Artists: Photography; Women Artists: Sculpture.* The slides are available from Harper & Row Media, 2350 Virginia Ave., Hagerstown, Md. 21740.
6. Emma Jung, *Animus and Anima*, 34–36.
7. Wolff, *Structural Forms*, 4.
8. The definition appears in C.G. Jung, *Civilization in Transition* (New York: Vintage 1965), 380; C.G. Jung, *CW* X, par. 28. (*The Collected Works of C.G. Jung*, trans. R.F.C. Hull, are published by Princeton University Press in the Bollingen Series XX and are hereafter cited as *CW* with volume and paragraph numbers following.) *Memories, Dreams and Reflections*, 380.
9. *CW* IX, part 1, par. 4.

10. C.G. Jung, *Dreams*, trans., R.F.C. Hull (Princeton, N.J.: Princeton Univ. Press, 1974), 95.
11. Erich Neumann, *The Great Mother*, 3–83, and Schema III.
12. Wolff's schema is the framework for Nor Hall, *The Moon and the Virgin* (New York: Harper & Row, 1980).
13. Wolff, *Structural Forms*, 4.
14. Jean Guitton, *The Madonna* (New York: Tudor, 1963.)
15. Ibid., 138.
16. Harris and Nochlin, *Women Artists*, 66.
17. Munro, *Originals*, 60. Munro's statement ignores the work of Käthe Kollwitz.
18. Adelyn Dohme Breeskin, *Mary Cassatt: A Catalogue Raisonné of the Graphic Work* (Washington, D.C.: Smithsonian Institution, 1979), 18.
19. Ibid.
20. *Mother About to Wash her Sleepy Child* (1880, oil on canvas, 39½ x 25 ¾ in.), pl. 8 in E. John Bullard, *Mary Cassatt: Oils and Pastels* (New York: Watson-Guptill, 1976), and Harris and Nochlin, *Women Artists*, fig. 89.
21. *Baby's First Caress* (1891, pastel on paper, 30 x 24 in.), pl. 15 in Bullard, *Mary Cassatt*.
22. *Baby Reaching for an Apple* (1893, oil on canvas, 39 x 25½ in.), pl. 17 in Bullard, *Mary Cassatt*.
23. *Breakfast in Bed* (1897, oil on canvas, 25⅝ x 29 in.), pl. 21 in Bullard, *Mary Cassatt*, and pl. 14 in Rubinstein, *American Women Artists*.
24. See *Reading "Le Figaro"* (1883, oil on canvas, 41 x 30 in.) and *Mrs. Robert Simpson Cassatt* (c. 1889, oil on canvas, 38 x 27 in.) pls. 10 and 14 in Bullard, *Mary Cassatt*.
25. Harris and Nochlin, *Women Artists*, 67.
26. Ibid., 276. *Mother and Child* (c. 1903, oil on cardboard, cradled, 28¼ x 20 in.), fig. 116.
27. Harris and Nochlin, *Women Artists*, 67.
28. *hon*, slide 77 in Petersen and Wilson, *Women Artists: Images—Themes and Dreams*.
29. Niki de Saint Phalle, *hon—en historia* (Stockholm: Moderna Museet, 1967).
30. *My Nurse and I* (1937, oil on sheet metal, 11¾ x 13¾ in.), slide 13 in Petersen and Wilson, *Women Artists: Images—Themes and Dreams*. Also see Hayden Herrera, *Frida: A Biography of Frida Kahlo* (New York: Harper & Row, 1983), plate X.
31. No one has explored this relationship better than Nancy Chodorow, "Family Structure and Feminine Personality," in Michelle Zimbalist Rosaldo and Louise Lamphere, eds., *Woman, Culture and Society* (Stanford: Stanford Univ. Press, 1974), 43–66.
32. See Herrera, *Frida*, 219–21, for a full interpretation of this painting, including the suggestion that it is a double self-portrait.

33. *Mother with Twins* (1924–1937, bronze, 30 in. high), fig. VI, 43 in Petersen and Wilson, *Women Artists: Recognition and Reappraisal.* The sculpture has several titles and exists in three forms. For a more complete discussion, see Estella Lauter and Dominique Rozenberg, "The Transformation of the Mother in the Work of Käthe Kollwitz," *Anima* 5, No. 2 (Spring Equinox 1979), 83–98; or Estella Lauter, *Women as Mythmakers: Poetry and Visual Art by Twentieth Century Women* (Bloomington: Indiana Univ. Press, 1984), ch. 2.

34. *The Mother* (1971, ceramic sculpture, 12 x 16½ x 9 in.), slide 60 in Petersen and Wilson, *Women Artists: Third World.*

35. *Macerena Esperanza* (1971, oil on canvas, 46 x 66 in.), slide 71 in Petersen and Wilson, *Women Artists: The Twentieth Century;* also pictured in Nemser, *Art Talk,* 321. Flack discusses her relationship with the painting in Nemser, *Art Talk,* 303–16, and in her "Louisa Ignacia Roldan," *Women's Studies* 6 (1978), 23–28.

36. Flack, "Louisa," 28.

37. *The Liberation of Aunt Jemima* (1972, mixed media, 11¾ x 8 x 3¾ in.), slide 78 in Petersen and Wilson, *Women Artists: The Twentieth Century.* Also see interview with Cindy Nemser, *Feminist Art Journal* 4, No. 4 (Winter 1975–76), 20.

38. *The Family* (1969, wood, plastic, terracotta and neon, 88 x 56 x 65 in.), slide 42 in Petersen and Wilson, *Women Artists: Images—Themes and Dreams.* A beautiful color reproduction with the egg-door open appears in Mary Lawrence, *Mother and Child* (New York: Crowell, 1975), 18.

39. *Celestial Pabulum* (1958, oil on masonite, 36¼ x 24⅜ in.), slide 73 in Petersen and Wilson, *Women Artists: Images—Themes and Dreams.* Also see Estella Lauter, "The Creative Woman and the Female Quest," *Soundings* 63, No. 2 (June 1980), 113–34; or Lauter, *Women as Mythmakers,* ch. 4.

40. See DuPlessis, "The Critique of Consciousness and Myth."

41. Emma Jung, *Animus and Anima,* 3, 4, 6, 9. Also see C.G. Jung, *CW* X, par. 2.

42. Emma Jung, *Animus and Anima,* 27.

43. Ibid., 28.

44. Ibid., 20.

45. See esp. Goldenberg, "Feminist Critique."

46. Fine, *Women and Art,* 19. *St. Anthony of Padua* (1662, oil) is fig. 1–11.

47. Harris and Nochlin, *Women Artists,* 109–10. *Portrait of Pietro Maria* (c. 1560, oil on canvas, 37¹³⁄₁₆ x 30 in.) is fig. 4.

48. Harris and Nochlin, *Women Artists,* 116. *Portrait of Paolo Morigia* (1596, oil on canvas, 34¾ x 31 in.) is fig. 8.

49. *George Washington* (n.d., pastel on grey paper, 9 x 11 in.), fig. 3–1 in Rubinstein, *American Women Artists.*
50. *The Young Husband: First Marketing* (1854, oil on canvas, 29½ x 24¾ in.), fig. 81 in Harris and Nochlin, *Women Artists.*
51. *Fi! Fo! Fum! (1858, oil on canvas, 37⅞ x 28⅝ in.), fig. 3–8 in Rubinstein, American Women Artists.*
52. *Old Man and Boy* (c. 1580s, oil on canvas), fig. 1–8 in Fine, *Women and Art.*
53. *The Jolly Toper* (1629, oil on canvas), fig. III, 40 in Petersen and Wilson, *Women Artists: Recognition and Reappraisal.*
54. See John Berger, *Ways of Seeing* (London: Penguin, 1972), ch. 3.
55. See Greer, *Obstacle Race*, ch. 7.
56. *Wizard* (1972, mixed media assemblage box, 13¼ x 11 x 1 in.), slide 68 in Petersen and Wilson, *Women Artists: Third World.*
57. *Self-Portrait as a Tehuana* (1943, oil on masonite, 24¾ x 24 in.), pl. XXI in Herrera, *Frida.*
58. Ibid., 361.
59. Ibid., 107.
60. *Thinking About Death* (1943, oil on masonite, 17¾ x 14½ in.), pl. XXII in Herrera, *Frida.*
61. *Sun and Life* (1947, oil on masonite, 15¾ x 19½), pl. XXXII in Herrera, *Frida.*
62. *The Love Embrace of the Universe, the Earth (Mexico), Diego, Me and Señor Xolotl* (1949, oil on canvas 27½ x 23¾ in.), pl. XXXIII in Herrera, *Frida.*
63. *Self-Portrait* (1923, oil on canvas, 46¼ x 26⅞ in.), fig. 9–4 in Fine, *Women and Art,* and fig. 5–19 in Rubinstein, *American Women Artists.*
64. *Vegetarian Vampires* (1962, oil on masonite, 33½ x 23½), fig. VII, 25 in Petersen and Wilson, *Women Artists: Recognition and Reappraisal.*
65. Janet Kaplan, "Remedios Varo: Voyages and Visions," *Woman's Art Journal* 1, No. 2 (Fall 1980/Winter 1981), 15; also see Lauter, "Creative Woman" or *Women as Mythmakers*, ch. 4, for a full treatment of Varo's protagonists.
66. Harris and Nochlin, *Women Artists,* 329. *The Angel of Anatomy* (1949, oil, 21⅝ x 13 ³⁄₁₆) is fig. 153.
67. *Noli Me Tangere* (1581, oil, 32 x 25 in.), col. pl. 5 in Harris and Nochlin, *Women Artists.*
68. *The Martyrdom of St. Eurosia* (18th century, oil on canvas, 23¼ x 15¾ in.), fig. 43 in Harris and Nochlin, *Women Artists.*
69. *The Fugitive* (after 1874, oil 22½ x 16 in.), fig. 4–14 in Fine, *Women and Art.*
70. *Pax Americana* (1973, acrylic on canvas, 60 x 38 in.), fig. 9–11 in Rubinstein, *American Women Artists.* It is also pictured with three other

paintings from Stevens' *Big Daddy* series in *Women's Studies* 3, No. 1 (1975), 83–87; it is accompanied by Lucy Lippard's "May Stevens' Big Daddies," 89–91, which is reprinted in her *From the Center* (New York: Dutton, 1976) 234–37.

71. *Kazakh* (1971, wood and leather, 16 in. high) is pictured in Nemser, *Art Talk*, 355.

72. *Joe Gould* (1933, oil on canvas, 39 x 29 in.) is pictured in Nemser, *Art Talk*, 146. *T.B. Case, Harlem* (1940, oil on canvas, 30 x 30 in.) is pictured in Nemser, *Art Talk*, 146; also fig. 150 in Harris and Nochlin, *Women Artists*.

73. *Memorial for Karl Liebknecht* (1919–20, woodcut, 13⅝ x 19½ in.), fig. VI, 47 in Petersen and Wilson, *Women Artists: Recognition and Reappraisal*; see also Munsterberg, *A History*, 115. *Mob Victim* (1944, oil) is slide 9 in Petersen and Wilson, *Women Artists: Third World*.

74. Chodorow, "Family Structure," 46. This is a central thesis of her book, *The Reproduction of Mothering: Psychoanalysis and the Sociology of Gender* (Berkeley: Univ. of California Press, 1978).

75. *Mum Bett* (1811, water color on ivory, 3 x 2 in.), slide 7 in Petersen, *American Women Artists: The Nineteenth Century*. *Portrait of Rosa Bonheur* (1898, oil 46 x 38½ in.), fig. 5–23 in Fine, *Women and Art*. *Susan B. Anthony* (1892, marble, 24 in. high), fig. 4–13; *Zenobia in Chains* (1859, marble, 49 in. high), fig. 3–25; *Hagar* (1868, marble, 52 in. high), fig. 3–26 in Rubinstein, *American Women Artists*.

76. Some of these images might well be characterized as personae, others as images of the Self. A great many, however, are essentially explorations of independence. Such images of women rarely occur in works by men, and when they do, as in Willem de Kooning's *Woman Acabonic* (1966, oil on paper on canvas, 80½ x 36 in.), pictured in Estella Lauter, "Homage to Anima: Some Cultural Implications of Willem de Kooning's Images of Woman," *Soundings* 59, No. 4 (Winter 1976), 426–46, they have a negative valence that is missing in the works by women.

77. Wolff, *Structural Forms*, 9.

78. Ibid., 10.

79. Ibid., 8.

80. Ibid.

81. Ibid.

82. Mary Esther Harding, *Women's Mysteries* (New York: Harper & Row, 1971), chs. 9, 10; but see p. 126 for Harding's judgment that the virgin is an unattractive model for a woman unless she serves Eros.

83. James Hillman, *Re-Visioning Psychology* (New York: Harper & Row, 1975), 36–38, 128–29, 139–41; and Christine Downing, *The Goddess: Mythological Images of the Feminine* (New York: Crossroad, 1981), 1–7.

84. *Hurricane* (1948–49, bronze), fig. 8–22 in Fine, *Women and Art.*
85. Fine, *Women and Art*, 176.
86. *Confessions for Myself* (1972, bronze painted black and black wool, 120 x 40 x 12 in.), fig. VII, 51 in Petersen and Wilson, *Women Artists: Recognition and Reappraisal*, and slide 80 in Petersen and Wilson, *Women Artists: Third World.*
87. Quoted by Petersen and Wilson, *Women Artists: Recognition and Reappraisal*, 143.
88. *Homage to my Young Black Sisters* (1969, cedar, 71 in. high), slide 71 in Petersen and Wilson, *Women Artists: Third World.* The best aticle on her work is Thalia Gouma-Peterson, "Elizabeth Catlett: 'The Power of Human Feeling and of Art'," *Woman's Art Journal* 4, No. 1 (Spring/ Summer 1983), 48–56. *She Number One* (1972, bronze painted black and black wool), slide 79 in Petersen and Wilson, *Women Artists: Third World.*
89. Erich Neumann, *The Archetypal World of Henry Moore* (Princeton: Princeton Univ. Press, 1959), 91–93.
90. *Outbreak* (1903, etching, 19⅞ x 23 in.), fig. 8–1 in Fine, *Women and Art.*
91. See for example, *Woman Thinking of the Past* in Lauter and Rozenberg, "Transformation," 85.
92. A similar work from the same period, *Wrapped in Silence* (1961, oil), is fig. VII, 29 in Petersen and Wilson, *Women Artists: Recognition and Reappraisal. La Pensierosa* can be seen in Constantine Jelenski, *Léonor Fini* (Lausanne, Switzerland: La Guilde du Livre et Clairefontaine, 1963).
93. See Estella Lauter, "Léonor Fini: Preparing to Meet the Strangers of the New World," *Woman's Art Journal* 1, No. 1 (Spring 1980), 44–49; also Lauter, *Women as Mythmakers*, ch. 6.
94. *Journey to the Sources of the Orinoco River* (1959, oil on masonite, 17¼ x 15½ in.), slide 74 in Petersen and Wilson, *Women Artists: Images— Themes and Dreams.*
95. See Lauter, "Creative Woman," and *Women as Mythmakers*, ch. 4. *To Be Born Again* (1960, oil on masonite, 31⅜ x 18½ in.) and *The Calling* (1961, oil on masonite, 39⅜ x 26¾ in.) are pictured in both sources. *Emerging Light* (1962, oil on masonite, 25½ x 11 in.), slide 67 in Petersen and Wilson, *Women Artists: Images—Themes and Dreams.*
96. *Artemesia Gentileschi* (1976, acrylic, 108 x 60 in.) is pictured in *Women's Studies* 6, 1 (1978), 75.
97. Biographical information is drawn from Fine, *Women and Art*, 14–17; Mary D. Garrard, "Artemesia and Susanna," in Norma Broude and Mary D. Garrard, *Feminism and Art History* (New York: Harper & Row, 1982), 147–72; Greer, *Obstacle Race*, ch. 10; Harris and Nochlin, *Women Artists*, 118–20.

98. *Self-Portrait as "La Pittura"* (1638, oil on canvas), fig. 1–10 in Fine, *Women and Art.*

99. *Judith and Maidservant with the Head of Holofernes* (1625, oil on canvas, 72½ x 55¾ in.), col. pl. 13 in Harris and Nochlin, *Women Artists.*

100. *Susanna and the Elders* (1610, oil on canvas, 67 x 47⅝ in.), fig. 10 in Harris and Nochlin, *Women Artists.* It is reproduced in color on the cover of Parker and Pollock, *Old Mistresses.*

101. *The Penitent Magdalene* (c. 1619–20, oil on canvas, 43¾ x 43 in.), fig. 11 in Harris and Nochlin, *Women Artists,* 121.

102. *Fame* (1632, oil on canvas, 50 x 38⅜ in.), col. pl. 14 in Harris and Nochlin, *Women Artists.*

103. Eleanor Maccoby et al., *The Development of Sex Differences* (Stanford: Stanford Univ. Press, 1974).

104. Chodorow, "Family Structure," 59–60.

iv

1. Mary Daly, *Beyond God the Father, Toward a Philosophy of Women's Liberation* (Boston: Beacon Press, 1973), 11.

2. Mary Daly, *Gyn/Ecology; The Metaethics of Radical Feminism* (Boston: Beacon Press, 1978), xiii–xiv. Although I had skimmed the preface, I deliberately put off reading *Gyn/Ecology* until this essay was finished to see if my conclusions showed any similarities to Daly's. Her book is full of interesting parallels to and further developments of my comments, giving evidence of the universality of the "Crones' Chorus." Her intent is to create a "written rebuttal of the rite of right research. It is part of the metapatriarchal journeying of women. . . . The acceptable/unexceptional circular reasonings of academics are caricatures of motion. The 'products' are more often than not a set of distorted mirrors, made to seem plausible through the mechanisms of male bonding. On the boundaries of the male-centered universities, however, there is a flowering of woman-centered thinking." (23).

3. Lewis Thomas, *The Medusa and the Snail* (New York: Viking, 1979), 39.

4. C.G. Jung, *Psychological Reflections* (New York: Harper & Row, 1953), 94.

5. Jung, *Psychological Reflections,* 97.

6. See Annis V. Pratt, "Archetypal Approaches to the New Feminist Criticism," *Bucknell Review* XXI, No. 1 (Spring 1973), 3–14.

7. See, for example, Lillian Robinson's "Dwelling in Decencies: Radical Criticism and the Feminist Perspective," *College English* 32, No. 8 (May 1971), 879–89.

8. Naomi R. Goldenberg, *Changing of the Gods: Feminism and the End of Traditional Religions* (Boston: Beacon Press, 1979), 62.

9. Ann Bedford Ulanov, *The Feminine in Jungian Psychology and in Christian Theology* (Evanston: Northwestern Univ. Press, 1971), x.

10. See Emma Jung and Marie-Louise von Franz, *The Grail Legend* (New York: Putnam's, 1970); M. Esther Harding, *Woman's Mysteries; Ancient and Modern* (New York: Bantam, 1971) and Marie Louise von Franz, *Problems of the Feminine in Fairy Tales* (Zurich: Spring Publications, 1972).

11. June Singer, "The Age of Androgyny," *Quadrant* 8, No. 2 (Winter 1975), 92, and a letter to the author, September 25, 1976.

12. Naomi R. Goldenberg, "A Feminist Critique of Jung," *Signs* 2, No. 2 (Winter 1976), 448.

13. Medusa is one example. See Annis V. Pratt, " 'Aunt Jennifer's Tigers': Notes Towards a Preliterary History of Women's Archetypes," *Feminist Studies* 4, No. 1 (Feb. 1978), 163–94.

14. Maud Bodkin, *Archetypal Patterns in Poetry* (London: Oxford Univ. Press, 1973), 305. Bodkin strongly dislikes the psychological dependence of Dante on the "Mother-Imago": "Within my own experience it is only as I relate the dialogue and description of the vision to the movement of the poem in its completeness that I can pass beyond the feeling of revulsion against what seems the dominance in the mind of Dante of the Mother-Imago" (178). Although she does not attribute her revulsion to any realization that such an obsession has less appeal (in the form of sublimated love for the spiritualized feminine) for women than men, she states that "the attempt to trace the form assumed in poetry by the archetypal images of man and woman suggested the inquiry whether one could find in the poetry of women writers any imaginative representation of man, related to the distinctive inner life of a woman in the same manner as an image of woman appearing in poetry shows relation to the emotional life of man." (290–91)

15. See Annis V. Pratt, *Archetypal Patterns in Women's Fiction* (Bloomington: Indiana Univ. Press, 1981), ch. 8.

16. C.G. Jung and C. Kerényi, *Essays on a Science of Mythology: The Myth of the Divine Child and the Mysteries of Eleusis,* trans. R.F.C. Hull (Princeton, N.J.: Princeton Univ. Press, 1950), 177; and as quoted in C. Kerényi, *Eleusis—Archetypal Images of Mother and Daughter,* trans. Ralph Manheim (New York: Schocken, 1971), xxi–xxxii.

17. Feminist critics have been passing Miller's statement around during the past several years, since it refreshingly validates both usual and more subtle methods of exclusion. I found it quoted by Carolyn Heilbrun, "Women, Men, Theories, and Literature," *Profession 81,* Selected Articles from the Bulletins of the Association of Departments of English and the Association of Departments of Foreign Languages

(New York: MLA, 1981), 25. Heilbrun quotes it from Sandra Gilbert, "What do Feminist Critics Want? or, A Postcard from the Volcano," *ADE Bulletin*, No. 66 (Winter 1980), 16–23, who quotes it from J. Hillis Miller, "The Function of Rhetorical Study at the Present Time," in *The State of the Discipline, 1970s–1980s* (Special Issue), *ADE Bulletin*, No. 62 (Sept.–Nov. 1979), 12.

18. Annette Kolodny, "A Map for Rereading: or, Gender and the Interpretation of Literary Texts," *New Literary History* XI, No. 3 (1980), 452.

19. Northrop Frye, *Fables of Identity: Studies in Poetic Mythology* (New York: Harcourt Brace & World, 1963), 57.

20. Northrop Frye, *Anatomy of Criticism* (Princeton, N.J.: Princeton Univ. Press, 1957), 102.

21. Frye, *Anatomy*, 112.

22. Frye, *Anatomy*, 6–7.

23. Northrop Frye, *The Critical Path: An Essay on the Social Context of Literary Criticism* (Bloomington, Indiana: Indiana Univ. Press, 1971), 24–25.

24. Frye, *Anatomy*, 187.

25. Frye, *Anatomy*, 200.

26. Northrop Frye, *The Secular Scripture: A Study of the Structure of Romance* (Cambridge, Mass: Harvard Univ. Press, 1976), 86. Frye does discuss heroines at this point and recognizes their virginity as the strength to survive by assuming "the position of the Goddess in the lower world." Frye, however, makes no further distinction between women heroes who identify with the goddess and male heroes who oppose her.

27. Nor Hall, *The Moon and the Virgin, Reflections on the Archetypal Feminine* (New York: Harper & Row, 1980), 11. For another interesting account of the relationship between women and nature see Susan Griffin, *Woman and Nature: The Roaring Inside Her* (New York: Harper & Row, 1978). Griffin provides a model for deconstructing patriarchal views of nature, women, and matter and reconstructing a more naturistic, holistic, and feminist mode of vision.

28. Sherry B. Ortner, "Is Female to Male as Nature Is to Culture?" in *Woman, Culture and Society*, ed. Michelle Zimbalist Rosaldo and Louise Lamphere (Stanford: Stanford Univ. Press, 1974), 73.

29. Frye, *Critical Path*, 131.

30. Frye, *Secular Scripture*, 119.

31. Northrop Frye, *Creation and Recreation* (Toronto: Univ. of Toronto Press, 1980), 27.

32. Frye, *Creation and Recreation*, 45.

33. Frye, *Secular Scripture*, 163.

34. Hall, *Moon and the Virgin*, 68. Hall seems to accept Pluto's rape of

Persephone as a necessary seduction or enrapturing rather than an essential violation of her integrity.

35. See Marija Gimbutas, "Women and Culture in Goddess-Oriented Old Europe" in Spretnak, ed., *The Politics of Women's Spirituality* (New York: Doubleday, 1982), 24 and passim.

36. Marija Gimbutas, *The Gods and Goddesses of Old Europe, 7000–3500 B.C.* (Berkeley: Univ. of California Press, 1974), 237.

37. Frye, *Anatomy*, 68.

38. Frye, *Secular Scripture*, 183. The full quote is interesting: "The imagination, as it reflects on this world, sees it as a world of violence and cunning, *forza* and *froda*. The typical agent of cunning is a woman, whose main instrument of will is her bed: in the *Iliad* even the greatest of goddesses, Hera, decoys Zeus in this way in an effort to aid the Greeks. Thus the *forza-froda* cycle is also that of Ares and Eros, both of which, for human beings, end in Thanatos or death. Ares and Eros are functionaries of Venus, whose alternative form is Diana of the triple will, the white goddess who always kills, and whose rebirth is only for herself."

39. See Northrop Frye, "Haunted by Lack of Ghosts, Patterns in The Imagery of Canadian Poetry," in *The Canadian Imagination: Dimensions of a Literary Culture*, ed. David Staines (Cambridge, Mass.: Harvard Univ. Press, 1977), 26–27, 35. See also Frye's *The Bush Garden: Essays on the Canadian Imagination* (Toronto: Anansi, 1971). I have dealt with one particular archetype in various Canadian fictions in "Affairs with Bears: Some Notes Toward Feminist Archetypal Hypotheses for Canadian Literature," (unpublished ms.)

40. See Claude Lévi-Strauss, Introd., *Myth and Meaning* (New York: Schocken, 1979).

41. Claude Lévi-Strauss, "The Structural Study of Myth," in *The Structuralists from Marx to Lévi-Strauss*, ed. Richard and Fernande De George (Garden City, N.Y.: Doubleday, 1972), 188.

42. Lévi-Strauss, *Myth and Meaning*, 17.

43. Leonard Michael Scigaj, "Myth and Psychology in the Poetry of Ted Hughes," Diss. University of Wisconsin 1977, pp. 35–36, with reference to Claude Lévi-Strauss, *Totemism*, trans. Rodney Needham (Boston: Beacon, 1963), 125.

44. Carol P. MacCormack, "Nature, Culture, and Gender: A Critique," in *Nature, Culture, and Gender*, ed. Carol P. MacCormack and Marilyn Strathern (Cambridge: Cambridge Univ. Press, 1980), 6–7.

45. Lévi-Strauss, "Structural Study of Myth," 179.

46. Claude Lévi-Strauss, *The Savage Mind* (Chicago: Univ. of Chicago Press, 1966), 125.

47. Claude Lévi-Strauss, *Structural Anthropology*, trans. Claire Jacobsen

254 | NOTES TO PAGES 126–137

and Brooke Grundfest Schoepf (London: Penguin, 1968), 61–62, as
cited in Juliet Mitchell, *Psychoanalysis and Feminism: Freud, Reich, Laing*
and Women (New York: Vintage, 1974), 371.

48. Frederic Jameson, *The Prison House of Language: A Critical Account of*
Structuralism (Princeton, N.J.: Princeton Univ. Press, 1972), 1–5.

49. Richard Webster, "Structuralism and Dry Rot," *The Observer* (February 1, 1981), 27.

50. Elizabeth Janeway, "Who Is Sylvia? On the Loss of Sexual Paradigms," *Signs* 5, No. 4 (Summer 1980), 573.

51. Adrienne Rich, *On Lies, Secrets and Silence: Selected Prose, 1966–1978*
(New York: Norton, 1979), 207. For an outline of methods similar to
those I suggest in this essay see Rich's "Toward a Woman-Centered
University" in the same volume.

52. Janeway, "Who Is Sylvia?," 575.

53. L.J. Jordanova, "Natural Facts: A Historical Perspective on Science
and Sexuality," in *Nature, Culture, and Gender*, ed. MacCormack and
Strathern, 65.

54. Carol Christ and Judith Plaskow, eds., Introd., *Woman-Spirit Rising:*
A Feminist Reader in Religion (San Francisco: Harper & Row, 1979), 7–9.

55. Nancy K. Miller, "Emphasis Added: Plots and Plausibilities in
Women's Fiction," *PMLA* 96, No. 1 (Jan. 1981), 36.

56. Joseph Campbell, *The Masks of God: Occidental Mythology* (New York:
Viking, 1964), 21–22.

57. Jane Ellen Harrison, *Mythology* (Boston: Jones, 1927), 60–62. See also
Themis: A Study of the Social Origins of Greek Religion (Cleveland: World,
1962) and *Prolegomena to the Study of Greek Religion* (Cambridge: Cambridge Univ. Press, 1922).

58. Campbell, *Masks of God*, 21.

59. Gimbutas, *Gods and Goddesses*, 238. At this writing a new edition
entitled *Goddesses and Gods of Old Europe, 6500–3500 B.C.* is planned for
publication by the same press. See also Elizabeth Fisher, *Woman's*
Creation: Sexual Evolution and the Shaping of Society (Garden City, N.Y.: Anchor-Doubleday, 1979).

60. Jean Bethke Elshtain, "Feminist Discourse and Its Discontents: Language, Power, and Meaning," *Signs* 7, No. 3 (Spring 1982), 618.

61. The researcher's name was Dr. Rosalinde Schindler, Wayne State
College of Lifelong Learning.

62. Carol Christ, "Spiritual Quest and Women's Experience," *Anima* 1,
No. 2 (Spring 1975), 6.

v

1. Samuel Noah Kramer, *The Sacred Marriage Rite: Aspects of Faith, Myth,*
and Ritual in Ancient Sumer, (Bloomington, Ind.: Indiana Univ. Press,

1969), 108–21; and Diane Wolkstein and Samuel Noah Kramer, *Inanna, Queen of Heaven and Earth: Her Stories and Hymns,* (New York: Harper & Row, 1983), 51–89.

2. Alexander Heidel, *The Gilgamesh Epic and Old Testament Parallels* (Chicago: Univ. of Chicago Press, 1946), 119–28.

3. Thorkild Jacobsen, *The Treasures of Darkness: A History of Mesopotamian Religion* (New Haven, Conn.: Yale Univ. Press, 1976), 55.

4. Kramer, *Sacred Marriage Rite,* 108.

5. Kramer, *Sacred Marriage Rite,* 112.

6. Wolkstein and Kramer, *Inanna,* 89.

7. Erich Neumann, "On the Moon and Matriarchal Consciousness," in *Fathers and Mothers: Five Papers on the Archetypal Background of Family Psychology* (Zurich: Spring, 1973).

8. Erich Neumann, "Psychological Stages of Feminine Development," *Spring: An Annual of Archetypal Psychology and Jungian Thought* (1959), 96.

9. Adrienne Rich, "Reforming the Crystal," in *Poems: Selected and New, 1950–1974* (New York: Norton, 1979), 228.

10. Carolyn G. Heilbrun, *Reinventing Womanhood* (New York: Norton, 1979), 37–50.

11. See, for example, Tillie Olsen, *Silences* (New York: Delta–Seymour Lawrence, 1979); Adrienne Rich, *Of Woman Born: Motherhood as Experience and Institution* (New York: Norton, 1974) and *On Lies, Secrets, and Silences: Selected Prose, 1966–1978* (New York: Norton, 1979); Heilbrun, *Reinventing Womanhood;* and Dorothy Dinnerstein, *The Mermaid and the Minotaur: Sexual Arrangements and Human Malaise* (New York: Harper & Row, 1977). Even Toni Wolff, in her essay "Structural Forms of the Feminine Psyche" explains her categories—mother, amazon, hetaira, medial woman—primarily in relation to the masculine. Although valid, these categories need to be understood more introvertedly, in terms of mothering, partnering, and mediating to our own feminine depths rather than just to outer, male partners.

12. See David R. Kingsley, *The Sword and the Flute: Kali and Krsna, Dark Visions of the Terrible and the Sublime in Hindu Mythology* (Berkeley: Univ. of California Press, 1975); and Beverley Zabriskie, "Isis, Ancient Goddess, Modern Woman," Diss. C.G. Jung Training Center, New York, 1980.

13. Jacobsen, *Treasures,* 36.

14. Heidel, *Gilgamesh Epic,* 134.

15. Perhaps the soul is considered feminine because so much female body-ego experience entails boundary penetration from within and without (e.g., menstruation, sexual intercourse, childbirth, lactation). This body experience prepares the ego for its capacity to be acted

upon, to let another exert influence upon it. And this penetration is analogous to the soul's penetration by the divine. In many cultures the worshipper is likened to a bride or wife of the god. Men are enjoined to emulate Radha or Christ's bride, and to submit to the transpersonal godhead. Women have also, in many cultures, generally taken charge of daily eating and excretory functions for some others. There is an analogy between these "lowly" activities and the careful tending of the soul's reception of the numinous above and below.

16. Jean Gebser, "The Foundations of the Aperspective World," extract in *Main Currents of Modern Thought* 29, No. 2 (1972) and 30, No. 3 (1973).

17. C.G. Jung, "The Psychological Aspects of the Kore," in C.G. Jung and C. Kerényi *Essays on a Science of Mythology. The Myth of the Divine Child and the Mysteries of Elusis* (New York: Harper & Row, 1949), 170.

18. Jacobsen, *Treasures*, suggests that the earliest form of her name was Ninanna(k), "Lady of the Date Cluster" (36).

19. See Rodney Collin, *The Theory of Celestial Influence* (New York: Weiser, 1954). The eight-year cycle of the planet Venus "appears to rule growth and the multiplication of mankind" (298). Studies have shown that the planet's periodicity correlates with major crop yields (276).

20. Samuel Noah Kramer, *From the Poetry of Sumer: Creation, Glorification, Adoration* (Berkeley: Univ. of California Press, 1979), 94.

21. The Throne-bed was made from a "world tree" cut down by Gilgamesh in her garden. For his help Gilgamesh received the *pukku* and *mikku*, royal emblems that later fell into the underworld and brought about his knowledge of mortality. (See Wolkstein and Kramer, Introd., *Inanna*, for a fuller discussion of this story, "Inanna and the Huluppu Tree.")

22. Jacobsen, *Treasures*, 137.

23. Kramer, *Poetry of Sumer*, 88.

24. Kramer, *Poetry of Sumer*, 97.

25. Jacobsen, *Treasures*, 138.

26. Kramer, *Sacred Marriage Rite*, 96.

27. Kramer, *Sacred Marriage Rite*, 59.

28. Jacobsen, *Treasures*, 141.

29. Karl Kerényi, *Athene: Virgin and Mother* (Zurich: Spring, 1978), 45.

30. Kerényi, "Kore," in Jung and Kerényi, *Science of Mythology*, 105.

31. Inanna describes her two sons: one "Who sings hymns to me/Who cuts my nails and smooths my hair" and one who "is a leader among men./He is my right arm./He is my left arm." (Wolkstein and Kramer, *Inanna*, 70, 71.) Mother and son are not lovers; Inanna's beloved consort is Dumuzi; and it is he whom she finally chooses to send as her substitute to the underworld. At a few points in the love poems she

refs to Dumuzi as son or brother (Kramer, *Sacred Marriage Rite*, 96–97), but this seems merely a Sumerian use of kinship words to express emotional closeness or respect. Such familial appellations are frequent in Sumer (and in tribal anthropology); thus Inanna also calls Ereshkigal "elder sister."

32. Heidel, *Gilgamesh Epic*, 50–52.
33. Kramer, *Poetry of Sumer*, 92.
34. Ezra 10:3–43.
35. See Rosaldo and Lamphere, eds., *Woman, Culture and Society*.
36. Edward C. Whitmont, *The Return of the Goddess* (New York: Crossroad, 1983).
37. *New York Times*, August 12, 1980, C7.
38. See C.G. Jung, "The Symbolic Life," in *CW* XVIII, pars. 630–31. (*The Collected Works of C.G. Jung*, trans. R.F.C. Hull are published by Princeton University Press in the Bollingen Series XX and are hereinafter cited as *CW* with volume and paragraph numbers following.)
39. Jacobsen, *Treasures*, 99.
40. Samuel Noah Kramer, *Sumerian Mythology: A Study of Spiritual and Literary Achievement in the Third Millenium B.C.* (New York: Harper & Row, 1961), 43–47.
41. Kerényi, "Kore," in Jung and Kerényi, *Science of Mythology*, 125.
42. "Inanna and the Huluppu Tree," in Wolkstein and Kramer, *Inanna*.
43. Jacobsen translates the line referenced in n42 as "Ereshkigal was given the *kur* as a prize." She becomes queen. With the separation of heaven and earth, the lower realm became her great dwelling and the place of a new fertility for her.
44. Similarly, the initiates into the Eleusinian Mysteries found comfort in Persephone and Demeter and the knowledge of eternal life gained through the mystery.
45. Swami Rama et al., *Yoga and Psychotherapy: The Evolution of Consciousness* (Honesdale, Pa.: Himalayan Institute, 1976), 226–31.
46. Depression is now two to six times more prevalent in women than men in the United States. See Maggie Scarf, *Unfinished Business: Pressure Points in the Lives of Women* (Garden City, N.Y.: Doubleday, 1980) for a lay review of the subject.
47. Sylvia Perera Massell, "The Scapegoat Complex," *Quadrant* 12, No. 2 (1979).
48. Patricia Berry, "The Rape of Demeter/Persephone and Neurosis," *Spring: An Annual of Archetypal Psychology and Jungian Thought* (1975).
49. Jane Ellen Harrison, *Prolegomena to the Study of Greek Religion* (Cambridge: Cambridge Univ. Press, 1922), 8–11.
50. Marie-Louise von Franz, *Shadow and Evil in Fairy Tales* (Zurich: Spring, 1974), 167.

51. Heidel, *Gilgamesh Epic*, 129.
52. Jacobsen, *Treasures*, 229.
53. Kramer, *Sacred Marriage Rite*, 114.
54. C.G. Jung, "Psychological Commentary on Kundalini Yoga" (Lecture 1, Oct. 1932), *Spring: An Annual of Archetypal Psychology and Jungian Thought* (1975), 2.
55. Linda Fierz-David's words apply aptly to Inanna, although the word "merging" would be more appropriate in her text than "relatedness":

> To live according to the principle of relatedness, to let oneself be entangled and to entangle others, is a necessity of nature for all women. . . . But as soon as the relatedness is carried on at the expense of one's own soul, as soon as the women flow over all too unreservedly into the world surrounding them . . . a powerful counter-current arises in them. . . . The spirit appears to them as death. . . . Over against overburdened life, *death* reveals itself to them *as the highest value* . . . herald(ing) to them the frightful necessity of rending all ties *in themselves* and giving up all related.iess in the world, in order to find the relationship to the spirit and therewith also to themselves. . . . They must . . . dare the leap into darkness. . . . Women, in the cold breath of the spirit realm, must experience also their own coldness . . . [in order to] deliver them from the compulsion of a relatedness that is in thralldom to nature.
> ("Psychological Reflections on the Fresco Series of the Villa of the Mysteries in Pompeii," 93–97)

56. von Franz, *Shadow and Evil*, 169.
57. Antonio T. de Nicolas, *Meditations through the Rig-Veda: Four-Dimensional Man* (Boulder, Colo.: Shambhala, 1978), 24.
58. Joseph Campbell, *Myths to Live By* (New York: Viking, 1972), 103–4.
59. This is part of the teaching of the Bhagavad-Gita.
60. Kramer, *Sacred Marriage Rite*, 116.
61. Jacobsen, *Treasures*, 58.
62. Kramer, *Sacred Marriage Rite*, 116.
63. Gertrude Ujhely, "Thoughts Concerning the *Causa Finalis* of the Cognitive Mode Inherent in Pre-Oedipal Psychopathology," Diss. C.G. Jung Training Center, New York, 1980. See also Dorothee Soelle, *Suffering*, trans. Everett R. Kalen (Philadelphia: Fortress, 1975).
64. Penelope Washbourne, ed., *Seasons of Women: Song, Poetry, Ritual, Prayer, Myth, Story* (San Francisco: Harper & Row, 1979), 52.
65. Quoted by Margaret W. Masson in "The Typology of the Female as a Model for the Regenerate: Puritan Preaching, 1690–1730," *Signs* 2, No. 2 (1976), 312.
66. Esther Harding, *Woman's Mysteries: Ancient and Modern* (New York: Harper & Row, 1976), 84.
67. Harding, *Woman's Mysteries*, 135–38.
68. This division of the two goddesses suggests an ancient, intuitive

awareness of brain functioning only recently confirmed scientifically by Paul MacLean and others. (See, for instance, Mary Long, "Ritual and Deceit," *Science Digest* (Nov.–Dec. 1980), 87–121.) The primitive, "reptilian" brain is responsible for self-preservation, violent aggression, dominance, and ritually repetitive display behaviors. These are roughly analogous to behavior patterns associated by the Sumerians with the figure of Ereshkigal. The limbic brain, with its prefontal neocortex processes, is responsible for functions that preserve the species: nurturance, empathy, social bonding. These are roughly analogous to behaviors associated with Inanna.

69. The major difference in masculine development is that until recently, and then often only in the second half of life, most men have not needed to go down into the repressed depths once they have initially freed themselves from their childhood and identified with the ideals of the culture, for they have been supported by the outside world. Increasingly, because there is no adequate masculine wholeness pattern that is collectively sanctioned to form a model of masculine ego development, and because the heroic ego ideal is coming to be inadequate, more and more men will have to dare the individual descents that will permit them to reclaim their repressed instincts.

70. Heidel, *Gilgamesh Epic*, 122–23.

71. Kramer, *Sacred Marriage Rite*, 113.

72. Kerényi, "Kore," in Jung and Kerényi, *Science of Mythology*, 139.

73. Kramer, *Sacred Marriage Rite*, 114.

74. Mircea Eliade, "Terra Mater and Cosmic Hierogamies," *Spring: An Annual of Archetypal Psychology and Jungian Thought* (1955), 35.

75. Eliade, "Terra Mater," 38.

76. Eliade, "Terra Mater," 39.

77. Neumann, *The Great Mother: An Analysis of the Archetype* (Princeton, N.J.: Princeton Univ. Press, 1955), 192–94.

78. Eliade, "Terra Mater," 39.

79. C.G. Jung, *The Visions Seminars, 1930–34.* 2 vols. (Zurich: Spring, 1976), 118–19.

80. To my knowledge, there is no awareness in Sumerian-Akkadian material of such energy and consciousness centers, but the careful ordering of garments makes such an interpretation plausible. In a similar interpretation, Joseph Campbell has suggested, in a lecture, that the seven-fold interlacement of the two serpents on the Babylonian Gudea cup (c2000 B.C.) may symbolize the kundalini and its chakras.

81. See S.P. Mason, *A History of the Sciences* (rev. ed., New York: Collier, 1962).

82. Apuleius describes his Roman initiation into the mysteries of Isis: "I

approach the confines of death. Having trod the threshold of Proserpina, I return through all the elements. At midnight I beheld the sun brightly shining. I was in the presence of the gods above and the gods below."

83. Wolkstein and Kramer, *Inanna*, 69.
84. Wolkstein and Kramer, *Inanna*, 61, 62.
85. Kramer, *Sacred Marriage Rite*, 166–67.
86. Wolkstein and Kramer, *Inanna*, 65.
87. Ibid., 64.
88. Edward C. Whitmont, "The Magic Dimension of Consciousness," *Spring: An Annual of Archetypal Psychology and Jungian Thought* (1956).
89. Kramer, *Sacred Marriage Rite*, 116.
90. Ibid.
91. Jung, *CW* XVIII, par. 631.
92. Kramer, *Sacred Marriage Rite*, 105.
93. Kramer, *Sacred Marriage Rite*, 118.
94. Kramer, *Sacred Marriage Rite*, 119.
95. Jacobsen, *Treasures*, 49–52.
96. Wolkstein and Kramer, *Inanna*, 74–89.
97. Kramer, *Sacred Marriage Rite*, 128.
98. Kramer, *Sacred Marriage Rite*, 63–66, 92, 100.
99. Kramer, *Sacred Marriage Rite*, 122.
100. Jacobsen, *Treasures*, 27–28.
101. Jacobsen, *Treasures*, 27.
102. James Hillman, "On Psychological Femininity," in *The Myth of Analysis* (New York: Harper & Row, 1972), 215–98.

vi

1. Adrienne Rich, "Transcendental Etude" in *The Dream of a Common Language* (New York: Norton, 1978), 76.
2. Harry Fiss, "Current Dream Research: A Psychobiological Perspective," in *Handbook of Dreams: Research, Theories and Applications*, ed. Benjamin B. Wolman (New York: Van Nostrand-Reinhold, 1979), 20–75.
3. Robert W. McCarley and Edward Hoffman, "REM Sleep Dreams and the Activation-Synthesis Hypothesis," *American Journal of Psychiatry*, 138, No. 7 (July 1981), 904.
4. J. Allan Hobson and Robert W. McCarley, "The Brain as a Dream State Generator: An Activation-Synthesis Hypothesis of the Dream Process," *AJP* 134, No. 12 (Dec. 1977), 1335–48.
5. Hobson and McCarley, "Brain as Dream State Generator," 1335.
6. Ibid.
7. James Hall, Letter, *AJP* 135, No. 5 (May 1978), 615.
8. Hobson and McCarley, "Brain as Dream State Generator," 1347.

9. Hobson and McCarley, Letter, *AJP* 135, No. 5 (May 1978), citing C.G. Jung, *Memories, Dreams, and Reflections*, ed. A. Jaffé, trans. Richard and Clara Winston (New York: Random, 1963), 161–62.

10. Hall, Letter, *AJP*, 615.

11. Susan Knapp, "Dreaming: Horney, Kelman, and Shainberg," in *Handbook of Dreams*, ed. Wolman, 344.

12. C.G. Jung, *The Collected Works*, VIII, XI, XII, XV, *(The Collected Works of C.G. Jung*, trans. R.F.C. Hull, are published by Princeton University Press in the Bollingen Series XX and are hereinafter cited as *CW* with volume and paragraph numbers following.)

13. J. Allan Hobson, "Film and the Physiology of Dreaming Sleep," *Dreamworks: An Interdisciplinary Quarterly* 1, No. 1 (Spring 1980), 13.

14. Carol Schreier Rupprecht, "The Martial Maid and the Challenge of Androgyny: Notes on an Unbefriended Archetype," *Spring: An Annual of Archetypal Psychology and Jungian Thought* (1974), 278.

15. Jolande Jacobi, *The Psychology of C.G. Jung* (New Haven, Conn.: Yale Univ. Press, 1973), 8.

16. See Thomas B. Kirsch, "The Relationship of the REM State to Analytical Psychology," *American Journal of Psychiatry* 124, No. 10 (April 1968), 1459–63; and McCarley and Hoffman, "REM Sleep Dreams," 904–11.

17. C.G. Jung, *CW* VIII, par. 849.

18. Kirsch, "Relationship of REM State," 1459.

19. C.G. Jung, *CW* VIII, par. 420.

20. C.G. Jung, *CW* IX, part 2, par. 29.

21. James Hall, *Clinical Uses of Dreams: Jungian Interpretations and Enactments* (New York: Grune & Stratton, 1977), esp. 115–16; and Edward Whitmont, "Reassessing Feminity and Masculinity: A Critique of Some Traditional Assumptions," *Quadrant* 13, No. 2 (Fall 1980), 109–22.

22. Hobson and McCarley, Letter, *AJP*, 617–18.

23. Edwin Kiester, Jr., "Images of the Night," *Science 80* (May–June), 43.

24. Knapp, "Dreaming," 343.

25. C.G. Jung, *CW* VIII, par. 408.

26. C.G. Jung, *CW* IX, part 1, par. 91.

27. Jung et al., *Man and His Symbols*, 58.

28. Philip D. Walls, Letter in *American Journal of Psychiatry*, 139, No. 11 (Nov. 1978), 1431.

29. See, for example, James Hillman, *The Myth of Analysis; Three Essays in Archetypal Psychology* (New York: Harper & Row, 1972); Naomi Goldenberg, *Changing of the Gods: Feminism and the End of Traditional Religions* (Boston: Beacon Press, 1979); Susan Griffin, *Woman and Nature; The Roaring Inside Her* (New York: Harper & Row, 1978);

Woman, Culture and Society, eds. Michelle Zimbalist Rosaldo and Louise Lamphere (Stanford: Stanford Univ. Press, 1974); *Nature, Culture, and Gender,* eds. Carol P. McCormack and Marilyn Strathern (Cambridge: Cambridge Univ. Press, 1980).
30. Rosalind Cartwright, *A Primer on Sleep and Dreaming* (Reading, Mass.: Addison-Wesley, 1978), 32.
31. Cartwright, *Primer,* 22.
32. Artemidorus Daldianus, *The Interpretation of Dreams,* trans. Robert J. White (Park Ridge, N.J.: Noyes, 1975), 24–25.
33. Edith Sheppard, "Dream Content-Analysis" in *Dream Psychology and the New Biology of Dreaming,* ed. Milton Kramer (Springfield, Ill.: Thomas, 1969), 228.
34. Calvin S. Hall, *The Meaning of Dreams* (New York: Harper and Bros., 1953); and "Strangers in Dreams: An Empirical Confirmation of the Oedipus Complex" in *Journal of Personality* 31 (1963), 337–45.
35. Calvin S. Hall and Bill Domhoff, "A Ubiquitous Sex Difference in Dreams," *Journal of Abnormal and Social Psychology* 66 (1963), 278–80.
36. Calvin S. Hall and Vernon Nordby, *The Individual and His Dreams* (New York: New American Library, 1972).
37. Hall and Nordby, *Individual and His Dreams,* 38.
38. Hall and Nordby, *Individual and His Dreams,* 32–33.
39. Hall and Nordby, *Individual and His Dreams,* 27.
40. Carol Gilligan, *In a Different Voice: Psychological Theory and Women's Development* (Cambridge, Mass.: Harvard Univ. Press, 1982), 1.
41. Kiester, "Images of the Night," 43.
42. Sheppard, "Dream Content-Analysis," 228–89.
43. Susana Ortiz, "Dreams in Pregnancy," Master's of Science in Nursing Thesis, Yale University 1979, p. 53.
44. Ortiz, *Dreams,* 68.
45. Ortiz, *Dreams,* 25–26.
46. Cartwright, *Primer,* 127.
47. Hall and Nordby, *Individual and His Dreams,* 101.
48. David Foulkes, "Children's Dreams," in *Handbook of Dreams,* ed. Wolman, 131–67.
49. Paul K. Feyerabend, *Against Method,* as cited in Hall, *Clinical Uses of Dreams,* 181.
50. James Hillman, *In Search: Psychology and Religion* (New York: Scribner's, 1967), 57.
51. Charles Rycroft, *The Innocence of Dreams* (London: Hogarth, 1979), 38–39.
52. Edward S. Casey, *Imagining: A Phenomenological Study* (Bloomington: Indiana Univ. Press, 1976).
53. Cartwright, *Primer,* 16–22; and Joanna Rohrbaugh Bunker, *Women: Psychology's Puzzle* (New York: Basic Books, 1979).

54. See Sue Cox, ed., *Female Psychology: The Emerging Self* (Chicago: Science Research Associates, 1976), 10–14; and Janet T. Spence, "Changing Conceptions of Men and Women: A Psychological Perspective," *Soundings: An Interdisciplinary Symposium* 64, No. 4 (Winter 1981), 466–84.

vii

1. Edwin Ardener, "Belief and the Problem of Women" and "The Problem Revisited," in *Perceiving Women* ed. Shirley Ardener (London: J.M. Dent, 1977), esp. 22–25.
2. Sue Cox, *Female Psychology: The Emerging Self* (Chicago: Science Research Associates, 1976), 4.
3. *Women's Studies Quarterly* 2, No. 2 (1974).
4. See Alice Rossi, "Life-Span Theories and Women's Lives," *Signs: Journal of Women in Culture and Society* 6, No. 1 (Autumn 1980), 4–32.
5. Jung's most successful explanation of this concept for a lay audience appears in his lectures to an audience in the United States later published as *Analytical Psychology: Its Theory and Practice* (New York: Random, 1968).
6. This concept has become controversial in French feminism because of Jacques Lacan's notions that the unconscious is a "prison house of language" and that women are barred from entering the symbolic realm that determines the dimensions of that house because they lack the castration complex, which in turn determines "the symbolic." See *Signs* 7, No. 1 (Autumn 1981) esp. 45–46; also Elaine Marks and Isabelle de Courtivron, *New French Feminisms: An Anthology* (New York: Schocken, 1981).
7. Edward S. Casey, "Toward an Archetypal Imagination," *Spring: An Annual of Archetypal Psychology and Jungian Thought* (1974), 1–32.
8. Edward C. Whitmont, "Reassessing Femininity and Masculinity: A Critique of Some Traditional Assumptions," *Quadrant*, 13, No. 2 (Fall 1980), 121.
9. Whitmont, "Reassessing," 112.
10. Whitmont, "Reassessing," 113. Whitmont cites Karen Elias-Button "Athena and Medusa," *Anima* 5, No. 2 (Spring 1979). Elias-Button also wrote "The Muse as Medusa," in *The Lost Tradition*, ed. Cathy Davidson and E.M. Broner (New York: Ungar, 1980), 193–206. The latter publication may be better known to feminist critics than archetypal psychologists.
11. Boston Women's Health Collective, *Our Bodies, Ourselves* (New York: Simon and Schuster, 1971).
12. Ortner, "Is Female to Male as Nature Is to Culture?" in *Woman,*

Culture and Society ed. Rosaldo and Lamphere (Stanford: Stanford Univ. Press, 1974), 67–88.

13. James Hillman, *The Myth of Analysis* (New York: Harper & Row, 1972), 215.
14. Hillman, *Myth of Analysis*, 218, and "Why 'Archetypal' Psychology?" *Spring: An Annual of Archetypal Psychology and Jungian Thought* (1970), 217.
15. Hillman, *Myth of Analysis*, 220.
16. Stephen Gould, *The Mis-Measure of Man* (New York: Norton, 1981).
17. Hillman, *Myth of Analysis*, 235.
18. Hillman, *Myth of Analysis*, 220–21.
19. Adrienne Rich, *Of Woman Born* (New York: Norton, 1976), 213.
20. Christine Downing, *The Goddess* (New York: Crossroad, 1981). See esp. her revaluation of Pallas Athene in ch. 5.
21. See Philip Slater, *The Glory of Hera* (Boston: Beacon, 1968).
22. Annis Pratt, *Archetypal Patterns in Women's Fiction* (Bloomington: Indiana Univ. Press, 1981), 3–12, 167–78.
23. Merlin Stone, *Ancient Mirrors of Womanhood*, I, II (New York: New Sibylline, 1979).
24. M. Esther Harding, *Women's Mysteries: Ancient and Modern* (New York: Harper & Row, 1971), 117–26, esp. p. 125 where the term "one-in-herself" is used.
25. Rich, *Of Woman Born*, 213.
26. Nor Hall, *The Moon and the Virgin* (New York: Harper & Row, 1980). Hall uses Wolff's theory to structure her book. See Estella Lauter's essay in this book for an account of Wolff's theory.
27. Erich Neumann, *The Great Mother*, trans. Ralph Manheim (New York: Pantheon Books, 1955). See Estella Lauter's essay in this book for an account of his theory.
28. Nancy Chodorow, *The Reproduction of Mothering: Psychoanalysis and the Sociology of Gender* (Berkeley: Univ. of California Press, 1978). See the critique of Chodorow in *Signs* 6, No. 1 (Autumn 1980).
29. Naomi Goldenberg, "Archetypal Theory and the Separation of Mind and Body—Reason Enough to Turn to Freud?" Paper presented at the American Academy of Religion, December 1982. This essay was to have been included in this volume but could not be finished in time because of the premature birth of Naomi's daughter Natalie.
30. Gloria Bonder, Director of the Centro de Estudios de la Mujer in Buenos Aires, presented her theory in a major address at the International Interdisciplinary Congress on Women in Israel, December 1981. The report on the Congress (Dec. 28, 1981–Jan. 1, 1982) appears in *Women's Studies Quarterly International Supplement* No. 2 (July 1982), 42–47.

31. Adrienne Rich, *The Dream of a Common Language* (New York: Norton, 1978), 77.

Bibliography

Note: This is not a bibliography of works cited; information concerning them is in the notes for each essay. Rather this is a list of books about women's experiences which provide the information and interpretations we need for the archetypal descent and ascent we recommend here.

Abel, Elizabeth, ed. *Writing and Sexual Difference*(Special Issue). *Critical Inquiry* 8, No. 2 (Winter 1981).

Ardener, Shirley, ed. *Perceiving Women*. London: J.M. Dent, 1977.

Bambera, Toni Cade. *The Black Woman*. New York: Signet, 1970.

Beauvoir, Simone de. *The Second Sex*. Trans. and ed. H.M. Parshley. New York: Knopf, 1953.

Bell, Roseann P., Bettye J. Parker, and Beverly Guy-Scheftall, eds. *Sturdy Black Bridges: Visions of Black Women in Literature*. Garden City, N.Y.: Doubleday, 1979.

Bernikow, Louise. *Among Women*. New York: Harmony Books, 1980.

Berry, Patricia. *Echo's Subtle Body*. Dallas: Spring Publications, 1982.

Bolen, Jean Shinoda. *Goddesses in Everywoman: A New Psychology of Women*. San Francisco: Harper & Row, 1984.

Castillejo, Irene Claremont de. *Knowing Women: A Feminine Psychology*. New York: Harper & Row, 1973.

Chesler, Phyllis. *Women and Madness*. Garden City, N.Y.: Doubleday, 1972.

Chicago, Judy. *The Dinner Party: A Symbol of Our Heritage*. Garden City, N.Y.: Doubleday, 1979.

———. *Embroidering Our Heritage: The Dinner Party Needlework*. Garden City, N.Y.: Doubleday, 1980.

———. *Through the Flower: My Struggle as a Woman Artist*. Garden City, N.Y.: Doubleday, 1975.

Chodorow, Nancy. *The Reproduction of Mothering: Psychoanalysis and the Sociology of Gender*. Berkeley: Univ. of California Press, 1978.

Christ, Carol. *Diving Deep and Surfacing: Women Writers on Spiritual Quest*. Boston: Beacon, 1980.

Christ, Carol, and Judith Plaskow. *Womanspirit Rising: A Feminist Reader in Religion*. San Francisco: Harper & Row, 1979.

Cox, Sue. *Female Psychology: The Emerging Self*. Chicago: Science Research Associates, 1976.

Daly, Mary. *Beyond God the Father: Toward a Philosophy of Women's Liberation.* Boston: Beacon, 1973.

———. *Gyn/Ecology: The Metaethics of Radical Feminism.* Boston: Beacon, 1978.

Davidson, Cathy N., and E.M. Broner, eds. *The Lost Tradition: Mothers and Daughters in Literature,* New York: Frederick Ungar, 1980.

Demetrakopoulos, Stephanie. *Listening To Our Bodies.* Boston: Beacon, 1983.

Diner, Helen (Berta Eckstein-Diener). *Mothers and Amazons: The First Feminine History of Culture.* New York: Julian Press, 1965.

Dinnerstein, Dorothy. *The Mermaid and the Minotaur: Sexual Arrangements and Human Malaise.* New York: Harper & Row, 1976.

Downing, Christine. *The Goddess.* New York: Crossroad, 1981.

Du Plessis, Rachel Blau. *Toward a Feminist Theory of Motherhood* (Special Issue). *Feminist Studies.* 4, No. 2 (June 1978).

Ehrenreich, Barbara, and Deirdre English. *Witches, Midwives, and Nurses: A History of Women Healers.* New York: Feminist Press, 1973.

Ellman, Mary. *Thinking About Women.* New York: Harcourt, Brace and World, 1968.

Fisher, Elizabeth. *Woman's Creation: Sexual Evolution and the Shaping of Society.* Garden City, N.Y.: Anchor-Doubleday, 1979.

Friedman, Susan. *Psyche Reborn: The Emergence of H.D.* Bloomington: Indiana Univ. Press, 1981.

Friedrich, Paul. *The Meaning of Aphrodite.* Chicago: Univ. of Chicago Press, 1978.

Gilbert, Sandra, and Susan Gubar. *The Madwoman in the Attic: The Woman Writer and the Nineteenth Century Literary Imagination.* New Haven: Yale Univ. Press, 1979.

———, eds. *Shakespeare's Sisters: Feminist Essays on Women Poets.* Bloomington: Indiana Univ. Press. 1979.

Gilligan, Carol. *In a Different Voice. Psychological Theory and Women's Development.* Cambridge, Mass.: Harvard Univ. Press, 1982.

Gimbutas, Marija. *The Gods and Goddesses of Old Europe, 7000–3500 B.C.* Berkeley: Univ. of California Press, 1974.

Goldenberg, Naomi. *The Changing of the Gods: Feminism and the End of Traditional Religions.* Boston: Beacon, 1979.

Griffin, Susan. *Pornography and Silence: Culture's Revenge Against Nature.* New York: Harper & Row, 1981.

———. *Woman and Nature: The Roaring Inside Her.* New York: Harper & Row, 1978.

Hall, Nor. *The Moon and the Virgin: Reflections On the Archetypal Feminine.* New York: Harper & Row, 1980.

Hannah, Barbara. *Striving Toward Wholeness*. New York: Putnam's, 1971.

Harding, M. Esther. *The Way of All Women*. New York: Harper & Row, 1971.

———. *Woman's Mysteries, Ancient and Modern*. New York: Harper & Row, 1971.

Harrison, Jane Ellen. *Mythology*. New York: Harcourt Brace, 1962.

———. *Prolegomena to the Study of the Greek Religion*. New York: Meridian, 1957.

———. *Themis: A Study of the Social Origins of Greek Religion*. Cleveland: World, 1962.

Heilbrun, Carolyn G. *Reinventing Womanhood*. New York: Norton, 1979.

———. *Toward a Recognition of Androgyny*. New York: Knopf, 1973.

Herrera, Hayden, *Frida: A Biography of Frida Kahlo*. New York: Harper & Row, 1983.

Horney, Karen. *Feminine Psychology*. Ed. Harold Kelman. New York: Norton, 1967.

Hubbard, Ruth, and Marian Lowe, eds. *Genes and Gender II*. New York: Gordian, 1979.

Janeway, Elizabeth. *Between Myth and Morning: Women Awakening*. New York: Morrow, 1974.

———. *Man's World, Women's Place: A Study of Social Mythology*, New York: Morrow, 1971.

———. *Powers of the Weak*. New York: Morrow, 1980.

Jelinek, Estelle C., ed. *Women's Autobiography: Essays in Criticism*. Bloomington: Indiana Univ. Press, 1980.

Jung, Emma. *Animus and Anima*. Zurich: Spring, 1974.

Keohane, Nannerl O., Michelle Zimbalist Rosaldo, and Barbara C. Gelpi, eds. *Feminist Theory: A Critique of Ideology*. Chicago: Univ. of Chicago Press, 1982.

Kolbenschlag, Madonna. *Kiss Sleeping Beauty Goodbye*. Garden City, N.Y.: Doubleday, 1979.

Kolodny, Annette. *The Land Before Her*. Chapel Hill, N.C.: Univ. North Carolina Press, 1983.

Kroll, Judith. *Chapters in a Mythology: The Poetry of Sylvia Plath*. New York: Harper & Row, 1976.

Langland, Elizabeth, and Walter Gove, eds. *A Feminist Perspective in the Academy: The Difference It Makes* (Special Issue). *Soundings: An Interdisciplinary Journal* 64, No. 4 (Winter 1981).

Lauter, Estella. *Women as Mythmakers: Poetry and Visual Art by Twentieth Century Women*. Bloomington: Indiana Univ. Press, 1984.

Leonard, Linda Schierse. *The Wounded Woman: Healing the Father-Daughter Relationship*. Boulder: Shambhala, 1983.

Lifshin, Lyn. *Ariadne's Thread: A Collection of Women's Journals.* New York: Harper & Row, 1982.

Lippard, Lucy R. *From the Center: Feminist Essays on Women's Art.* New York: Dutton, 1976.

―――. *Overlay: Contemporary Art and the Art of Prehistory.* New York: Pantheon, 1983.

MacCormack, Carol P., and Marilyn Strathern, eds. *Nature, Culture and Gender.* Cambridge: Cambridge Univ. Press, 1980.

Marks, Elaine, and Isabelle de Courtivron, eds. *New French Feminisms.* New York: Schocken, 1981.

Mazow, Julia Wolf, ed. *The Woman Who Lost Her Names: Selected Writings by American Jewish Women.* San Francisco: Harper & Row, 1980.

Miller, Jean Baker, ed. *Psychoanalysis and Women.* Baltimore, Md.: Penguin, 1973.

―――. *Toward A New Psychology of Women.* Boston: Beacon, 1976.

Mitchell, Juliet. *Psychoanalysis and Feminism: Freud, Reich, Laing, and Women.* New York: Vintage, 1974.

Moers, Ellen. *Literary Women.* Garden City, N.Y.: Doubleday, 1976.

Monaghan, Patricia. *Women in Myth and Legend.* London: Junction, 1981.

―――. *The Book of Goddesses and Heroines.* New York: Dutton, 1981.

Ochshorn, Judith. *The Female Experience and the Nature of the Divine.* Bloomington: Indiana Univ. Press, 1981.

Ostriker, Alicia. *Writing Like a Woman.* Ann Arbor, Mi.: Univ. of Michigan Press, 1983.

Parker, Roszika, and Griselda Pollock, eds. *Old Mistresses: Women, Art and Ideology.* New York: Pantheon, 1982.

Perera, Sylvia Brinton. *Descent to the Goddess: A Way of Initiation for Women.* Toronto: Inner City Books, 1981.

Pomeroy, Sarah. *Goddesses, Whores, Wives, and Slaves: Women in Classical Antiquity.* New York: Schocken, 1975.

Pratt, Annis. *Archetypal Patterns in Women's Fiction.* Bloomington: Indiana Univ. Press, 1981.

Rich, Adrienne. *Of Woman Born: Motherhood as Experience and Institution.* New York: Norton, 1976.

Rigney, Barbara. *Madness and Sexual Politics in the Feminist Novel.* Madison: Univ. of Wisconsin Press, 1978.

Rosaldo, Michelle Zimbalist, and Louise Lamphere, eds. *Woman, Culture and Society.* Stanford, Calif.: Stanford Univ. Press, 1974.

Ruether, Rosemary Radford. *New Woman/New Earth.* New York: Seabury, 1975.

―――. *Sexism and God-talk: Toward a Feminist Theology.* Boston: Beacon, 1983.

Sherfey, Mary Jane. *The Nature and Evolution of Female Sexuality*. New York: Vintage, 1972.

Sherman, Julia A. *On the Psychology of Women: A Survey of Empirical Studies*. Springfield, Ill.: Thomas, 1971.

Singer, June. *Androgyny: Toward a New Theory of Sexuality*. Garden City, N.Y.: Doubleday, 1976.

Slater, Philip. *The Glory of Hera: Greek Mythology and the Greek Family*. Boston: Beacon, 1968.

Spacks, Patricia Meyer. *The Female Imagination*. New York: Knopf, 1975.

Spretnak, Charlene. *Lost Goddesses of Early Greece: A Collection of Pre-Hellenic Myths*. Berkeley, Calif.: Moon Books, 1978.

Spretnak, Charlene, ed. *The Politics of Women's Spirituality*. Garden City, N.Y.: Anchor-Doubleday, 1982.

Stewart, Grace. *A New Mythos: The Novel of the Artist as Heroine, 1877–1977*. St. Alban's, Vermont: Eden Press, 1979.

Stone, Merlin. *Ancient Mirrors of Womanhood*. Vols. I, II. New York: New Sibylline Books, 1979.

———. *When God Was a Woman*. New York: Harcourt Brace Jovanovich, 1978.

Strouse, Jean, ed. *Women and Analysis*. New York: Dell, 1974.

Ulanov, Ann. *Receiving Woman: Studies in the Psychology and Theology of the Feminine*. Philadelphia: Westminster, 1981.

Washbourn, Penelope. *Becoming Woman: The Quest for Wholeness in Female Experience*. New York: Harper & Row, 1977.

———. *Seasons of Woman*. New York: Harper & Row, 1979.

Williams, Juanita H. *Psychology of Women: Behavior in a Biosocial Context*. New York: Norton, 1977.

———, ed. *Psychology of Women: Selected Readings*. New York: Norton, 1979.

Wolkstein, Diane and Samuel Noah Kramer. *Inanna: Queen of Heaven and Earth*. New York: Harper & Row, 1983.

Wolff, C. *Love Between Women*. New York: Harper & Row, 1971.

Wolff, Toni. *Structural Forms of the Feminine Psyche*. Zurich: C.G. Jung Institute, 1956.

Woolf, Virginia. *A Room of One's Own*. Harmondsworth, U.K.: Penguin, 1945.

Index

Mary Cassatt *(cont.)*
About to Wash Her Sleepy Child,
52
Catlett, Elizabeth: *Homage to My
Young Black Sisters,* 77
Ceriddwen, 144
child, 52, 55, 58, 59
Chodorow, Nancy, 60, 72, 81,
235; *The Reproduction of
Mothering,* 210
Chomsky, Noam, 12
Christ (Jesus), 58, 70, 72, 112,
113, 115, 116, 148, 149, 161,
179, 183, 256n
Christ, Carol, 23, 36, 129, 135
code, 95, 119, 121, 125, 130, 131,
147, 232
collective unconscious, 4, 17, 24,
27, 74, 101, 107, 119, 127, 188,
195, 198, 211, 221, 223, 225,
241n
colloquy, 187, 218, 219; *see also*
conversation, dialogue
conscience, 155
consciousness, 63, 142, 143, 144,
150, 151, 154, 157, 159, 164,
166, 171, 174, 175, 185, 187,
193, 194, 208, 209, 211, 216,
225, 234, 242n; collective, 157,
209, 221, 223; matriarchal, 149
consciousness-raising, 95, 220
conversation, 25–26, 43; *see also*
colloquy, dialogue
Cox, Sue, 224
creation, 169
creativity, 20, 47, 116, 142, 144,
146, 157, 159, 160, 174, 183,
184, 193, 198, 211, 232; of
women, 46
culture, 62, 74, 75, 80, 108, 110,
111, 112, 114, 116, 117, 118,
119, 122, 123, 124, 127, 209,
219, 225, 228, 236, 259n;
dominant, 221, *see also*
patriarchal perspective,
patriarchy; "muted," or
"wild," 14, 112, 221, 237

Daly, Mary, 19, 35, 43, 93, 250n
Dante Alighieri, 251n; *Divine
Comedy,* 102
daughter(s), 139, 140, 141, 146,
147, 148, 158, 163, 165, 168,
171, 173, 177, 178, 181, 182,
212, 213
death, 143, 152, 159, 168, 172,
184, 253n, 258n, 260n
Demeter, 76, 77, 102, 113, 114,
115, 141, 144, 257n
Demeter/Kore
(Demeter/Persephone), 55, 97,
105, 112, 113, 114, 116, 140
demonic power, 143, 148, 155,
163, 176, 185
demons, 138, 178, 179, 181
depression, 153, 154, 165, 167,
172, 215, 257n
dialectic, 37, 120, 130
dialogue, 227; *see also* colloquy,
conversation
Didion, Joan, 104
Dionysus, 155, 185
dominants, 41
Downing, Christine, 76; *The
Goddess,* 231, 235
dreaming, 167, 190, 197
dreams, xi, 3, 16, 21, 22, 33, 46,
47, 97, 98, 100, 127, 138, 147,
148, 152, 153, 156, 160, 164,
165, 168, 172, 181, 183, 184,
186, 187–219, 220, 225, 232, 233
Dumuzi (Tammuz), 138, 145, 167,
177, 180, 181, 184, 185, 256n;
Dumuzi's Dream, 180
DuPlessis, Rachel Blau, 11

Economics, 83, 221
ego, 4, 72, 96, 109, 139, 142, 143,
158, 178, 185, 194, 196, 203,
214, 224, 233; -ideal 152, 255n,
259n
Eleusinian Mysteries, 171, 257n
Elias-Button, Karen, 227
Eliot, George, 103, 115
Elshtain, Jean, 134

Hobson and McCarley *(cont.)* 188, 191, 193, 195, 197, 198, 200, 205, 206, 217
holistic thinking, 22, 94, 106, 122, 186, 191, 193, 197, 200, 208, 234, 252n
Horney, Karen, 198
Hosmer, Harriet: *Thomas Hart Benton*, 65; *Zenobia in Chains*, 73, 78
human experience, 37, 50, 197
human identity, 200, 235

id, 4
ideologies, 17, 60
image(s), 39, 46, 50, 60, 64, 65, 72, 76, 82, 141, 144, 152, 186, 187, 195, 197, 199, 207, 213, 225, 237; and behavior, 83, 216–17
imagination, 50, 167, 215, 221, 225, 253n; active, 211, 225
Inanna, 20, 76, 137, 138, 141, 143, 144–49, 151, 154, 155, 157, 158, 160, 161, 164–74, 176, 178–80, 182, 184, 185, 223, 228, 235, 256n, 258n, 259n; /Ishtar, 142, 144, 147, 162, 167, 172, 176
independence, 53, 76, 217, 248n
independent woman, 18, 48, 72, 78, 80, 164
individuation, 4, 33, 155, 193, 224
inductive method, 6, 19, 94, 108, 126
initiation(s), 140, 142, 167, 171, 184
instinct, 28, 157, 199, 259n
interdisciplinary approach, 3, 94, 136, 188, 194, 198, 222, 232, 237
internalization, 24, 25, 27
Isis, 76, 141, 259n
Izanami, 137

Jacobi, Jolande, 7, 29; *The Psychology of C.G. Jung*, 195
Jaffe, Aniela, 7
Jameson, Frederic, 125
Janeway, Elizabeth, 127, 128
Jerome, Saint, 229
Job, 179
Johnson, Adelaide: *Susan B. Anthony*, 73
Jones, Lois Mailou: *Mob Victim*, 72
Jordanova, L.J., 128
Joseph, 58
journey, 106, 142, 149, 166, 172, 233; *see also* quest, rebirth journey
Judith, 73, 79
Jung, Carl Gustav, i, xii, 4, 5, 6, 7, 8, 12, 18, 21, 23, 26, 28, 29, 30, 31, 32, 34, 35, 37, 41, 44, 46, 49, 50, 53, 69, 82, 93, 96, 106, 107, 109, 111, 112, 114, 118, 120, 121, 124, 125, 126, 135, 155, 170, 186, 188, 191, 192, 195, 196, 197, 198, 208, 214, 215, 217, 223, 224, 225, 227, 234, 240n, 241n, 243n, 263n; *The Archetypes and the Collective Unconscious*, 49; *Aspects of the Feminine*, 5; *Civilization in Transition*, 48; *Collected Works*, 7, 189; *Man and His Symbols*, 7, 46, 199; *Memories, Dreams and Reflections*, 48; *Symbols of Transformation*, 101
Jung, Emma, 34, 35, 36, 46, 48, 63, 70, 72, 99; *Animus and Anima*, 41
Jungian psychology, 5, 7, 8, 10, 62, 187, 234; *see also* analytical psychology
Jungian theory, xi, 6, 17, 18, 19, 21, 27, 32, 44, 81, 82, 98, 193
Jungian thought, xii, 35, 46, 48, 63, 82, 107, 166, 191, 195, 211, 212, 223, 224, 226, 235
Jungians, 23, 26, 28, 37, 38, 40, 41, 44, 47, 48, 51, 56, 62, 81, 99, 198, 225

Kahlo, Frida, 61; *The Love Embrace*

Frida Kahlo *(cont.)*
  *of the Universe, the Earth
  (Mexico), Diego, Me and Señor
  Xolotl,* 68; *My Nurse and I,* 55,
  61; *Self-Portrait as a Tehuana,* 67;
  Sun and Life, 68; *Thinking About
  Death,* 68
Kali, 141, 157
Kaplan, Janet, 69
Kaufman, Sue: *Diary of a Mad
  Housewife,* 104
Klumke, Anna: *Rosa Bonheur,* 73
Kolbenschlag, Madonna, 6; *Kiss
  Sleeping Beauty Good-bye,* xi
Kollwitz, Käthe, 61; *Karl
  Liebknecht,* 72; *Mother with
  Twins,* 56, 61; *Outbreak,* 77; *Seed
  Corn Must Not Be Ground,* 56;
  Tower of Mothers, 56
Kolodny, Annette, 106
Kramer, Samuel, 139, 233
Kundalini Chakras, 172, 259n

Laçan, Jacques, 235, 263n
Lama, Giulia: *The Martyrdom of
  St. Eurosia,* 70
language, xi, 12, 14, 26, 35, 46,
  47, 49, 60, 74, 187, 233, 263n
Laurence, Margaret: *The Diviners,*
  105
Lauter, Estella, xi, 13, 17, 21, 227,
  231, 234
Lessing, Doris, 104; *The
  Four-Gated City,* 105
Lévi-Strauss, Claude, 18, 19, 93,
  96, 118–27, 130, 227
Lewis, Edmonia: *Hagar,* 73
Leyster, Judith: *The Jolly Toper,* 66
literary criticism, 93–136, 237
literature, xiii, 28, 81, 95, 100,
  106, 117, 127, 220, 232, 234
Logos, 6, 9, 154, 157, 226, 228
Lowell, Robert: "Near the
  Ocean," 133
Luckmann, Thomas: *The Social
  Construction of Reality,* 24

McCarley, Robert W., 21, 188,
  189, 196
McCarthy, Mary, 103; *The Group,*
  104
McCormack, Carol: *Nature,
  Culture and Gender,* 123, 129
magic, 99, 142, 150, 159, 166, 175
male, 63, 72, 105, 133, 140, 151,
  162, 174, 198, 200, 201, 204,
  209, 214, 216, 218, 220, 235;
  and female, 51, 228;
  experience, 15, 39, 97;
  strangers, 64, 70, 209
man, 5, 135, 214, 218, 229, 241n,
  251n
Manning, Olivia, 103
Marisol, Escobar: *The Family,* 58,
  61
marriage, 115, 124, 139, 154, 163
Mary, 51, 52, 58, 65, 141, 228
Mary Magdalene, 70, 73
masculine, 5, 8, 48, 62, 63, 64,
  67, 69, 71, 72, 76, 98, 99, 109,
  118, 130, 132, 133, 136, 139,
  147, 150, 154, 162, 163, 167,
  174, 182, 185, 187, 198, 218,
  221, 222, 255n; development,
  105, 259n; within the female,
  64, 69, 71, 72; *see also* animus
Mather, Cotton, 159
medieval period, 73
medium, 18, 42, 51, 74, 255n
Medusa (Gorgon), 111, 125,
  132–33, 141, 157, 176, 213, 227,
  232, 251n
men, 48, 63, 72, 97, 98, 122, 124,
  125, 127, 139, 143, 166, 199,
  203, 205, 206, 207, 209, 210,
  216, 217, 224, 259n
Mercurius, 174
"methodolatry," 93
Metis, 117
militance, 58, 61, 63, 73, 77, 80
Miller, J. Hillis, 106
Miller, Jean Baker: *Toward a New
  Psychology of Women,* 41, 43
Miller, Nancy K., 130

Feminist Archetypal Theory has been set on the Linotron 202N in ten point Palatino with two points of spacing between lines. Palatino Italic has been used as display. The book was designed by Laury Egan, composed by Williams of Chattanooga, printed offset by Thomson-Shore, Inc., Dexter, Michigan, and bound by John H. Dekker & Sons, Grand Rapids, Michigan. The paper on which the book is printed bears the watermark of S.D. Warren and is designed for an effective life of at least three hundred years.

THE UNIVERSITY OF TENNESSEE PRESS : KNOXVILLE